# THE SYSTEMATIC THOUGHT
# OF HANS URS VON BALTHASAR

# The Systematic Thought of Hans Urs Von Balthasar

## *An Irenaean Retrieval*

*Kevin Mongrain*

*A Herder & Herder Book*
The Crossroad Publishing Company
New York

The Crossroad Publishing Company
481 Eighth Avenue, New York, NY 10001

Printed in the United States of America

Library of Congress Cataloging-in-Publication Data

Mongrain, Kevin.
    The systematic thought of Hans Urs von Balthasar : an Irenaean
retrieval / Kevin Mongrain.
        p. cm.
    "A Herder and Herder book."
    Includes bibliographical references and index.
    ISBN 0-8245-1927-2 (alk. paper)
    1. Balthasar, Hans Urs von, 1905– I. Title.
BX4705.B163 M66 2002
230'.2'092—dc21
                                        2002006506

1   2   3   4   5   6   7   8   9   10      06   05   04   03   02

# Contents

# Abbreviations

| | |
|---|---|
| AH | *Against Heresies* |
| GL1 | *The Glory of the Lord: A Theological Aesthetics: Volume I: Seeing the Form* |
| GL2 | *The Glory of the Lord: A Theological Aesthetics: Volume II: Studies in Theological Style: Clerical Styles* |
| GL3 | *The Glory of the Lord: A Theological Aesthetics: Volume III: Studies in Theological Style: Lay Styles* |
| GL4 | *The Glory of the Lord: A Theological Aesthetics: Volume IV: The Realm of Metaphysics in Antiquity* |
| GL5 | *The Glory of the Lord: A Theological Aesthetics: Volume V: The Realm of Metaphysics in the Modern Age* |
| GL6 | *The Glory of the Lord: A Theological Aesthetics: Volume VI: Theology: The Old Covenant* |
| GL7 | *The Glory of the Lord: A Theological Aesthetics: Volume VII: Theology: The New Covenant* |
| LA | *Love Alone: The Way of Revelation* |
| LTSH | *Liberation Theology in Light of Salvation History* |
| MWR | *My Work: In Retrospect* |
| MP | *Mysterium Paschale* |
| OPSC | *The Office of Peter and the Structure of the Church* |
| SI | *The Scandal of the Incarnation: Irenaeus Against the Heresies* |
| THdL | *The Theology of Henri de Lubac* |
| TD1 | *Theo-Drama: Theological Dramatic Theory: Volume I: Prolegomena* |
| TD2 | *Theo-Drama: Theological Dramatic Theory: Volume II: The Dramatis Personae: Man in God* |
| TD3 | *Theo-Drama: Theological Dramatic Theory: Volume III: The Dramatis Personae: The Person in Christ* |
| TD4 | *Theo-Drama: Theological Dramatic Theory: Volume IV: The Action* |
| TD5 | *Theo-Drama: Theological Dramatic Theory: Volume V: The Last Act* |
| TDPT | *Theo-Drama and Political Theology* |
| TKB | *The Theology of Karl Barth* |

| | |
|---|---|
| *TL1* | *Theologic: Volume One: The Truth of the World* (English translation of *Theologik: Erster Band: Wahrheit Der Welt*) |
| *TL2* | *Theologik: Zweiter Band: Die Wahrheit Gottes* |
| *TL3* | *Theologik: Dritter Band: Der Geist Der Wahrheit* |

# Acknowledgments

I would like to express my deep gratitude to Cyril O'Regan for all his advice and assistance in the writing of this book. His comments on the manuscript were always remarkably sagacious and apotropaic through and through. He has been an infinite source of scholarly insight into von Balthasar's project as well as a brilliant guide in the art of rhetoric.

I also owe a debt of gratitude to David Kelsey and George Lindbeck for their involvement in this project, and for all they have done in its support.

I would also like to thank John Jones and Michael Parker at Crossroad-Herder for believing in the merits of this project, diligently editing and commenting on the manuscript, and nourishing me with many words of affirmation and encouragement.

My gratitude is also extended to Tony Sciglitano, Erich Rutten, Tom Bolin, and Steve Heymans, all of whom have been valued dialogue partners on von Balthasar, and all things theological.

This book could not have been written if not for the philosophical and theological training I received from Rene McGraw, O.S.B., and Bill Cahoy at St. John's University in Collegeville, Minnesota. My intellectual debts to them both are beyond calculation.

Finally, I would like to express gratitude to my wife, Becky Bacon. She did excellent work proofreading the chapters of the manuscript, and she offered extremely wise editorial suggestions. This book would be twice as long and half as intelligent if it were not for her rigorous efforts to hold me to the principle that more is not necessarily better. Also, and just as important, her love, patience, and understanding were indispensable to me throughout this entire process.

Church Father(s) — influential
~~doctrines~~ theologians who
developed what the Christian
ought to believe
- formative to Christian
doctrine
- "classic" → tells us something about
the human condition

Aquinas
neo scholasticism — an attempt
to explain philosophy
↳ highly abstract

v.B. - we've lost sight in the "glory of the
Lord"

3
Transcendentals
= True, good, and beautiful

# The Systematic Thought of Hans Urs von Balthasar

Much of the dynamism for reforming the Catholic Church prior to the Second Vatican Council (1962–1965) came from the work of creative theologians who sought to reform Catholic theology by returning it to its roots in the writings of the church fathers. Theologians such as Henri de Lubac, Yves Congar, Jean Daniélou, Louis Bouyer, and, in his own way, Karl Rahner worked to retrieve for the modern church the wisdom of ancient Christianity's highly sacramental and liturgical sensibility. The teachings of Vatican II were in large part inspired by this project in theological retrieval.[1] Hans Urs von Balthasar (1905–1988) shared the same basic vision of and strategy for ecclesial reform as the *ressource- ment* theologians who inspired Vatican II. Throughout his life this Swiss polymath fiercely and relentlessly advocated the idea that modern Catholic theology needed to correct and transform itself through an in-depth assimilation of ancient Christian theology's fundamental commit- ment to the regulatory control of concepts by symbols. He dedicated all his gifts for scholarly virtuosity to articulating, defending, and elaborat- ing on this basic idea. Sadly and ironically, unlike the writings of most of his reformist *ressourcement* allies, von Balthasar's brilliant and stag- geringly erudite evangelism on behalf of the *ressourcement* ideal never caught the attention of a wide readership in mainstream academic the- ology. In this work I will present an analysis of von Balthasar's system- atic theology. My hope is that this presentation will persuade readers that his uniquely sophisticated articulation of the *ressourcement* vision deserves the attention of theologians today.

## Intellectual Biography

It is impossible to understand von Balthasar's thought without realizing that he began his intellectual career as an angry dissident from the neoscholastic status quo in Catholic academic theology.[2] He received his education in Catholic neoscholasticism during his Jesuit seminary train-

1

ing from 1931–1933; this experience permanently soured him toward academic theology. As I will explain in more detail in chapter 2, von Balthasar considered neoscholasticism nothing but a species of secular rationalism and hence a perversion of Catholic theology. He believed neoscholasticism's myopic obsession with late mediaeval philosophy and its insistence on the centrality of abstract and neutral rationality in theology sowed the seeds of much heterodox mischief in the church. His encounter with neoscholastic theology was so distasteful that he never pursued a doctorate in academic theology, nor did he ever hold a university professorship.[3] Von Balthasar's later description of his experience in the Jesuit seminary as a "languishing in the desert of neoscholasticism," and his consequent righteous rage against the neoscholastic status quo, reveals the adversarial agenda of his post-seminary intellectual career.[4] He wrote:

> My entire period of study in the Society was a grim struggle with the dreariness of theology, with what men had made out of the glory of revelation. I could not endure this presentation of the Word of God. I could have lashed out with the fury of a Samson. I felt like tearing down, with Samson's strength, the whole temple and burying myself beneath the rubble. But it was like this because, despite my sense of vocation, I wanted to carry out my own plans, and was living in a state of unbounded indignation.[5]

During and after his seminary training he became increasingly convinced of his vocation to defend the Catholic faith by challenging what he believed was neoscholasticism's narrow intellectualism. He pursued this goal by returning to the eclectic scholarly interests that had characterized his preseminary university education.[6] Throughout his life these interests became ever more wide-ranging, reaching into all periods of Eastern Orthodox and Protestant theology, medieval and modern Jewish theology, European philosophy, psychology, literature, poetry, and drama. During his time as a university student and a seminarian he encountered two men whose thought gave him the intellectual tools that enabled him to unite his eclectic scholarly interests into a coherent alternative to neoscholasticism. The first was Erich Przywara, and the second—and by far more important—was Henri de Lubac.

Von Balthasar corresponded and met periodically with Przywara during his university and seminary training. Przywara's doctrine of analogy had a major influence on his thinking, and it helped set the agenda for his extremely formative dialogue with Karl Barth.[7] Przywara functioned for von Balthasar as an important model of intellectual dissent from the neoscholastic status quo. He insisted that his students master the classics of scholastic philosophy, but not so they could be idolized in themselves as monuments to a long-past golden age of Catholic theology. On the contrary, Pryzwara sought to transcend the static intellectualism of the neoscholastics by bringing medieval Catholic philosophy into constructive dialogue with modern philosophy.[8] Przywara showed von Balthasar that it was possible and necessary to bring Thomistic metaphysics and German Idealism into a mutually corrective conversation.[9] Even when he later began to question some of the directions this project took in Przywara's writings, as well as in the work of Joseph Maréchal and Karl Rahner, he never abandoned his belief that the project itself was worthwhile. Von Balthasar came to believe that properly carrying out Pryzwara's project required distinguishing what was theologically valid in Thomas from the confusions and distortions of Thomas's neoscholastic admirers. This required reading Thomas in the context of the tradition as a whole, which meant first of all studying in depth the patristic sources Thomas drew from for the content of his theology. This was the lesson he learned from Henri de Lubac.

From 1933 through 1937 von Balthasar studied patristic theology with de Lubac at the Jesuit theologate in Fourvière, near in Lyons. During this time in France he also collaborated with Daniélou, Henri Bouillard, Gaston Fessard, and other scholars in research projects on the church fathers. This research led to a number of ground-breaking books on long-neglected ancient Latin and Greek theologians, and many of its results eventually were integrated into the monumental *ressourcement* volumes *Sources Chrétiennes* and *Théologie*. Von Balthasar's own research eventually resulted in books and articles by him on the Greek fathers Irenaeus, Origen, Gregory of Nyssa, Clement of Alexandria, Evagrius of Pontus, Dionysius, and Maximus Confessor.[10] This time with the best and brightest patristic scholars in France was clearly the most formative intellectual experience of von Balthasar's life. As Edward Oakes aptly puts it, under de Lubac's influence von Balthasar "fell in love with the Church Fathers" during this time.[11] Peter Henrici has correctly asserted, "It was from him [de Lubac] that he learned what theology really was and could be."[12] De Lubac freed von Balthasar from what Gerald McCool has referred to as neoscholasticism's "search for a unitary method" in Catholic theology by opening for him the vast pluralistic world of patristic theology.[13]

It is not surprising, therefore, that von Balthasar later unequivocally took sides with de Lubac against Pope Pius XII and his neoscholastic advisers when de Lubac's 1946 book, *Surnaturel,* on the relationship between nature and supernatural grace, which its opponents referred to dismissively as teaching *"la nouvelle théologie,"* was impugned and censored by the Vatican. The Vatican and its theological allies had been suspicious of the *ressourcement* theologians throughout the late 1930s and 1940s, seeing in their writings a whole host of dangers: anti-intellectualism, irrationalism, fideism, relativism, evolutionism, symbolism, subjectivism, immanentism, Romanticism, Hegelianism, Existentialism—in short, the *ressourcement* movement was nothing but a resurgence of all the Modernist heresies and their wrong-headed philosophical assumptions.[14] In 1950, acting under the intellectual influence of well-respected neoscholastic theologians such as Réginald Garrigou-Lagrange and Marie-Michel Labourdette, Pope Pius XII silenced de Lubac, and, in his encyclical letter *Humani Generis*, called into question the orthodoxy of the ideas and methods associated with the *ressourcement* movement in general and the *nouvelle théologie* in particular. From von Balthasar's perspective, this controversy was both inevitable and welcome. He saw de Lubac's theology of grace as a direct challenge to the neoscholastic status quo in Catholic theology, and hence he interpreted the *nouvelle théologie* controversy as the chance to end the neoscholastic hegemony in academic theology.[15] He later framed the issue in the *nouvelle théologie* controversy in these stark terms: "With *Surnaturel* . . . a young David comes onto the field against the Goliath of modern rationalization and reduction to logic of the Christian mystery."[16] I will discuss some of the details of this controversy below, and in chapter 2 I will discuss von Balthasar's basic agreement with de Lubac. For the moment I want to highlight that, for von Balthasar, the specific issues in the *nouvelle théologie* debate symbolized a fundamental disagreement between Catholic intellectuals about the proper relationship between concept (*Begriff*) and symbol (*Vorstellung*) in theology. He was not alone in thinking about the issue in this way.

Even if Pius XII and his neoscholastic supporters were mistaken in thinking that the *ressourcement* movement was simply repeating Modernist heresies, they in fact had reason to suspect that de Lubac and his movement were involved in a subversive project to undermine Pope Leo XIII's teaching in *Aeterni Patris* (1879) that scholastic theology in general, and Thomist theology in particular, ought to enjoy pride of place in Catholic intellectual life.[17] De Lubac's neoscholastic critics were right to recognize that he and his *ressourcement* movement were not doing scholarly research on the church fathers for its own sake; the *ressourcement* movement was hostile toward *Aeterni Patris*'s vision of a unitary scholastic method in theology, and, perhaps more important, its presuppositions about the primacy of concept over symbol in theology. They sought to provide theological dissidents with a vast array of resources from the patristic era for challenging *Aeterni Patris* on both counts. The issue for de Lubac and his school was not that Thomas

Aquinas's theology was inherently and irredeemably flawed (although Daniélou came close to asserting this,[18] and, as I will show in chapter 2, von Balthasar seems to have thought that the methodological assumptions employed by Thomas were too dangerous to be a serious theological option in the contemporary context). Rather, the main focus in de Lubac's work was on challenging Thomas's modern imitators by raising questions about whether they actually read him correctly. There was a dual purpose in this critical project: de Lubac wanted both to rehabilitate Thomas as a Catholic intellectual and prevent the particular theological methods of high mediaeval scholasticism from having hegemonic status in contemporary Catholic theology by showing the dangers latent in this approach to things.[19]

De Lubac's concern in undertaking this dual task was to reassert what he believed were ancient Christianity's assumptions about the regulative primacy in theology of sacramental and liturgical symbolism over neutral, abstract concepts. In asserting the centrality of the symbolic in theology, de Lubac never denied the necessary role of philosophical abstraction and rational concepts in theology. Rather, his concern was getting the order of priority straight.[20] When the order of priorities is reversed, as in neoscholasticism, then the result is a "shabby theology" that confuses faith with science, and experiential wisdom with factual knowledge.[21] He describes how this confusion occurs in the history of Catholic theology in a chapter of his book *Corpus Mysticum*, entitled "From Symbolism to Dialectic."[22] In this chapter, as Joseph Komonchak explains, de Lubac "describes a shift in the notion of theology from that spiritual understanding of the faith characteristic of the Fathers, 'those geniuses of ontological symbolism,' to the 'Christian rationalism' foreshadowed in Berengarius, carried on in Abelard and Anselm, vainly resisted by Bonaventure, but triumphant in St. Thomas."[23] De Lubac believes that this shift was necessary to deal with new cultural and intellectual challenges to the faith, but nevertheless he laments the theological loss when, in his words, "symbolic inclusions" become "dialectical antitheses."[24] He writes,

> The dialectical mode of thought has so imposed itself in modern times that people have wound up thinking that it defines thought itself, that before its appearance there was only an era of "compilation," that without it, in any case, intelligence could not have been truly active and "creative." . . . In reality, the dialectical theology of the Middle Ages at its acme replaced another mode of thought which, if it too is taken at its acme, should not a priori be declared to be inferior: the symbolic theology of the Fathers. One theology succeeds another, and, inevitably, in accord with the laws of life, it is unjust or uncomprehending towards it.

But, despite what is naively thought, it is not simply *theology* which is born after the incubation of a long "prehistory."[25]

Clearly de Lubac thinks that the replacement of "the symbolic theology of the Fathers" by "dialectical theology" is a net loss for Catholicism. As Komonchak rightly points out, however, this does not mean he rejects the notion that *dogma* progressively develops. Rather, it means he rejects the neoscholastic claim that high scholastic theology, Thomistic or otherwise, represents some kind of pinnacle of *theological* development.[26] Because theology does not necessarily develop, it is possible for contemporary theologians to treat theological methods and assumptions in the recent past as inadequate in comparison with theological methods and assumptions from the distant past; when necessary, the latter can, and ought to be, retrieved to correct the former.

What then did de Lubac mean by "the symbolic theology of the Fathers," and in what sense would reviving it provide an alternative vision to the dialectical methods of scholasticism and neoscholasticism? Part of the answer is given in his 1938 book, *Catholicism: Christ and the Common Destiny of Man*. In this book, which is a classical example of *ressourcement* theology, de Lubac culled from a wide range of ancient Christian sources what he believed was the coherent theological perspective underlying all patristic thought. The genius of patristic thought lay in its ability to hold in paradoxical unity Judaism's belief in God's elusive transcendence outside time and Christianity's belief in God's incarnation in time. This ability is a sign of genius not because it is the product of human intellectual creativity but rather because it is the product of spiritual education by God in and through symbolic realities. All of pre-Easter history, de Lubac argues, was a process of divine pedagogy preparing the Jews for the paradox of God's incarnation in one man, and all post-Easter history is a process of divine pedagogy training the human race to recognize and accept the paradox of the God-Man's incarnation in the social body of the church.[27] The institutional church is paradox *par excellence* because its symbolic sacramental and liturgical system is the site of the on-going incarnation of Judaism's monotheistic God in universal human history. As such the church is itself the curriculum of God's pedagogy. As this pedagogy proceeds, humanity learns to practice a type of spiritual communalism in which the personal uniqueness of individuals grows in direct proportion to the unity of the global ecclesial community.[28] In this sense the church's sacramental system is a lesson in the paradoxical unity-in-difference of the Trinity.

Maintaining this complex nexus of paradoxes was the central goal in all of the early church's doctrinal battles. As de Lubac sweepingly puts it, "the whole of dogma is nothing but a series of paradoxes, disconcerting to natural reason and requiring not an impossible proof but reflective justification."[29] De Lubac considers it the basic characteristic of all non-Christian forms of mysticism that they oppose Christianity's belief in the paradoxical unity of time and eternity.[30] Moreover, insofar as sacramental Christianity is the tool of God's pedagogical training in this paradoxical unity, non-Christian forms of mysticism oppose it. The institutional church in particular makes no sense to non-Christian forms of mysticism because they either collapse the difference between God and creation into a system of rationalist monism, or they ossify it into a dichotomous dualism. The former results in an abstract, anti-institutional universalism in which one collective soul or one cosmic spirit unites all people and things. The latter results in a sectarianism in which spiritual elites separate themselves from the carnal masses in the hope of escaping from the finite, temporal world. In both cases a pessimistic and bleak view of temporal life replaces the church's progressive optimism about history. Moreover, both are essentially atheistic because, de Lubac assumes, to deny the monotheistic God of incarnational paradox is to have no God at all. For de Lubac, the church's greatest enemy is the non-Christian "sage" who looks at all the complexity and multiplicity in reality, all the light and shadow, and tries to explain them in one totalitarian theory of everything: the non-Christian "sage . . . may well be deluded for a space by the thought that he is the master of the world rhythm . . . or that he captures it all in the net of his aesthetic contemplation."[31] Even though the focus of the discussion here is on non-Christian types of mysticism, de Lubac intends his point about the consequences of rejecting Christianity's belief in the paradoxical unity of time and eternity to apply analogously to other intellectual systems in history as well. For example, in *Catholicism* de Lubac also presents a far-reaching critique of secular humanism (Marxism is his primary target) as assuming the "monotonous" worldview of non-Christian forms of mysticism.[32] The implicit point in this text, however, with its avalanche of citations from patristic sources, its vigorous arguments for the paradoxical nature of dogma, and its insistence on the primarily sacramental nature of the church as the on-going incarnation of Christ's Body in history, is that modern Catholicism, under the tutelage of neoscholasticism, is suffering from amnesia about its patristic heritage.

One particularly debilitating symptom of this amnesia, de Lubac thinks, is the way in which neoscholastic theologians have taught Catholics to think about the relationship of nature and grace, or nature and the supernatural. De Lubac's book on this subject, *Surnaturel*, earned him the censure of Pope Pius XII, who in 1950 silenced him and put his writings on the Index.[33] On the surface the *"nouvelle théologie"* of *Surnaturel* does not today seem like the stuff of controversy; as Komonchak notes, even in 1946 the book was a challenging read because it "presumed an acquaintance with many little-known authors and with apparently esoteric questions and developments in theology."[34] Nevertheless, de Lubac's thesis about the heterodoxy of neoscholasticism's theology of the relationship between nature and grace, and, by implication, its theology of creation and redemption, hit a nerve.[35] De Lubac provoked the neoscholastics by calling their theology "timid" and suggesting that they not only betrayed the genuine theology of Thomas Aquinas, but also the Catholic tradition as a whole by setting nature and supernature into a dichotomous relationship.[36] More provocative still, de Lubac's method of critique presupposed that theology could evolve and devolve, and that established theological concepts were not immutable but contingent and reformable.[37] This assumption seemed to strike at the foundations of neoscholasticism's belief in the notion of fixed first principles in theology.

In *Surnaturel* de Lubac essentially tells the story of how theological concepts evolve and devolve. He maintained that the church fathers always understood human nature as inherently "paradoxical" because it was created to transcend itself toward God; human nature was created in the "image" of God, which meant that it had an intrinsic desire to surpass itself and find its ultimate fulfillment in its creator.[38] Human nature could attain the "likeness" of God if it responded to the vision of God's glory presented to it in God's gracious acts of revelation in history. These acts activate in the human heart a supernatural desire for the transcendent and thereby lead its human recipients beyond the capacities of their own nature into a union with the God of infinite love.[39] This too was the teaching of Thomas, de Lubac argues, at least before it was perverted by the later Thomist tradition in a misguided effort to explain and defend the autonomy and freedom of the created realm with a hypothetical, theoretical construct called "pure nature."[40] Over time this theoretical construct calcified into a rigid metaphysical necessity, so that by the twentieth century neoscholastic theologians were arguing, completely at odds with Thomas and the church fathers, de Lubac contended, that this construct was essential for defending the pure gratuity of grace. In this conceptual system, the gratuity of grace began to appear as something "miraculously" bestowed on the created order as a wonderful supplement to its already completed nature.[41] The animating rationale behind this effort was intrinsic to Thomas's own methodological assumptions about the role pre-Christian, revelation-neutral Aristotelian notions of "nature" could play in theology.[42] Thomas's use of Aristotle, de Lubac believed, was a genuine theological evolution;

Thomas's brilliant mind was able to hold in tension the patristic anthropology, with its highly sacramental view of human nature as created to be a vessel of grace, and Aristotelian naturalism. But in the hands of Thomas's later disciples this balance was lost, and Thomas's Aristotelian assumptions were given too much weight. As a result, Catholic theology underwent a long period of devolution in which it increasingly gave more and more validity to the mistaken notion that anthropology could be conducted apart from theology, philosophy apart from religion.[43] This notion, de Lubac charged, was forgetful of the patristic tradition's teaching that human beings are unique in creation because they have a supernatural desire for union with God. Moreover, in opposition to the extrinsicist "two-storey"-house model of nature-supernature common in neoscholasticism, de Lubac insisted that theologians committed to the doctrine of the incarnation, which presupposes a highly symbolic-sacramental anthropology, cannot allow a theory of "pure nature" to be the dominant, regulative concept in theology. However good the intentions of the neoscholastics, they were paving a dangerous road for Catholicism. Theories of pure nature, he argued, not only are unnecessary for defending God's freedom, they have a toxic effect on theology by making it impossible to see what the church fathers and Thomas himself understood about the sacramental potential of human nature when it encounters the grace of God in the Body of Christ.[44] Any explanatory effort to disentangle nature and grace only creates unnecessary intellectual puzzles and, worse, subverts Catholicism's sacramental and liturgical sensibility.

De Lubac's vision of a modern church suffering amnesia about its identity as a fundamentally sacramental and liturgical religion was one that von Balthasar essentially accepted and expanded for his own purposes. I will assume throughout this study that von Balthasar's own interpretation of the patristic consensus—the "symbolic theology of the Fathers," their fusion of Christology and ecclesiology, their sacramental anthropology—was essentially a repetition of de Lubac's interpretation of it in *Catholicism* and *Surnaturel*. More specifically, the major thesis I would like to argue here is that von Balthasar granted Irenaeus of Lyons privileged status as the quintessential patristic figure whose theology is the standard by which all other patristic theologies should be judged. Nevertheless, the basic logic guiding von Balthasar's exaltation and retrieval of Irenaeus remains strictly within the parameters of de Lubac's theology in *Catholicism* and *Surnaturel*. These books provided von Balthasar with the panoramic theological perspective that he would spend the rest of his life supplementing and emending with his own wide-ranging scholarly pursuits. I have already noted his partisan allegiance to de Lubac's theological vision in *Surnaturel.* He had a similar allegiance to *Catholicism,* which he translated into German, calling it a "beautiful work" and "a fundamental book for us. . . ."[45] In his study of de Lubac he describes *Catholicism* as a "programmatic" book with "seminal importance" that led him "to the task of constructing out of the origins (that always lie open to us), yet without historicism, a theology of true synthesis."[46] As I will suggest below, and argue throughout the remainder of this work, von Balthasar believed this true synthesis was essentially indebted to the theology of Irenaeus. Von Balthasar's Irenaean reading of de Lubac and de Lubacean reading of Irenaeus supplied him with both his constructive theological agenda and the critical perspective that he invariably applied to all modern systems of thought, Christian or otherwise. For example, he claims he learned from de Lubac "the philosophical mysticism of Asia and the phenomenon of modern atheism. . . ."[47] It is important to note that he learned these not on their own terms, but as anti-monotheistic ("atheistic") and anti-sacramental paradox ("Gnostic") rivals to his Irenaean reading of de Lubac's patristic consensus. Before beginning this argument, however, there are still several relevant details from von Balthasar's intellectual biography that need to be put on the table.

In 1936 von Balthasar was ordained to the priesthood. In 1939 his superiors in the Jesuit order gave him the option of either going to Rome to work as a professor at the Gregorian University or to Basel for a post as a chaplain in the university there.[48] In a life-defining move, von Balthasar opted against an academic career and for a career in pastoral ministry. In addition to his work as student chaplain, he continued his own scholarly research and writing. During this time von Balthasar became a serious reader of Karl Barth's theology. He and Barth knew each other and were by their own accounts mutually impressed. A great deal has been written about Barth's formative influence on von Balthasar's thinking.[49] There is no doubt he was fascinated by Barth's theology. His influence on von Balthasar, however, has been greatly overestimated. I will argue in this book that he was fascinated with Barth's theology only to the extent that he saw it as a friendly rival to de Lubac's program of theological reform. Insofar as Barth was conforming to the patristic consensus, von Balthasar lauded him. Insofar as he deviated from it, von Balthasar judged him deficient and in need of correction. His engagement with Barth's theology was something of a dress rehearsal for his many later projects in the critical application of de Lubac's paradigm to modern theology.

During this same period of time von Balthasar met Adrienne von Speyr, a woman who profoundly changed the direction of his life.[50] She was a physician with no theological training who had fallen away from practicing the Protestant faith of her youth. Von Balthasar became her spiritual director, and in 1940 she converted to Catholicism under his guidance. She was, to say the least, a charismatic figure. Apparently she was the recipient of many types of paranormal experiences, many of which von Balthasar claims to have witnessed.[51] Her esoteric mysticism entranced him, and her Johannine interpretation of Ignatian spirituality captured his theological imagination. He became consumed with the task of transcribing and propagating her theology and biblical commentaries, most of which she derived from her Marian experiences.[52] Together they founded a lay community, The Community of St. John,[53] and a publishing house, Johannnes Verlag. The latter was primarily founded to publish von Speyr's books. Under her influence, von Balthasar left the Jesuit order in 1950 to devote himself entirely to his collaborations with von Speyr. This move meant that he was forbidden by canon law to hold a professorship in a Catholic university. Cut off now from both academic employment and the financial support of the Jesuits, von Balthasar eventually moved in with von Speyr and her husband, Werner Kaegi, a professor of history at the University of Basel. In addition to his continuing research and writing, von Balthasar stayed busy managing his secular institute and trying to prevent his publishing house from going bankrupt. He earned money by giving retreats and theology lectures around Germany.[54]

From this time until his death, von Balthasar's intellectual life was almost completely occupied with writing his own books, editing, publishing, and propagating von Speyr's books, and seeking ecclesiastical recognition of her theology. These tasks were for him all part of one common project. Remarkably, he claimed that her theology "laid the basis for most of what I have published since 1940," and therefore his works and hers were "two halves of a whole" and thus could not be separated or understood apart from each other.[55] More remarkably, he insisted that most of his own books were not simply expressions of his own convictions, but rather "a translation of what is present in more immediate, less technical fashion in the powerful works of Adrienne von Speyr. . . ."[56] These are extremely dubious claims whose lack of self-evidence troubled even von Balthasar himself.[57] As a general rule, interpreters should defer to the explicit opinions of authors when they comment on their own writings. In the case of his claims about de Lubac's influence on his theology, this rule should be respected. In the case of von Balthasar's odd claims about von Speyr's influence on his theology, however, this rule should be suspended. The assumption guiding my reading of von Balthasar is that von Speyr's influence on his theology was deforming rather than constructive, derived rather than original; von Speyr is essential for psychologically understanding von Balthasar but completely dispensable for theologically understanding him. Defending the scholarly validity of this assertion is beyond the scope of the present study. My hope is that the interpretation I am putting forward here will give scholars the tools for refuting von Balthasar's misleading claims about her role in shaping his theology.

After von Speyr's death in 1967, in addition to publishing her works, von Balthasar spent most of his intellectual energy finishing and publishing the centerpiece of his scholarly corpus, a vast trilogy that totals fifteen volumes in the English translation.[58] In 1969 he was appointed to the International Theological Commission, and in 1971 he helped the second Synod of Bishops draft its document on the spirituality of priesthood. In 1972 he founded the theological journal *Communio* in an attempt to defend a *ressourcement* interpretation of Vatican II. In the postconciliar period he became alarmed at the trends he saw developing. Given the *ressourcement* movement's difficult struggle in the decades before Vatican II to reconnect the contemporary church with its patristic inheritance, von Balthasar was galled by what he considered the superficiality and ignorance of the church fathers shown by many "progressive" postconciliar theological movements. It seemed to him that many in the theological academy were blind to the real theological sources of Vatican II, and hence were systematically distorting its teachings.[59]

## Von Balthasar's Tepid Reception in the Theological Academy

In 1984 John Paul II bestowed on von Balthasar the prestigious International Paul VI Prize, and then, in 1988, named him a cardinal.[60] Throughout the 1970s and 1980s he received numerous awards and honorary degrees from several Catholic universities in Europe and America. Nevertheless, the mainstream theological academy has been slow to engage his works in serious study. As David Tracy observed over twenty-five years ago, von Balthasar's proposals received a "stunningly silent response" from his theological contemporaries.[61] It is remarkably difficult to interpret the exact motives for this "stunningly silent response." As Tracy's point suggests, theologians did not write about von Balthasar, not even to fault or chastise him. Hence we can only guess at the reasons why he was ignored. There are several possibilities. First of all, his central proposals were not widely known in the English-speaking theological academy because most of his books were not translated.

At the time of his death only about a quarter of his trilogy had been translated into English. Several of his shorter books and essays were available in translation, but they gave only a fragmentary picture of his complex theology. Second, he wrote too much to be assimilated during his lifetime. He produced an absurdly massive body of writings—he published tens of thousands of pages of text—which displays such a vast range of scholarly interests that the central point often becomes submerged.[62] His vertigo-inducing level of erudition does not easily yield anything as straightforward as a core thesis or a self-evident thread of logic. De Lubac praised him as "perhaps the most cultivated man of his time."[63] This was certainly meant as a compliment, but it was precisely his highly cultivated, omnivorous intellect that prevented him from communicating his best theological ideas clearly and directly. Moreover, because he was an independent scholar who never earned a doctorate in theology or held a university professorship, von Balthasar did not have a cadre of graduate students to explain and defend his theological system in the theological academy. During his life only a small number of Catholic theologians took on the challenging task of working through his dauntingly immense works.

Third, although it is impossible to make certain claims on this matter, it seems reasonable to assume that, given the general unpopularity within the theological academy of the positions von Balthasar took on certain controversial issues, there might have been an unspoken consensus among some Catholic academic theologians that he had betrayed the reformist cause which he had espoused before Vatican II, and that he was now too "conservative" to bother reading.[64] In addition to his apparently "traditionalist" interest in retrieving premodern theologians, after the Council he began writing books and essays stridently opposing many "progressive" causes in the church. For example, he suggested there were anti-Catholic ideological motives behind such popular causes as liberation theology and ecumenism among world religions. Moreover, he sided with the Vatican in opposition to women's ordination, artificial contraception, and optional clerical celibacy. In arguing his positions on all these issues he sometimes demonstrated self-righteous contempt for theological opinions different from his own; when his intellectual advice was not heeded, he could be a nasty and bitter polemicist.[65] Suspicion of his ideas only grew as self-styled "conservatives" nostalgic for Tridentine Catholicism appropriated von Balthasar as an intellectual champion of their causes. His image as a reactionary was also fostered by the fact that most of the English translations of his books were published by a company whose catalogue is filled with books written by theologically, politically, and culturally conservative Catholics.

In the fifteen years since von Balthasar's death, most of his trilogy was translated into English, and several fine expository studies of his work have appeared.[66] These studies tend to be primarily exegetical and descriptive overviews of his work. Nevertheless they represent an important step forward in von Balthasar studies. These studies make it obvious that his thought is far too intellectually complex and theologically sophisticated to classify simplistically according to the partisan labels of postconciliar Catholicism. The virtue of these expository studies, however, is also their vice. They limit their scholarly usefulness by either presenting a pastiche of themes from von Balthasar's work or by simply describing sequentially the contents of his trilogy. Their failure to rank themes according to a hierarchy of importance and then to systematically analyze the whole in light of this hierarchy is a major flaw. Failure to identify the dominant themes in his theology that conceptually regulate the entire system make it impossible to raise critical questions about its overall coherence, internal consistency, and rhetorical balance.

Fortunately a new, critical phase of von Balthasar studies is underway. This new phase is analytical in the sense that it attempts to make decisions about von Balthasar's conceptual priorities, regulative themes, and privileged theological, philosophical, and literary sources.[67] These decisions allow for the possibility of an internal critique that evaluates von Balthasar's thought on its own terms. Several von Balthasar scholars are already moving Catholic theology in this direction with impressive results.[68] Of course not all attempts at internal critique are equally successful. Success in such an endeavor depends on the degree to which one's analysis of the whole is accurate. Many attempts at internal critique fail to persuade because their analyses either overlook or misunderstand the core theological commitments animating von Balthasar's intellectual project. At the risk of overgeneralization, I will classify the erroneous interpretations into two basic sets.[69]

The first set of erroneous interpretations claims that von Balthasar's theological system is monistic, and the second set claims that it is dualistic. Those who assert the former tend to read his theology as being primarily committed either to the totalizing circle of Plotinus's *exitus-reditus* metaphysics, or to the monological system of Hegel's pantheistic-trinitarian theory of history. In either case this type of interpretation can only maintain its claim that von Balthasar's theology is monistic by explaining away a large amount of textual data. As I will argue throughout this book, there are many passages in which he contrasts his theology with Plotinian and Hegelian systems and asserts an irreducible *difference* between God and world, eternity and time, infinity and finitude, the trinitarian persons, human persons and human communities, Christian and non-Christian, male and female, and so on.[70] For the monistic interpreters, doing an internal critique means systematically reading all of von Balthasar's claims for difference either as signifying only that difference has a provisional status before the eschaton or as the presence of a dissembling rhetoric that must be expunged from his theology before it can make sense.

Those who assert that von Balthasar's theology is primarily committed to dualism tend not to expunge data from his writings to frame their argument for internal coherence. But like the monistic interpreters, their starting point is the assumption that von Balthasar's theology is mired in Neoplatonic assumptions. In this case, however, "Neoplatonic" means not speculative monism but static Gnostic dichotomies between matter and spirit, time and eternity, body and soul, individual and community, reason and faith, earth and heaven, and so on. In this interpretation internal critique means the process of demonstrating how consistently von Balthasar's dualism leads him into asserting difference and then reneging on his assertion by collapsing one pole into the other. Hence these interpreters frequently assert that his thought "minimizes" or "fails to do justice to" some essential theological theme. In some cases those who argue this case grant that von Balthasar's intentions are profoundly antidualistic. They might even acknowledge that he intends to affirm the sacramental potential of matter, the spiritual aspects of bodily existence, the centrality of faith to human reason, the inescapably dramatic nature of salvation history, the inevitably political mission of the church, the indispensability of community in the development of the self, the real autonomy of earth in its interrelation to heaven, and the complementarity of the different genders. Yet when these interpreters grant these points, they usually then add that that there is a dichotomous logic driving his system that is incongruent with his good intentions. Von Balthasar subverts his own intellectual goals, the argument goes, because he is simply too fascinated by Gnostic mysticism, too obsessed with the apolitical piety of private, individual souls, too fixated on the interior life of the eternal Trinity, and too concerned with the timeless life of heaven above the temporal earth. Some authors soften the critique by avoiding the claim that his theology actually is dualistic, and instead assert only that his theology "risks" or is in "danger" of falling into some kind of dualism. Analyses that assert dualism yield internal critiques that present his theology as a confused, crypto-Jansenism. It can only be salvaged by radically rewriting it to inject the balanced perspective it cannot generate internally.

*[margin note: Dualistic = neoplatonic]*

### Thesis, Method, and Outline of the Book

The aim of this book is to offer a different analysis of von Balthasar, that, in turn, yields a different internal critique. In other words, the aim is to understand how von Balthasar's mind works, and thereby create the possibility of evaluating his theological claims by his own standards. The working assumption of my analysis is that de Lubac's theology is the general source of the internal logic in von Balthasar's theology in the sense that it determines his conceptual priorities, regulative themes, and privileged theological, philosophical, and literary sources. His assimilation of de Lubac's belief that the pedagogical mission of the church in history is to train humanity in the monotheistic-sacramental paradox accounts for both the wide-frame perspective noticed by the monistic interpretation and the binary tendency noticed by the dualistic interpretation. My thesis is that von Balthasar came to see Irenaeus of Lyons's theology of the mutual glorification of God and humanity in Christ as the best articulation of the theological vision presented by de Lubac. Irenaeus, read through de Lubac's lens, therefore became von Balthasar's primary critical resource from the patristic archive for reforming contemporary Catholic theology and challenging various modern intellectual movements in theology, culture, and politics.

My thesis is limited in two ways. First, I am not attempting to demonstrate that von Balthasar's theology is in fact Irenaean. That claim would require a comparative analysis of von Balthasar and Irenaeus's texts. Rather, I am arguing that von Balthasar *thinks* his theology is Irenaean. In other words, he consciously identifies Irenaeus's thought as the purest expression of the patristic consensus and builds the theology of his trilogy around it. I am not concerned with the question of whether his reading of Irenaeus is accurate or idiosyncratic. My method will be to examine what von Balthasar explicitly claims about Irenaeus's theology in several of his texts, and then, focusing primarily on his trilogy, analyze how these claims closely match what he argues in his own voice about theological norms and the criteria for measuring theological deviance from them. Second, my thesis is limited by my distinction between the internal logic of von Balthasar's theology, on one hand, and his philosophical theology of logic, on the other hand. Focus on the latter would involve a close study of the three volumes that constitute the third part of his trilogy, *Theologik*.[71] My interest in the internal logic of his theology, however, is broader and more general than the philosophical theology of logic presented in *Theologik*. I contend that von Balthasar advocates something that can be referred to as "doxa-logic," which is for him a normative theological discourse that can function as a corrective for some trends in contemporary theology. In making this argument, however, my point is that von Balthasar advocates a distinctive theological style with certain definite conceptual priorities, regulative themes, and privileged sources from the Christian tradition.

Reading von Balthasar's theology as an attempted retrieval of Irenaeus and an advocacy of a particular set of theological norms can provide an extremely useful hermeneutic resource for identifying the elements of incoherence, inconsistency, and, possibly, heterodox rhetoric in his thought. Several commentators have noticed von Balthasar's interest in Irenaeus, but few treat this interest as anything more than an expression of his interest in patristic theology in general, and none treats it as a resource for internal critique.[72] This is unfortunate because an Irenaean reading of von Balthasar can redeem the most salient aspects of many of the various criticisms of his work that have been offered, particularly those that detect Gnosticism in some of his ideas. My goal is to open the possibility of internal critique, and in the concluding chapter I will suggest a few lines it might take.

The method of my analysis differs from the general practice used by the expository scholars. Most of these studies read the trilogy sequentially, arguing that his theological aesthetics (beauty), theodramatics (goodness), and theologic (truth) ought to be read as a linear progression. Von Balthasar chose this ordering of the transcendentals as a conscious challenge to the ordering of Kant's trilogy (reason, ethics, aesthetics), and therefore it ought to be respected. This is a valid point, but its merit is limited. First, the three parts of the trilogy are not pure discussions of beauty, goodness, or truth. Each part does accent one of the transcendentals, but each covers the others in great detail as well. Second, von Balthasar himself insisted that he was not presenting a rigidly systematic account of the transcendentals. In volume one of *Theologic* he writes,

> The circumincession of the transcendentals suggests the necessity of, and therefore excuses, a new discussion of issues that, at least in part, we have treated in the previous panels of our triptych. After all, there is simply no way to do theology except by repeatedly circling around what is, in fact, always the same totality looked at from different angles. To parcel up theology into isolated tracts is by definition to destroy it.[73]

I will take him at his word on this point. There is a great deal of repetition, with various nuances, throughout the trilogy. Therefore I will range around the trilogy to discuss a series of interconnected theological themes. My argument that von Balthasar understood his project primarily as a retrieval of Irenaeus will determine the structure of my analysis.

## Notes

1. Of course it is impossible to interpret the teachings of the Second Vatican Council exclusively in terms of any one particular theological school. Nevertheless, a strong case can be made that the proposals of thinkers like de Lubac, Rahner, Daniélou, Congar, and Bouyer were generally ratified by the Council and integrated into its teachings. For example, see *Lumen Gentium*'s teachings that it is the nature of the church to be a "sacrament" of Christ, who is himself the visible image of the invisible God on earth (see paras. 1, 2, 8, 9, 48). *Gaudium et Spes* (paras. 42 and 45) and *Sancrosanctum Concilium* (paras. 2 and 5) make similar claims. Perhaps the most important expression of this ancient Christian sacramental and liturgical sensibility comes in *Sancrosanctum Concilium*'s remarkable assertion that "the liturgy is the summit toward which the activity of the church is directed; at the same time it is the font from which all her power flows" (para. 10).

2. See Fergus Kerr's excellent discussion of von Balthasar's hostile intellectual attitude toward neoscholasticism, "Foreword: Assessing this 'Giddy Synthesis,'" in *Balthasar at the End of Modernity*, ed. Lucy Gardner, David Moss, Ben Quash, and Graham Ward (Edinburgh: T&T Clark, 1999), 1–13.

3. Von Balthasar asserted the following in an interview in 1976: "You address me as a theologian or a theological writer, but I never got my doctorate in theology; by nature and upbringing I am a Germanist." "Geist und Feuer: Ein Gespräch mit Hans Urs von Balthasar," *Herder Korrespondenz* 30 (1976): 75–76. Cited in Edward T. Oakes, *Pattern of Redemption: The Theology of Hans Urs von Balthasar* (New York: Continuum, 1994), 73.

4. Cited in Peter Henrici, "Hans Urs von Balthasar: A Sketch of His Life," in *Hans Urs von Balthasar: His Life and Work*, 12. See also Henrici's intellectual biography of von Balthasar in his essay, "Hans Urs von Balthasar: His Cultural and Theological Education," in *The Beauty of Christ: An Introduction to the Theology of Hans Urs Von Balthasar*, ed. Bede McGregor, O.P. and Thomas Norris (Edinburgh: T&T Clark, 1994), 10–22.

5. Cited in Henrici, *Hans Urs von Balthasar*, 13.

6. As a university student in Zurich, Vienna, and Berlin von Balthasar showed a keen interest in the overlapping religious concerns of ancient philosophy, medieval theology, modern European philosophy, literature, music, and psychoanalysis. Plotinus, Kierkegaard, Goethe, Nietzsche, Freud, and Mahler framed many of the issues that dominated his thinking. He eventually wrote a doctoral dissertation on the theological themes in modern German literature. See Henrici, *Hans Urs von Balthasar*, 9–11.

7. See Oakes, *Pattern of Redemption*, 15–44. See also Medard Kehl, "Hans Urs von Balthasar: A Portrait," in *The Von Balthasar Reader*, ed. Medard Kehl and Werner Löser (New York: Crossroad, 1982), 17–22.

8. Henrici, *Hans Urs von Balthasar*, 13.

9. Kehl, "Hans Urs von Balthasar," 19.

10. See *MWR*, 11–12, 48–49, 107–9.

11. Oakes, *Pattern of Redemption*, 3.

12. Henrici, *Hans Urs von Balthasar*, 13. Von Balthasar's account of de Lubac's theology in *THdL* is essentially an overview of the fundamental themes in his own theology. Medard Kehl gives a concise outline of von Balthasar's debts to de Lubac in his biographical essay, "Hans Urs von Balthasar: A Portrait" in *The Von Balthasar Reader*, 31–42.

13. Gerald A. McCool tells the story of the nineteenth-century rise and twentieth-century fall of neoscholasticism's search for a unity method in Catholic theology. See his detailed and fascinating studies, *Nineteenth-Century Scholasticism: The Search for a Unitary Method* (New York: Fordham University Press, 1989), and *From Unity to Plurality: The Internal Evolution of Thomism* (New York: Fordham University Press, 1989). I would suggest that von Balthasar's rejection of a single, monolithic theological method in his little book on theological pluralism ought to be read as a manifesto expressing the theological ideals he learned from de Lubac. See his *The Truth Is Symphonic: Aspects of Christian Pluralism* (San Francisco: Ignatius Press, 1987).

14. The exact details of this critique are beyond the scope of the present work. Interested readers should consult the following sources: Aidan Nichols, "Thomism and the Nouvelle Théologie," *The Thomist* 64/1 (January 2000): 1–19; Joseph A. Komonchak, "Theology and Culture at Mid-Century: The Example of Henri de Lubac," *Theological Studies* 51/4 (December 1990): 579–602; Gerald McCool, *From Unity to Plurality*, 200–233.

15. See Fergus Kerr, "Assessing this 'Giddy Synthesis,'" in *Balthasar at the End of Modernity*, 2–5.

16. *THdL*, 63. Later in this same text he writes that the issue in *Surnaturel* was not "merely . . . overcoming theologically the poison of Jansenism that had smoldered for centuries in French intellectual life but rather with the poison (intended as an antidote) of a rationalism become worldwide, which treated man (and the angels), as if (following Aristotle) it was true that 'the natural desire does not extend beyond what lies in the natural capacities.' What was devised by theologians to protect the order of grace turns, according to an inner logic, into a closed order of nature for which the 'supernatural' can only be something 'superadded' exteriorly and thus can be dispensed with." *THdL*, 66.

17. For a discussion of *Aeterni Patris* and its place in nineteenth- and twentieth-century Catholic theology, see McCool, *Nineteenth Century Scholasticism*, 226–40, and *From Unity to Pluralism*, 5–38. The neoscholastic defenders of *Aeterni Patris* rightly sensed that the *ressourcement* theologians were involved in an implicit act of dissent from papal teaching. Expressing what came to be the standard neoscholastic point of view, in 1936 one alarmed neoscholastic theologian wrote to Marie-Michel Labourdette, the editor of the *Revue Thomiste*, to complain that "a concerted enterprise of destabilization of the Scholastic method was at work in France." This letter is cited by Aidan Nichols in "Thomism and the Nouvelle Théologie," 8.

18. See Nichols's discussion of Daniélou's inflammatory 1946 *ressourcement* manifesto, "Les oriéntations présentes de la pensée religieuse," in "Thomism and the Nouvelle Théologie," 4–6.

19. For the point about overcoming the hegemony of scholasticism, see especially Nichols, "Thomism and the Nouvelle Théologie," 10–11; Komonchak, "Theology and Culture," 581–84, and McCool, *From Unity to Pluralism*, 208–30.

20. See, for example, de Lubac's 1930 essay, "Apologetics and Theology," which is translated into English and reprinted in his *Theological Fragments*, trans. Rebecca Howell Balinski (San Francisco: Ignatius Press, 1989), 91–104.

21. De Lubac, "Apologetics and Theology," 92–95.

22. I am indebted to Joseph Komonchak's essay "Theology and Culture," 589–90 for this reference to "From Symbolism to Dialectic" and the interpretation of it that follows.

23. "Theology and Culture," 589. The passages cited from de Lubac here are found in *Corpus mysticum: L'Euchariste et l'église au moyen âge: Etude historique* (Paris: Aubier, 1944; 2d ed., 1949), 248–77.

24. "Theology and Culture," 590. See also McCool, *From Unity to Pluralism,* 212.

25. De Lubac, *Corpus mysticum*, 366–67; cited in "Theology and Culture," 590.

26. "Theology and Culture," 590.

27. See *Catholicism: Christ and the Common Destiny of Man*, trans. Lancelot C. Sheppard and Elizabeth Englund (San Francisco: Ignatius Press, 1988), 48–81, 137–216, 326–50. See also de Lubac, *The Mystery of the Supernatural*, trans. Rosemary Sheed (New York: Herder and Herder, 1967), 154ff.

28. *Catholicism*, 326–66.

29. *Catholicism*, 327. See also de Lubac, *The Mystery of the Supernatural*, 131–241, and passim.

30. *Mystery of the Supernatural*, 137–64.

31. *Mystery of the Supernatural*, 140; see also 137–47.

32. Compare for example *Catholicism*, 140 and 358–61.

33. See McCool, *From Unity to Pluralism*, 224–25. See also Nichols, "Thomism and the Nouvelle Théologie," 1–22.

34. Komonchak, "Theology and Culture," 580.

35. For de Lubac's statement of his position see his *The Mystery of the Supernatural*, 131–241, and passim. This text is a translation of *Le mystére du surnaturel* (1965), which is itself a revised version of his *Surnaturel*. See also his *Augustinianism and Modern Theology* (New York: Crossroad/Herder & Herder Publishing, 2000).

36. De Lubac, *Surnaturel: Etudes historiques* (Paris: Aubier, 1946), 437; cited in Komonchak, "Theology and Culture," 584.

37. McCool, *From Unity to Pluralism*, 210–11.

38. For a discussion of this and the following points, see de Lubac's 1965 revised and expanded edition of *Surnaturel, The Mystery of the Supernatural*, trans. Rosemary Sheed (New York: Herder and Herder, 1967), 131–80. See also his *A Brief Catechesis on Nature and Grace* (San Francisco: Ignatius Press, 1984), 9–53.

39. See *The Mystery of the Supernatural*, 272–311.

40. De Lubac, *Surnaturel*, 137–39; see also his *Augustinianism and Modern Theology*, 126–27; both texts are cited in Komonchak, "Theology and Culture," 585.

41. Komonchak, "Theology and Culture," 586.

42. *Surnaturel*, 434–35; cited in Komonchak, "Theology and Culture," 587–88.

43. See, for example, *Surnaturel*, 173–75; cited in Komonchak, "Theology and Culture," 587.

44. *Surnaturel*, 25–47, 242–71. See also *A Brief Catechesis on Nature and Grace*, 20–41.

45. *MWR*, 15, 49.

46. *THdL*, 35, 43.

47. *MWR*, 48; *THdL*, 28–29, 45–59.

48. See Henrici, *Hans Urs von Balthasar*, 14–18.

49. For an introduction to the themes and issues in this field of commentary, see Edward Oakes, *Pattern of Redemption*, 45–71.

50. Von Balthasar discusses his relationship with von Speyr in *Our Task: A Report and a Plan*, trans. John Saward (San Francisco: Ignatius Press, 1994).

51. See Johann Roten's uncritical review of von Balthasar's strange fascination with von Speyr in Roten's essay "Two Halves of the Moon: Marian Anthropological Dimensions in the Common Mission of Adrienne von Speyr and Hans Urs von Balthasar," in *Hans Urs von Balthasar: His Life and Work*, 65–86. Among other oddities, Roten reports that von Balthasar personally witnessed von Speyr's "countless visions, bilocations, emanations of light, ecstasies, and exterior stigmatizations" (68). At one episode von Speyr helped von Balthasar hold hands with Christ (70). At another episode she bestows on von Balthasar the gift of a bandage that the Virgin Mary had used to wrap a cut on von Speyr's hand; von Balthasar carried the bandage with him in a little knit bag for the rest of his life.

52. Von Balthasar published at least sixty volumes based on von Speyr's dictation. He described their working relationship between 1944–1960 as follows: "Almost invariably she dictated for twenty minutes or half hour each afternoon. . . . [S]he would read the version, close her eyes, reflect for a few seconds and then begin to dictate continuously, usually very quickly, so that being a poor stenographer, I followed only with difficulty and frequently had to ask her to pause for a moment. . . . Soon she was so accustomed to dictating that she spoke fluently, and in the last year what she dictated was often ready for direct publication. I later made a fair copy of all that had been dictated, making insignificant changes . . . but nothing of her thought was ever changed." *First Glance at Adrienne von Speyr* (San Francisco: Ignatius Press, 1981), 98–99; cited in Roten, "Marian Anthropological Dimensions," in *Hans Urs von Balthasar: His Life and Work*, 71.

53. For a discussion of this community and von Balthasar and von Speyr's vision for it, see *The Von Balthasar Reader*, 43–44, and 300. See also Maximilian Greiner, "The Community of St. John," in *Hans Urs von Balthasar: His Life and Work*, 87–101.

54. For a account of this period in his life, see Henrici, *Hans Urs von Balthasar*, 22–24.

55. *MWR*, 89.

56. *MWR*, 105–6.

57. His claim that she strongly influenced his books and that he learned his theology from her, he notes, "is an assertion that can only be verified at a later time" (*MWR*, 107).

58. The first seven volumes of the trilogy are a theological aesthetics, *The Glory of the Lord*. The next five volumes are a theodramatics, *Theo-Drama*. The last three volumes are a theological-metaphysical ontology, *Theologik*.

59. See, for example, his book *Who Is a Christian* (New York: Newman Press, 1968), and *MWR*, 51–58. See also Henrici, *Hans Urs von Balthasar*, 36–39.

60. This latter honor embarrassed him, and he initially declined it but was ordered by the pope to accept. He died before the ceremony officially making him a cardinal. See Henrici, *Hans Urs von Balthasar*, 41.

61. David Tracy, *Blessed Rage for Order: The New Pluralism in Theology* (New York: Seabury, 1975), 79.

62. For a complete bibliography of von Balthasar's works, see *Bibliographie, 1925–1990* (Einsiedeln: Freiburg, 1990). For a bibliography that contains most of the English translations of von Balthasar's works, see *Hans Urs von Balthasar: His Life and Work*, ed. David L. Schindler (San Francisco: Communio Books/Ignatius Press, 1991), 299–305.

63. Henri de Lubac, "A Witness of Christ in the Church," *Communio* (Fall, 1975): 230.

64. This point is made by Medard Kehl in "Hans Urs von Balthasar: A Portrait," *The Von Balthasar Reader*, 4–6.

65. The most notorious example of this tendency is von Balthasar's grotesquely unfair polemic against Karl Rahner's doctrine of the anonymous Christian in *The Moment of Christian Witness*, trans. Richard Beckley (New York: Newman, 1969). In a highly critical discussion of this book, Frans Jozef van Beeck contends that von Balthasar's arguments are not properly theological, but instead are merely "the product of anger born out of anxiety" (*God Encountered: A Contemporary Catholic Systematic Theology: Volume Two/1: The Revelation of the Glory* [Collegeville: Liturgical Press, 1993] 6–7). He then offers a psychoanalytical sketch of von Balthasar in an attempt to explain why he wrote this polemical work. Van Beeck explains that von Balthasar's theology has "substantial weaknesses . . . mostly of the 'symptomatic' kind" (6). A "symptomatic" weakness means for van Beeck "biases that are symptoms of individual author's unstated personal agendas. . . . Intelligence and learning, we have discovered, are not the same as self-awareness or mental health; capable theologians have this in common with most other men and women, that they enjoy only limited access to their motives and, hence, that their insights may be twisted by psychodynamics that are less than entirely sound or constructive" (*God Encountered: A Contemporary Catholic Systematic Theology, Volume One: Understanding the Christian Faith* [San Francisco: Harper and Row, 1989], 79). Van Beeck's point is probably valid, but his method is unfair. Rather than offering psychological critique of von Balthasar, it is more scholarly and intellectually responsible to offer an internal critique of his own texts.

66. In addition to the volume of essays in *Hans Urs von Balthasar: His Life and Work*, see *The Beauty of Christ,* ed. Bede McGregor, O.P. and Thomas Norris; *The Analogy of Beauty: The Theology of Hans Urs von Balthasar*, ed. John Riches (Edinburgh: T&T Clark, 1986); Oakes, *Pattern of Redemption;* Angelo Scola, *Hans Urs von Balthasar: A Theological Style* (Grand Rapids, MI: Eerdmans, 1995); Aidan Nichols, *The Word Has Been Abroad: A Guide Through Balthasar's Aesthetics* (Washington D.C.: Catholic University of America Press, 1998); idem, *No Bloodless Myth: A Guide Through Balthasar's Dramatics* (Washington D.C.: Catholic University of America Press, 2000); idem, *Say It Is Pentecost: A Guide Through Balthasar's Logic* (Washington D.C.: Catholic University of America Press, 2001).

67. Perhaps the best example of this type of approach is *Balthasar at the End of Modernity*. Each essay in this collection practices internal critique to deal with the question of whether von Balthasar's theology can be counted as postmodern.

68. A fine example of this new, more sophisticated von Balthasar scholarship is Mark A. McIntosh's study, *Christology from Within: Spirituality and the Incarnation in Hans Urs von Balthasar* (Notre Dame: University of Notre Dame Press, 1996). Cyril O'Regan has also published several analytical-critical essays on von Balthasar's theology. See his "Von Balthasar and Thick Retrieval: Post-Chalcedonian Symphonic Theology," *Gregorianum* 77/2 (1996): 227–60; "Balthasar and Eckhart: Theological Principles and Catholicity," *The Thomist* 60 (April 1996): 203–39; "Newman and von Balthasar: The Christological Contexting of the Numinous," *Eglise et Théologie* 26 (1995): 165–202; "Balthasar: Between Tübingen and Postmodernity," *Modern Theology* 14 (July 1998): 325–53.

69. What follows are two composite descriptions of general types of interpretation. There are no absolutely pure types, and therefore I will not cite any representative examples of each type at this point because to do so would inevitably result in a caricature of the cited author. Throughout this work I will cite the specific passages from actual authors that I consider instances of the relevant elements from the composite types discussed here.

70. Rowan Williams is correct to argue that von Balthasar is a primarily a theologian of difference for whom the point of theological speech is maintaining "simultaneity and reciprocity." See his "Afterword: Making a Difference," in *Balthasar at the End of Modernity*, 173–79.

71. Readers interested in *Theologik* would do well to begin with Aidan Nichols's excellent study, *Say It Is Pentecost: A Guide through Balthasar's Logic*.

72. Aidan Nichols is a notable exception. He correctly asserts that Irenaeus is the "favoured" patristic theologian in von Balthasar's theology (*Say It Is Pentecost*, 74).

73. *TL1*, 8.

# PART ONE

# VON BALTHASAR'S RETRIEVAL OF IRENAEUS

# Chapter I

# True Gnosis and the *Corpus Triforme*

Of the many things von Balthasar learned from de Lubac, one of the most important was that he should read the actual texts of the church fathers. This led him to rediscover Irenaeus of Lyons. Irenaeus's *Against Heresies* completely captivated von Balthasar, and eventually its assumptions permeated all areas of his thinking. He became convinced that Irenaeus's theology was the purest expression of the patristic consensus, and therefore all theological roads should lead from and return to him. He believes Irenaeus illustrates premodern Christian theology at its most theologically rich and spiritually profound. Patristic thinkers other than Irenaeus certainly have had an important influence on von Balthasar's theology, but all the luminaries of the patristic theological tradition he holds up as exemplars are for him only moons to Irenaeus's sun. Attentive reading of von Balthasar's trilogy is necessary, however, because it is easy to overlook the presence of the Irenaean paradigm amidst the panorama of theologies he discusses. He does not explicitly identify Irenaeus as the most important patristic figure for interpreting his theology. Moreover, the order of his argument for unifying beauty, goodness, and truth does not follow an obvious Irenaean pattern, nor do his forays into aesthetic and dramatic theory have an Irenaean precedent. Nevertheless, it is possible to show that his fundamental theological paradigm is crafted from what he believes was Irenaeus's theological perspective. Irenaeus is thus the indispensable key for interpreting the retrieval of the patristic consensus in von Balthasar's trilogy.

In addition to brief commentaries scattered throughout the trilogy, von Balthasar wrote three essays on Irenaeus. These commentaries and essays provide the template for reading his work as a whole. The first essay is an introduction to an anthology of passages from *Against Heresies*, the second essay is in the second volume of *The Glory of the Lord*, and the third essay is a long excursus on Irenaeus's theology in *Against Heresies* in the second volume of *Theo-Drama*.[1] All three essays ought to be read together as a statement of von Balthasar's Irenaean interpretation of the patristic consensus. Like patristic theology in general, this perspective advocates the fundamentally doxological and sacramental nature of Christian existence. Irenaeus distinguishes himself, however, by recognizing more clearly than any other church father the need to defend doxological sacramentality from deformation by various types of Gnostic antisacramentality.

Of course Irenaeus is not the only possible patristic resource for interpreting von Balthasar's theology in his trilogy.[2] In a discussion of his work to retrieve figures from the ancient tradition who are "essential, and, indeed, indispensable" for understanding Christianity in "our all-forgetting age," von Balthasar names not only Irenaeus but also Origen, Gregory of Nyssa, Augustine, Dionysius the Areopagite, and Maximus Confessor.[3] Asserting the presence of a massive Irenaean influence on von Balthasar is not meant to eclipse the importance of any of these other figures on his thought. Nor does it imply that every aspect of his theology can be directly and exclusively accounted for by his debts to Irenaeus's theology; von Balthasar draws more from its basic vision than from its details, which he grants are sometimes imprecisely articulated.[4] Yet understanding that his basic vision is Irenaean provides a hermeneutic key for understanding the theological measure he applies in his positive evaluations and retrievals of other thinkers. For example, he asserts that Irenaeus's theology "is at once markedly anti-Gnostic and pre-Alexandrian, that is to say, not as yet Platonizing. . . . Christian thought is imbued [by Irenaeus] with a good spirit; one can only regret that succeeding ages did not give more careful attention to this beginning."[5] Even when von Balthasar is not explicitly discussing Irenaeus in his trilogy, his theological system is nevertheless conceptually pervasive. When he praises theologians it is because they follow Irenaeus's theological precedents and work out details he left undeveloped, and when he criticizes theologians, both those he greatly admires and those he despises, it is because he judges that they are deviating from an Irenaean theological norm.[6]

A close reading of the trilogy reveals that one foundational Irenaean theme, and several corollary subthemes, continually recur and regulate the project as a whole. My discussion of these themes in this chapter is merely introductory—in subsequent chapters I will provide deeper analyses of their structural function in the internal logic of von Balthasar's trilogy. The foundational theme is Irenaeus's paradoxical and doxological theology of the mutual glorification of God and creation. There are four subthemes that emerge from this foundation. The

first subtheme is Irenaeus's distinction between a "true gnosis" centered ①
on the doxological paradox and a "false gnosis" centered on the Gnostic rejection of doxological paradox. The second subtheme is a *corpus* ②
*triforme* interpretation of true gnosis. The doctrine of the *corpus triforme* sees the Body of Christ as a temporal sacrament symbolizing the
Word's incarnation in a three-phase historical process. The first phase of
the incarnation occurred in the old covenant; the second phase occurred
in Jesus of Nazareth; and the third phase is currently unfolding in the ③
new covenant. The third subtheme is a metanarrative theology of divine
pedagogy that reads all human history as an education in recognizing
and becoming part of the *corpus triforme*. The fourth subtheme is a dra- ④
matic interpretation of post-Easter history in which the participants in
the third phase of the incarnation battle with their Gnostic enemies.

### True Gnosis and the Doxological Paradox

Von Balthasar praises Irenaeus as "theology's founding father and a ✓
paradigmatic figure in its history" and he lauds his writings as "the birth
of Christian theology."[7] Irenaeus's greatness as a theologian lies in his
"dedication to reality" and commitment to the principle that faith
focuses on "things as they are."[8] For him, von Balthasar writes, "The
primary aim is not to think, to impose Platonic intellectual or even
mythical categories on things, but simply to *see* what *is*."[9] Irenaeus is
not opposed to thinking per se but instead to thinking outside the context of experience. Von Balthasar explains that Irenaeus sees humanity
as childlike in that it "acquires wisdom only slowly by experience."[10]
The word *experience* is "constantly recurring" in Irenaeus's writings
because he believes that "[t]he concept of something acquired by experience is more solid and less open to doubt than a conclusion from a
hypothesis."[11] Facts and experience always take primacy for him over
detached "intellectual hypotheses" and neutral explanatory schemes.
The facts of revelation, and the experience of God it makes possible, are
accessible to everyone, even the simple: "whoever wants to can see the
truth" because it is given to humanity to be experienced. All that is
required is a willingness to accept "without fear" or "prejudice" God's
truth in its "openness and simplicity, its availability to general inspec-
tion," its "clarity" and "directness," its "plainness."[12] Irenaeus insisted
that theology should not allow itself to drift into "abstraction" when
presenting revealed truth, but rather it should strive to preserve "the
irrefutability and irresistibility of its internal obviousness."[13] For
Irenaeus, von Balthasar writes, "God has communicated himself and
made himself knowable, and this knowledge (gnosis) of God is real,

indeed the most real of all forms of knowledge. . . ."[14] Von Balthasar valorizes Irenaeus for constantly pointing to this type of "true gnosis" to deflate the pretentiousness of the "learned" and the "wise" who puff themselves up with "false gnosis," making themselves intellectually proud and numb to the profound experiential truth of the Gospel message. He writes, "For him, therefore, holiness is greater than gnosis."[15] In other words, true gnosis is to know the limits of theory, abstraction, and speculation in theology; for Irenaeus, to know less is to know more.

In Irenaean theology, von Balthasar explains, the foundational fact is "the mutual glorification of God and man" in Christ.[16] The most obvious clue that von Balthasar models his own constructive theology on Irenaeus's doctrine of mutual glorification is the title of the first part of his trilogy, *The Glory of the Lord*. This title is an oblique reference to the first half of Irenaeus's teaching that "the glory of God is a living man, and the life of man is the vision of God" (*AH* 4.20.7). He gives a further clue by referring to the second half of Irenaeus's teaching in the title of the first volume of *The Glory of the Lord*, *Seeing the Form*. At first this talk of the obviousness of revealed glory may seem like pious rhetoric, and perhaps even fideism. However, von Balthasar sees great sophistication in it. Irenaeus's theology is not irrational or anti-intellectual. Rather, it is profoundly perceptive because it recognizes that the human experience of God in Christ is an experience of both an irreducible otherness and an intimate closeness. In other words, Irenaeus understood that Christ reveals the paradoxical totality of reality as the creator and the creation mutually glorifying each other's freedom and difference across an ontological divide that cannot be explained in theories, whether they be based on dichotomous dualism or pantheistic monism:

> [T]he totality can only come into view where there is acceptance of (that is, in faith) the One who is bearing witness to himself. This is because the God who, in the testimony, is bearing witness to himself—for he is the prime Witness—remains sovereignly free, even when revealing himself; but he is so free that he is able to create beings who are themselves free, whose freedom he can bring to perfection by his own free self-revelation and self-giving. Thus we can indeed express this totality in the words "*Soli Deo Gloria*" provided we add that God's grace glorifies itself in his creation and revelation (Eph 1:6, 12, 14), that "the God of love did not need man, but man needed the glory of God" (*AH,* IV, 16, 6), that it is "the glory of man to abide in the service of God" (*AH,* IV, 14, 1), because "the glory of man is God" (*AH,* III, 20, 2); and for that very reason the "living man" who has been led to perfect freedom "is the glory of God" (*AH,* IV, 20, 7). Thus the starting point for beholding this (ever-greater) totality is that primal relationship between God and the world (man) that leaves

God, the Creator and Redeemer . . . free to allow free, created beings to exist.[17]

Irenaeus matters to von Balthasar, therefore, because he is a theologian of paradoxical unity-in-difference. He is a Christian theologian—one who dares to speak of God—but he nevertheless retains a rigorous commitment to ontological difference even when speaking of the unity of God and humanity in Christ. Moreover, Irenaeus insists not only that the "totality" of reality is fully revealed in the scandalous particularity of the incarnation but also that this revelation guarantees the different natures and genuinely unique personal identities of both the divine revealer and the created recipients of revelation.

Irenaeus's definition of faith is "seeing" this paradoxical unity-in-difference of God and creation in Christ.[18] Von Balthasar makes this point in the second volume of *Theologik, Die Wahrheit Gottes*, in the context of a discussion of religious paradox. Von Balthasar argues that true religious contemplation preserves the unity-in-difference between visible form and invisible splendor, knowing and not-knowing, positive revelation and negative mystery, and divine presence and divine transcendence. He credits Irenaeus with offering one of the clearest statements of how the paradox of the incarnate Word combines all these paradoxes:

Nobody has formulated this paradox more clearly than Irenaeus in his well known theses: "According to his splendor it is impossible to know God, for it is impossible that the Father can be measured. However, as regards His love, which shows us the way to God through obedience to his Word, we constantly learn the ever-greater immense splendor of God." Somewhere else Irenaeus says that God can be called a spirit that contains all reality, "but this Spirit is unlike the human spirit." Equally, Irenaeus writes, one could call God light, "but this light is not like the light which is innate to human nature. . . . God can be named according to these terms in regard to his love, but he is sensed as exceeding them in his splendor." [Irenaeus continues:] "According to his splendor he is unknown to all who have been made by him, for none has searched out his exalted height, . . . but as regards his love, he can always be known in the one through whom he created all things. Now this one is his Word, our Lord Jesus Christ, who in the last times was made a human among humans." The unveiling of God's splendor does not mean that God is totally exposed to a human gaze. However, neither does it imply that God's unveiling is only partial, as Irenaeus tries to show in the following way, "of course his Word protects the invisibility of the Father so that man never becomes a despiser of God; however, the Word protects the invisibility in such a way that humans are always given something that draws them towards God; he shows God to humans by dispensing many hints so that they do not lose all sense of God, completely fall away from him, and thus cease to exist."[19]

The theological program of saying and unsaying implied by this passage is remarkably complex. Irenaeus's method is to express paradox in terms of a christocentric doctrine of the *analogia entis*.[20] On von Balthasar's reading, for Irenaeus the incarnation teaches that analogy is always superior to both dichotomy and univocity in theological speech. The invisible God of the Jews remains invisible and transcendent even when he becomes fully known and present to humanity through the visible incarnation of the Word. Moreover, humanity learns the monotheistic lesson that the finite, temporal cosmic order is good in itself because it was both created and redeemed through an infinite, eternal, and uncreated divine Logos.[21] In becoming a perfect human being God revealed that created human beings were made in God's own image and can fulfill their creaturely potential through union with God. According to Irenaeus, Jesus also remained fully human in his union with God: the eternal Son experienced the full reality of finitude and death.[22] In other words, on von Balthasar's reading, Irenaeus was a Chalcedonian thinker long before Chalcedon. His assertion of the Chalcedonian paradox of "fully human and fully divine" is the basis of Irenaeus's doxological theology of the mutually affirming yet ontologically asymmetrical relationship between God and the creation.

Von Balthasar believes that an important point follows from Irenaeus's doctrine of the doxological paradox. The human being is a body-soul composite in its very nature as created, and consequently the redemption of the created order by the uncreated God will include the redemption of the whole human person without undoing its ontological status as created and finite. Von Balthasar consistently emphasizes this point as central to Irenaeus's understanding of true gnosis.[23] For Irenaeus, he writes, there is "[n]o natural salvation, no 'divine core' in man, no overlap between God and the world."[24] Therefore, the redemption of the created order in Christ implies not the negation but rather the healing of humanity in its finitude and creatureliness, and hence the perfection of the sensory, physical nature of human persons.[25] According to this Irenaean doxological conception of redemption, human persons have a central place in the cosmic order. They are the unique site of God's self-glorification, which occurs when they receptively open themselves in obedience to the artistic work of God the Father through his two hands, the Son and Spirit.[26] This Irenaean doxological conception of redemption is intrinsic to the New Testament's version of monotheism, von Balthasar believes, because it holds that God affirms humans in their human nature as finite, and humans in turn affirm God in God's nature as the divine artist of creation and redemption.[27]

## Distinguishing True Gnosis and False Gnosis

In Irenaeus's theology the opposite of true gnosis is false gnosis, or Gnosticism. Von Balthasar sees many modern theological trends as modern variants of second-century Gnostic doctrines, and he intends his entire theological project as a contemporary reprise of Irenaeus's project in *Against Heresies*.[28] Given the level of importance he attaches to the theological diagnosis and critique of Gnosticism, it is a major hermeneutic difficulty that von Balthasar does not present a maximally coherent definition of it. On the contrary, he often tends to use the terms "Gnostic" and "Gnosticism" more in a strategic and rhetorical sense than in a precise scholarly or historical sense. Throughout the trilogy he generally uses the terms "Gnostic" and "Gnosticism" to refer to types of religious thought that prioritize a priori knowledge over a posteriori concrete, particular historical experience. He broadly characterizes Gnosticism as a religious discourse that prioritizes explanatory theories about reality, focusing on human nature and/or the cosmos, over monotheistic christocentrism.[29] Rather than carefully defending this characterization with a detailed argument demonstrating that all types of religious thought that are neither monotheistic nor christocentric, or one but not the other, can be reduced to a theological common denominator under the heading "Gnosticism," von Balthasar simply assumes this is the case and proceeds accordingly.[30] Given the remarkable variety of nonmonotheistic and nonchristocenric religions, it is not surprising that von Balthasar's category "Gnostic" is extremely broad, general, and imprecise. His assertions about which religious movements and/or spiritual practices are in fact "Gnostic" generally require far more qualification and justification than he often supplies. Nevertheless, his strategic and rhetorical approach does have at the very least a minimal degree of conceptual coherence, and hence should not be dismissed without consideration.[31] If it is possible and theologically desirable to speak paradoxically of God and the world as fundamentally different yet mutually affirming, then it is reasonable to suggest that some religions, or elements of some religions, might fail to speak of the God-world relation in this way. Moreover, it is fair to assert from a Christian perspective that some religions are theologically deficient and deserving of critique. A doxological and sacramental critique, which is positive about both God and world, would fault religious claims made from a dichotomous perspective that deny the world's goodness and perhaps even deny God's goodness. From this admittedly extremely general position von Balthasar tries to formulate a theologically precise interpretation of Gnosticism capable of sharpening the contrast between monotheistic christocentrism and false gnosis. I will summarize this interpretation in six points.[32] The first two points focus on his assumption that there is an anti-Judaic bias in Gnosticism, and the remaining four focus on his assumption that there is an anti-Christian bias in Gnosticism. Of course these biases are not cleanly separated in von Balthasar's thinking because he believes Judaic monotheism and Christian christocentrism cannot, and should not, be separated. Therefore all six of his interpretive points can be summarized in his frequent accusation that Gnosticism attempts a "disincarnation" of human religion.[33]

First, Gnosticism prefers as the starting point for religious reflection a priori myths or speculative theories over the historically contingent events of the biblical narratives. Von Balthasar sometimes uses the terms "mythological" and "speculative" interchangeably because he assumes mythology is simply abstract theory disguised in a narrative form. Theory disguised as myth is easy to expose, he believes, because myth always relativizes the contingent events of history by interpreting them as disposable shells containing universal, ahistorical truths. These truths are always anthropocentric and/or cosmocentric but never authentically theocentric in a monotheistic sense. Consequently, the divine in Gnostic religions is a theoretical construct containing human elements such as tragedy, pain, and psychosis, and cosmic elements such as birth, death, seasonal cycles, and organic growth. It is an absolute axiom in all Gnostic religions, von Balthasar assumes, that an absolutely transcendent, omnipotent, infinite, and free God does not exist. This accounts for the profoundly anti-Judaic bias in most Gnostic theologies. Judaism holds that God entered history at a specific point in time to choose the Hebrew race as his assistants in a universally relevant process of human redemption. The logic of Gnosticism compels it to flatly reject all these Jewish claims as impossible.

Second, von Balthasar assumes that Gnosticism rejects the belief that the divine transcends the categories of human thinking, and hence believes that the divine can be conceptually mastered in a priori theories. This explains why Gnosticism always seeks to attain a perspective above the divine and the nondivine and thereby rationally explain or mythologically narrate their interactions. Such grandiose totalizing visions leave no room for the unexplainable Judaic paradoxes of a God who is both Other and non-Other, absent and present, infinite and finite, and eternal and temporal. Gnostic religions, contrary to what they might deceptively claim, consistently opt for the second pole in these paradoxes but never the first. In some cases this option takes form as metaphysical spirit-matter dualism, and in other cases it takes form as metaphysical pantheistic monism. In either case, von Balthasar contends, the extremes meet, and a Manichean scorn for all that is finite, material, and temporal results. The dualists see that which is nondivine as real but evil, and the monists see that which is nondivine as illusory and hence evil. When humans think they have captured the divine and the nondivine in a synoptic gaze, it is inevitable that they will interpret them in an inversely proportional relationship. Given that Gnostics construct the divine from human and cosmic elements, this dichotomous approach is a contradiction that accounts for many of the internal disagreements among various Gnostic sects.[34]

To illustrate these two points let us return for a moment to von Balthasar's reading of Irenaeus's aesthetic analogy of God as an artist who shapes creation and redemption with his two hands, the Son and the Spirit. Irenaeus's strict commitment to paradox in his doctrine of true gnosis prevents his aesthetic analogies from crystallizing into explanatory theories. It is sometimes easy to lose sight of this point in von Balthasar's enthusiastic presentation of Irenaeus's wide-frame perspective. He praises Irenaeus for his "all-embracing doctrine of history" that contextualizes "everything that happens" from creation to eschaton according to a trinitarian metanarrative of salvation history.[35] However, he damns Irenaeus's archnemesis, Valentinus, for assuming that poetic myths can synoptically include "everything" and thus achieve "philosophical and religious completeness."[36] The difference is that Irenaeus's grand holistic vision is based on authentic Johannine theology, whereas Valentinian Gnosticism's grandiose vision is not. Like the author of John's Gospel, von Balthasar explains, Irenaeus sees all of reality in light of the monotheistic God's trinitarian self-revelation in the incarnate Word. God's trinitarian self-revelation reveals that God's own inner being is characterized by paradoxical unity-in-difference; the oneness of God refers both to God's singularity and God's interior unity. God's activity in history would be no less respectful of difference and no less intent on unity than God's own trinitarian being. So when Irenaeus interprets history as a symphonic metanarrative flowing from creation through eschaton, his monotheistic trinitarianism allows him to avoid lapsing into an explanatory theory that puts God and world on the same ontological plane.[37] The ordered "beauty" of "Christ-form" in Irenaeus's theological aesthetics is qualitatively different than Valentinian Gnosticism's aesthetic theology. In Irenaeus, von Balthasar writes, we have an "illustration of the same historical law which governs the history of thought from Plato onwards: it is only the turning away from the 'aesthetic' and its conquest which provides the power and opens the eyes to see real beauty."[38] Because he is a biblical monotheist, however, Irenaeus understands and obeys this law better than Plato (and better than many of the church fathers). Irenaeus is a quintessentially antispecula-tive theologian, who rigorously maintains that humans cannot form a concept of God because there is an ontological difference between God and creation. Unlike Valentinian Gnosticism, von Balthasar contends, Irenaeus's metanarrative "everything" respects analogy and avoids uni-vocity. For Irenaeus, God the Father is like an artist and human history is like wet clay: the Father shapes the wet clay with his two hands, the Son and the Spirit.[39]

The third point in von Balthasar's interpretation of Gnosticism is that it is inherently disdainful of the Christian claim that the eternal God entered time, became incarnate in a human being, suffered, died, and was resurrected as a spiritual body. For Irenaeus, disdain is the defining characteristic of false gnosis. Von Balthasar asserts that for Irenaeus "all heresy can be reduced to the common denominator of a denial that the Word became flesh."[40] Moreover, for Irenaeus, von Balthasar contends, when this disdainful attitude toward the doctrine of the incarnation is coupled with an a priori metaphysics that disallows the possibility of a revelation of the eternal in time and spirit in matter, it becomes inevitable that the texts of the Hebrew and Christian Scriptures will undergo radical reinterpretation. These reinterpretations usually retain many elements of the canonical Scriptures but are revised so that they no longer retain the paradoxical form of monotheistic christocentrism.[41]

This leads to the fourth point of von Balthasar's interpretation. In order to preserve a doctrine of redemption, Gnosticism gives rise to a variety of alternative religious systems, all of which attempt to look behind the Christ presented by the canonical Scriptures and the church in order to explain the meaning of redemption in terms of a priori meta-physical laws.[42] In dualistic systems Christ saves by helping souls escape the material world. In monistic systems Christ saves by offering enlight-enment about the illusory nature of all differences. In either case, it is perfectly logical to see Christ as simply one of many possible teachers offering disciples one of many possible paths to salvation. Von Balthasar assumes that all types of Gnosticism view redemption as the attainment of an exclusively worldly and purely human religious knowledge by some type of technique. There is no real "salvation" in the strong sense because humans save themselves through their knowledge. The knowl-edge attained differs widely in content: one learns how to resign oneself to fate by embracing a tragic sense of life; another learns how to avoid fate and tragedy by freeing the soul from the body; still others learn how to gain control over fate and prevent tragedy through the use of tech-niques for controlling nature. In any case, there is no sense of divine love breaking into history from the outside to save humanity from fate.

Because Gnostic systems lack this sense, their doctrines of redemption are always on the verge of nihilism.[43]

The fifth point in von Balthasar's interpretation of Gnosticism is that in its abstract theories of redemption, the meaning of Christ is not the glorification of creation but instead the negation of creation in its materiality, temporality, and multiplicity. Often Gnostic religions merge the biblical stories of creation and fall so that the existence of the finite, material world can be interpreted as an accident or a mistake that Christ must rectify.[44] Christ points beyond the temporal realm of history toward a more ultimate, and thus more spiritually relevant, eternal realm of ahistorical existence to which humanity ought to return by decreating themselves.

Finally, the sixth point is that the spiritual practices derived from Gnostic theories of redemption can be highly elitist and extremely ascetic because they hold that salvation depends on attaining knowledge and mastery of special techniques for the soul to escape from the body and/or the realm of illusion. Their elitism tends to make Gnostic religions secretive and insular in contrast to the public and open nature of the church.[45] Hence for Gnostics the visible, institutional church could never really be the Body of Christ but rather is always the obstacle to knowledge of the true spiritual Christ.

### True Gnosis as Seeing and Participating in the *Corpus Triforme*

The next subtheme von Balthasar retrieves from Irenaeus is one that Irenaeus himself never explicitly formulated, but only presupposed. The theme is a *corpus triforme* interpretation of the incarnation. In the next chapter I will explain von Balthasar's aesthetic understanding of "form" (*Gestalt*). However, for the moment the term "form" should be interpreted as a sacramental symbol that expresses the unity-in-difference of God and creation. In von Balthasar's use, the Latin term *corpus triforme* means the one Word of God in three continuous, overlapping sacramental incarnations. The original source of the idea of a *corpus triforme* is Alexandrian Christology, which seems to have derived the concept from Origen.[46] Alexandrian *corpus triforme* Christology taught that the Body of Christ is a multidimensional phenomenon that includes Scripture, Eucharist, and church.[47] Von Balthasar basically accepts this theology of the incarnation but considers the tripartite Scripture-Eucharist-church articulation too potentially reductive because it risks setting the three embodiments of the one Word in opposition as three different bodies of Christ.[48] He argues that the three elements of the

CORPUS TRIFORME — SCRIPTURE, EUCHARIST, AND CHURCH

Body of Christ "are intertwined with one another and overlap" as "perceptible expressions" of the one Word.[49] His appeal for complexity and capaciousness is very revealing. A careful reading of von Balthasar's trilogy shows that he is undertaking a massive project to rehabilitate the doctrine of the *corpus triforme* by presenting it in its Irenaean version. His overarching goal is to preserve Irenaeus's emphasis on the organic "unfolding" of the one Body of Christ in a "multiplicity" of incarnational forms throughout history.[50] For Irenaeus, he explains, "Christ is both the fruit of the long organic development of the ages of the world and the one who descends freely from above; as both the fruit of the world and the fruit of the Father he has brought heaven and earth together and united the Spirit with man."[51] My contention is that this Christology spans von Balthasar's trilogy. Following what he takes to be Irenaeus's position, he sees the eternal Word's incarnation as a temporally extended "body" that includes both the old and new covenants. That is to say, he does not think that the life of Jesus, the writings of the New Testament, and the church's post-Easter sacramental worship tell the whole story of the incarnation. The writings of the Old Testament are part of the canon of Holy Scripture, he believes, because they testify to the first phase of the Word's incarnation. The life, death, and resurrection of Jesus constitute the second phase of the incarnation, and the development of the church—including the New Testament and eucharistic worship—constitutes the third phase of the incarnation. In this Irenaean version of *corpus triforme* Christology favored by von Balthasar, the phases of the incarnation occur in a chronological sequence, but the later phases are not ontologically separate from, nor do they supersede, the earlier ones. The incarnation is a cumulative process that can only be adequately understood if it is seen in its historical totality as the redemptive work of the Trinity in history. In other words, the Jewish community and the Christian community are linked by the life, death, and resurrection of Jesus as two phases of God's on-going incarnational process in history. All three phases are the human "form" of God in history, or the Word's *corpus triforme*.

Von Balthasar recognizes that Irenaeus never used the term *corpus triforme*, but he believes that Irenaeus's Christology constantly assumed and implicitly taught the dynamic historical concept to which this term refers. He believes this because he finds in Irenaeus the pervasive presence of three doctrines that are *corpus triforme* Christology's logical corollaries. He writes,

> Irenaeus is brought, by the very form of his thought . . . , to note the continuity above all between reality and ideal, between nature and grace, the work of the Father (creation) and the work of the Son and Spirit (the order

of salvation), between Adam and Christ, Old and New Covenant, world and Church. It is this point that is the source of his sober truth, his warming goodness and glowing beauty.[52]

The three Irenaean *corpus triforme* corollaries that are the most important to von Balthasar are: (1) the unity-in-difference of nature and grace expressed in the doxological doctrine of the redemption through deification of the creation *qua* creation; (2) the unity-in-difference of the old and new covenants expressed in the biblical canon of Old and New Testaments; (3) and the unity-in-difference of Christ and church expressed in the doctrine of a directly proportional relationship between the flourishing of the institutional church and the Holy Spirit's work in history. Von Balthasar both begins and ends his excursus on Irenaeus in *TD2* with a discussion of these corollaries. He begins the excursus by explaining that Irenaeus argues throughout the five books of *Against Heresies* for

> the unity of God and the economy of his Word (from Creation to the Incarnation); . . . the unity of history (as a unity of both Testaments); . . . the unity of mankind that has been achieved by Christ's Resurrection and the perfection of the world in and through God. . . . In all the books Irenaeus speaks of the unity of the individual human being, the unity of the human race and the (pneumatic and institutional) unity of the Church, in dependence upon Christ.[53]

He closes the excursus by discussing Irenaeus's teaching on the continuity between "creation and redemption," between the "historical ages" of the Old and New Covenants, and between "Christ-Spirit and the Church."[54] The presence of these continuities in Irenaeus necessarily means he assumes a *corpus triforme* doctrine of the incarnation. In other words, the presence of the corollaries indicates the presence of the axiom. One would only hold all of these views about continuity if one also thought of the incarnation as a three-phase process. As christological corollaries, all three sets of continuity are paradoxical because in each case the unity in question is a unity-in-difference. Therefore, on von Balthasar's reading, *corpus triforme* Christology fits in the Irenaean category of "true gnosis." In subsequent chapters I will discuss in detail the presence of the *corpus triforme* corollaries in von Balthasar's theology, suggesting in each case that the Irenaean doctrine of true gnosis determines his understanding of them.

### Divine Pedagogy: Training in the *Corpus Triforme*

Another subtheme from Irenaeus's theology that von Balthasar finds worthy of retrieval is his image of God as a teacher who leads humanity through a religious training process.[55] Von Balthasar finds this idea extremely compelling for two reasons. First, the image of God as a teacher with a gradual religious curriculum for humanity strongly affirms the process of history as the indispensable means and permanent context of revelation. This affirmation is the necessary presupposition for the entire *corpus triforme* doctrine of the incarnation, but it is especially relevant to the first corollary on the unity-in-difference of nature and grace. Von Balthasar contends that the absence of a pedagogical interpretation of history causes theologians who otherwise claim to believe in the doctrine of the Word's incarnation in Christ and redemption through deification to lose their theological bearings and drift into other-worldly thinking. Von Balthasar thinks this is particularly evident in Alexandrian theology.[56] For example, in his study of Origen, whom he considers an advocate of an insufficiently Irenaean version of *corpus triforme* Christology, von Balthasar offers this criticism: "The Alexandrian idea of the incarnation always reminds one of the action of a ball which, thrown from great height, in an instant strikes against the ground only to spring up from the earth with tremendous force and return to its starting point."[57] In contrast, he argues, the doctrine of the incarnation should be "compared with a wave of the sea which, rushing up on the flat beach, runs out, ever thinner and more transparent, and does not return to its source but sinks into the sand and disappears."[58] This latter image captures the difference von Balthasar sees between Irenaeus's theology of divine pedagogy and Alexandrian Neoplatonic theology. Contrary to the Alexandrian theological tendency, Irenaeus's theology of divine pedagogy assigns ultimate religious importance to the process of human history, and hence it forecloses all tendencies within Christian theology to minimize the value of temporal existence. The doctrine of divine pedagogy, von Balthasar agrees, allows a christocentric theology of salvation history to include and validate much of the content of Israel's history, as well as the general historical trajectory of all non-biblical religions. Given the mistaken association of von Balthasar's theology with Neoplatonic thought, his retrieval of the doctrine of divine pedagogy is a particularly important point.[59]

Second, von Balthasar sees that Irenaeus's doctrine of divine pedagogy is related to both his doxological theology of mutual glorification and his *corpus triforme* Christology. For Irenaeus, humans were created with the capacity to receive and express the creator into the created order.[60] Doxology is therefore natural but must nevertheless be learned because, in the fallen world, it is not automatic or self-evident. Moreover, humans need slow, gradual training in how to receive the divine Word in God's on-going incarnational process. This is training in dox-

ology because God's incarnation always maintains the unity-in-difference of the divine and the human. Indeed, throughout his volumes on
the old and the new covenants in *The Glory of the Lord*, von Balthasar
argues that God's efforts to train humanity in doxological receptivity to
the Word were piecemeal, painful for both students and teacher, and full
of catastrophic setbacks. Irenaeus understood the complexity of this historical training process because he understood the difficulty of spiritual
growth. Irenaeus believed that the Jewish God incarnates himself only
to the extent that his creaturely vessels soften themselves and submit to
being impressed by his hands.[61] The more open humanity is to God,
both as individuals and collectively, the greater the momentum of the
incarnational process in history. Humanity was built by God with a
capacity for God's indwelling, and hence was made to learn how to
incarnate God in a variety of human forms. The Jewish God who
teaches humans to activate their incarnational receptivity, Irenaeus
argues, conducts his lessons slowly with patience and gentleness. This is
because God wants time to become accustomed to dwelling in humans,
and humans need time to become accustomed to being indwelt by
God.[62] All three elements of *corpus triforme* required long periods of
"preliminary training": the old covenant was a *paidagōgos eis Christon*
while the Son waited patiently for his full historical moment to come.[63]
The church too is still in the process of training in receptivity to the Holy
Spirit; the incarnate presence of the Son in the church will gradually
undergo "intensification" until the eschaton.[64] Irenaeus thought the
church would eventually succeed in fully incarnating God in the entire
created order, but he did not think that this process would be smooth,
straight, and uninterrupted. He saw the Gnostic infiltration of the
church as a major obstacle to be overcome in this process; indeed, God's
curriculum of receptive obedience entailed learning how to properly
resist the Gnostic rebellion against training in monotheistic christocentrism. Von Balthasar remarks that for Irenaeus, "Gnosis was the opponent Christian thought needed in order fully to find itself."[65] This
opponent is both external and internal to the church but also internal to
each human heart. Irenaeus believed that learning to recognize it and
overcome it, even if this means interior crucifixion or actual martyrdom,
is the key to the church's genuine historical progress.[66]

### False Gnosis and the Dramatic Battle
### for the *Corpus Triforme*

The final subtheme von Balthasar retrieves from Irenaeus is a dramatic
interpretation of history in which the sacramental church of the *corpus*

*triforme* does battle with its Gnostic enemies. This theme dominates his theology in *Theo-Drama*. In *Theo-Drama* he analogically deploys dramatic theory to argue that conflict between the adherents of true gnosis and the adherents of false gnosis fundamentally characterizes history.[67] Just as the dramatic tension of a play results from the competition and struggle between protagonists and antagonists, so too the dramatic tension of salvation history results from the competition between Christ's disciples and his enemies' conflicting symbolic systems, contradictory claims of absolute truth, and rival conceptions of the good.[68] God's trinitarian revelation in Christ renders history a "battlefield" on which the faithful struggle to defend God's revelation against those who attempt to erase it and replace it with their own, purely human conceptions of the divine.[69] He sees this same dynamic at work with regard to Gnostic reinterpretations of the *corpus triforme*. Irenaeus's critique of his Gnostic contemporaries provides von Balthasar with a way to understand the strategy modern theologians use in their hostile reinterpretations of the *corpus triforme*. While disdaining its core beliefs in monotheism and the incarnation, Gnosticism attempts to retain some external elements of the *corpus triforme*. In the process it produces Christologies that resemble metaphysical philosophy more than doxological sacramentality. Because Christianity must come first before Gnostic thinkers can plagiarize and pervert the basic elements of its Christology, von Balthasar often refers to Gnostic religion as "post-Christian." Von Balthasar notes that Irenaeus clearly recognized that Christianity cannot avoid conflict with Gnostics who put God and humanity on the same ontological plane. Indeed, Irenaeus illustrated this in his own theological struggle against the various types of second-century Gnosticism. Von Balthasar takes Irenaeus's struggles as the point of departure for his own understanding of the "theodramatic war" inaugurated by the incarnation:

> Thus, with the advent of the grace of Christ, there is a heightening of the danger implied in freedom; in other words, the severity of judgment is increased. Now what is at stake is an eternal Yes or No (*AH*, IV, 28, 2; IV, 36, 4). Only after Christ does there arise that concentration of satanic and anti-Christian powers in world history (V, 25, 1; V, 26, 2; V, 27, 1-2, V, 29, 2). Thus the eschatological saving events do not overtake and supersede the drama of existence: they actually raise it to its real stature. If Christ, in his own temptation "recapitulated the warfare we wage with our enemy" (V, 21, 1), he has not dispensed us from fighting our own battle.[70]

Even prior to God's revelation in Christ, von Balthasar explains, history was already a battlefield insofar as God endeavored to educate a sinful, recalcitrant Israel in the doxological monotheism. The prophets exemplified the doxological ethos, and as a consequence, they frequently found themselves in an embattled relationship with the Israelite social and political order that similarly refused to internalize and practice God's law. Von Balthasar maintains that Israel's hostility toward the prophets not only continued into the new covenant but was exacerbated by God's provocative entry into the created order in the incarnation. Thus he characterizes the "theodrama" of salvation history in terms of a "Yes or No to the Incarnation of the Son of the Father"—a Yes or No to the mystery of Christ and its power to draw persons into active lives of discipleship.[71] Because Jesus claimed to be the sole source of absolute meaning and thus the only mediator of salvation, his mission was met by an extreme contempt that the New Testament authors considered an expression of humanity's sinfulness.[72] Von Balthasar contends the incarnation provokes contempt because it challenges human sinfulness by making it clear that only Jesus Christ, and not human nature in general, is divine and our salvation is totally dependent on him, not on our own unaided rational or spiritual resources.[73] This sinful hostility toward Jesus manifests itself as a concerted effort to obstruct Jesus' mission by redefining the meaning of salvation according to a rival set of values. The primary characteristic of this rival system is willed deviance from an aesthetic, sacramental, and doxological ethos. This deviance is motivated by two factors: (1) a preference for disembodied religiosity, and (2) a refusal to accept the idea that true human freedom comes only through the grace offered in Christ.[74] Confronted with this resistance to his mission, von Balthasar argues, Jesus must have understood himself to be "conducting a war" on behalf of the Father's doxological vision for creation.[75] Working from many new Testament texts, and from his reading of the book of Revelation in particular, von Balthasar makes the case that this theodramatic conflict between Christ and his enemies intensifies after Easter into a conflict between the sacramental church and anti-ecclesial forces dedicated to the inherently reactionary project of negating the incarnation.[76]

According to von Balthasar this conflict sets the pattern for all post-Easter history. He argues that over the course of time there was an "increasing polarization" between the church's mission and "the satanic counter-strategy" of its enemies; this conflict eventually became a full "theodramatic war" between the Christ-church and the Antichrist.[77] This war illustrates, von Balthasar asserts, that there is a stark dichotomy between history before Christ and history after him, with the latter being a state of perpetual warfare between the Christian protagonists and the "post-Christian" antagonists. Indeed, this state of perpetual warfare is "the fundamental law of post-Christian world history."[78] He insists that the church, insofar as it carries out its mission of sacramentally extending the incarnation into history, will always and necessarily be engaged in "the most bitter struggle" with those who assert a No to the incarnation and who attempt to subvert it with disincarnating "counterdesigns."[79] The church is inevitably drawn into the "theodramatic war" because it cannot avoid challenging Gnosticism's hostile reinterpretations of Christ.

Throughout *Theo-Drama*, von Balthasar discusses the theologies of the post-Christian antagonists of the *corpus triforme* in terms of the six points of Gnostic discourse outlined above. Moreover, he also refines the category of false gnosis by highlighting its anti-Judaic "epic" theology of history. Corresponding to the two types of Gnosticism, there are two extreme types of "epic" theology constantly vying for supremacy in post-Christian religion. Von Balthasar describes these two types of "epic" theology as follows:

> At one extreme, there is the mythological view in which God (or the gods) is embroiled in the world drama, which, with its own laws of operation, thus constitutes a third level of reality above God and man; at the other extreme, God is seen as dwelling in philosophical sublimity above the vicissitudes of the world, which prevent him from entering the dramatic action.[80]

Von Balthasar believes Irenaeus was familiar with and critical of both poles of epic theology.[81] Few shared Irenaeus's perceptiveness, however, because epic theology concealed itself well. True to their Gnostic identity, epic theologians did not announce their disdain for biblical revelation and preference for abstract speculation. Instead they postured as adherents of biblical revelation, assigning themselves the task of being its objective narrators.[82] Von Balthasar charges that the idea that revelation can be narrated objectively is post-Christian in that it assumes God's interactions with humanity can be surveyed from a higher, neutral perspective. As a result of this assumption, epic theologians eviscerate the historicity of the Christ-event and encourage a detached ethos of "calm resignation" in the face of history's tragedies and tumult.[83] Moreover, there is a strong proclivity in epic theology to ground this ethos of resignation in an anthropological theory that equates a timeless dimension of existence with the spiritual core of human nature. This anthropology obviously fosters a nondramatic interpretation of existence because it valorizes the resigned passivity of a pure spiritual interiority over active involvement with the ultimately illusory persons and events in history.

The Christian answer to epic theology is therefore a dramatic theology of existence. Von Balthasar revives the ancient philosophical images of the "theater of the world" and the "world stage" in order to interpret salvation history and the battle between true and false gnosis as a dramatic form. According to von Balthasar these images express a central philosophical and religious theme latent in all of Western theater from ancient Greece through today: the ultimate meaning of humanity's existence in history can be interpreted in terms of a "dramatic play before the eyes of the gods."[84] He uses the theme of "dramatic tension" to analogically indicate the highly dramatic, agonistic struggle between Christianity and its historical rival, post-Christian Gnosticism. Dramatic tension helps distinguish true from false gnosis for two reasons. First, dramatic tension presupposes a theatrical form that orders both dramatic action and narrative meaning within a temporal horizon. Second, dramatic tension presupposes that there are rival players acting out a conflict. Although von Balthasar does think this understanding of existence has its dangers,[85] he also thinks it can be an extremely valuable resource for applying Irenaeus's distinction between true and false gnosis in a Christian theology of history. He believes that this defensive weapon must be unsheathed today. Epic theology has been increasingly prevalent in modern Christian discourse; the dominant intellectual assumptions in the West have deep roots in ancient Gnosticism. Indeed, he considers modern post-Christian discourse a thinly disguised reprise of ancient Gnostic rejections of Jesus' claim to be the fulfillment of all pre-Christian religion.[86] Yet in rejecting this claim Gnostic thinkers in the second century did not completely ignore Jesus. Rather they radically reinterpreted him according to anti-Judaic and anti-incarnational assumptions.[87] Von Balthasar is convinced that this practice continues today. But the dramatis personae from the second century's battles are no longer easily recognizable. The protagonists and antagonists in the battle for the *corpus triforme* are often so tangled together in modern theological debates that only a trained eye can distinguish them. Irenaeus had such an eye in the second century, von Balthasar believes. He praises him for drawing "clear lines" between Christianity and Gnostic theologies.[88] Von Balthasar thinks he too sees clearly the true identities of today's combatants in the theodramatic war. Like Irenaeus, he assigns himself the task of defining them.

### Notes

1. See *SI*, 4–11; *GL2*, 31–94; and *TD2*, 140–49.

2. It would be reductive to completely ignore nonpatristic thinkers as influences on his theology. For example, there are nine nonpatristic figures whose theological "styles" are anthologized in *GL2* and *GL3*. Each could conceivably function as a resource for interpreting his theology. They are Anselm, Bonaventure, Dante, John

of the Cross, Pascal, Hamann, Soloviev, Hopkins, and Péguy. Although Ignatius of Loyola is missing from the anthology of *GL2* and *GL3*, he too must be counted as a major influence. For a very persuasive and insightful discussion of the influence of Maximus Confessor and Ignatius of Loyola on von Balthasar's theology, see Mark A. McIntosh, *Christology from Within: Spirituality and the Incarnation in Hans Urs von Balthasar* (Notre Dame: University of Notre Dame Press, 1996). If primacy and overall regulative influence are the issues, however, then Irenaeus's theology has a level of importance that seems to surpass all these theologians in providing the interpretive paradigm for von Balthasar's theology.

3. *MWR*, 67.

4. Von Balthasar acknowledges that Irenaeus's theology "may not be worked out to the last technical detail. . . ." (*SI*, 11).

5. *GL2*, 17.

6. For instance, he argues that "Immediately after [Irenaeus's] death, the clear lines which he drew become blurred. Tertullian, who had written a powerful treatise 'On the Flesh of Christ', defected to the 'spiritual Church' of the Montanists, thereby subscribing to one of the fundamental principles of Gnosticism. Not long after, the great Alexandrians Clement and Origen attempted to annex to Christian theology as much as they could of the speculative property of Gnosticism, and behind that, of Middle Platonism" (*SI*, 8).

7. *SI,* 8; *GL2*, 31.

8. *GL2*, 45.

9. Ibid.

10. Ibid., 78.

11. Ibid., 78–79.

12. Ibid., 49.

13. Ibid., 50, 43.

14. Ibid., 60.

15. Ibid., 44.

16. Ibid., 74. For Irenaeus "the central fact of the Incarnation of the Word" is the perfection of humanity and the created order in their finite particularity; here "the greatest thing possible is achieved: the total glorification of God and of man in God (*AH* 4.17.6)." *TD2*, 149.

17. *TD2*, 118.

18. See *GL2*, 45, 48. See also *TD2*, 141–42. Von Balthasar argues that the "leitmotif" of *Against Heresies* is that "God, who is ever-greater, who, 'according to his greatness and his ineffable glory . . . is incomprehensible, and who, according to his almighty power, even grants the divine vision to those who love him' (*AH*, IV, 20, 5). . . . Both aspects are necessary, neither render the other superfluous. The Father must remain invisible, 'lest man should come to despise God, and so that he sees space ahead of him for his further progress'; but he must not remain so invisible 'that man, totally deprived of God, should cease to be himself' (*AH*, IV, 20, 7). The invisible Father renders himself visible in his Word and Son, who reveals him to us as the loving Father and Creator of all things . . ." (141).

19. *TL2*, 63–64. See also *TL1*, 143–44; *GL2*, 46.

20. *TD2*, 141, 146.

21. *GL2*, 39, 65–66. Cf. *TD2*, 146–47.

22. *TD2*, 143–44.

23. *GL2*, 58, 64–66, 74.

24. Ibid., 62.

25. Von Balthasar contends in *Theologik* that Irenaeus interpreted the bodily resurrection of Christ in these terms in order to oppose all spiritualizing interpretations of redemption as an escape from the body: "Irenaeus emphasizes against spiritualizing Gnostics the worth of the flesh. 'Christ goes with his flesh to heaven in order to recapitulate all things and to resurrect all human flesh.' (*Adv. Haer.* I, 10, 1)" (*TL2*, 276).

26. "In his anti-Gnostic theology Irenaeus put the living man at the center of everything, not as a microcosm of it, but as God's primary dialogue partner. Man is God's work of art, formed by the Father through the hands of his Son and Spirit from the beginning of salvation history. (Irenaeus: 'The angels are not the center of creation, but rather they play an accompanying and serving role.') This dialogue completes itself slowly and steadily through the ages, so that humans, who are in themselves weak and 'in need of God's glory,' can participate in God's glory and become 'living persons to the glory of God'" (*TL1*, 207).

27. *GL2*, 74–75.

28. See *SI*, 4–11. He refers to "the continuing relevance of the second-century struggle against Gnosticism" and asserts that Gnostic assumptions currently permeate both Western culture and Western Christianity. He writes, "The Word of God first clashed with the Gnostic myth in the second century, and nowhere more dramatically than in the work of Irenaeus. Given the fantastic forms of the mythology of the time it all seems exotically remote. In fact, when we look more closely we can see that we are dealing with a confrontation which has never ended and is constantly assuming new forms. The confusion [in Gnosticism] between the spirit of man and the Spirit of God characterizes all of mankind's more ambitious religious and philosophical speculations and mysticisms." (*SI*, 4–5; cf. 8). See also *TD4*, where von Balthasar draws an analogy between the ecclesial and theological situation in the late twentieth century with Irenaeus's second-century struggle against Gnosticism: "The situation is somewhat similar to Irenaeus' campaign against Gnosticism, but it is more acute insofar as the Gnostic sects that claim to have the correct interpretation are no longer outside the Church: they are inside her, claiming to have the proper scientific tools and to be in authentic communication with all religions and world views. . . . A 'battle of the Logos' within the *Catholica* herself is today unavoidable" (*TD4*, 460).

29. The adjective "monotheism" is a necessary qualifier because von Balthasar believes that Gnostic thinkers often claim to be christocentric, but their interpretation of "Christ" turns out to be based more on monistic or dualistic assumptions than on biblical ones.

30. In this sense he is following Henri de Lubac's rhetorical practice in *Catholicism* of categorizing all religions in history as either "biblical" or "pagan." This simplistic categorization makes it difficult to interpret religions such as Islam, which is monotheistic but not christocentric, and Mormonism, which is christocentric but not monotheistic.

31. For example, it is simply too dismissive to suggest, as does Frans Jozef van Beeck, that von Balthasar's "arrogant, uninformed disparagement of 'Eastern' forms of prayer, lumped together for mere polemical convenience, is best forgotten" (*God Encountered: A Contemporary Catholic Systematic Theology: Volume Two/1: The Revelation of the Glory* [Collegeville: Liturgical Press, 1993], 7).

32. The following sketch is a synthesis constructed from my reading of the trilogy as a whole. For a concise discussion containing many elements in my synthesis, the reader should start with *The Scandal of the Incarnation*, 1–7. Then for examples

from the *The Glory of the Lord* where von Balthasar uses the terms "gnosis," "Gnostic," and "Gnosticism" in the general sense under discussion here, the reader should see *GL1*, 133, 138–39, 504, 618; *GL2*, 33–44, 59, 62; *GL4*, 31, 37–38; *GL6*, 324, 342; and *GL7*, 13–14, 86–87, 103–4, 105–6, 107, 111–12, 129, 178, 214–15, 293–94, 449, 453–54, 473, 482, 497, 510.

33. See *TD4*, 145, 411, 412, 445, 452.

34. *GL2*, 41.

35. Ibid., 148, 140. Of course, Irenaeus is not the first Christian to identify faith with a panoramic knowledge of God, world, and redemption. Von Balthasar traces the identification of holistic "gnosis" with faith to the New Testament theologies of Paul and John (*GL1*, 131–36). For both Paul and John, von Balthasar contends, gnosis belongs to the content of faith as "the interior understanding of faith, the insight into the mystery of faith itself" (ibid., 136). He also points to Alexandrian theology in general, and in Origen's theology in particular, as teaching a doctrine of faith as true gnosis (*GL1*, 136–39).

36. *GL2*, 37.

37. See *GL2*, 43, 60–62, 66, 76–77.

38. *GL2*, 32.

39. See ibid., 73, 82, 71, 77.

40. *GL2*, 42; cf. *GL4*, 37; *GL7*, 105–7, 111–12, 400, 453–54, 473, 510–13.

41. Von Balthasar argues that Irenaeus recognized that Gnostic thought used the "tools and materials of the Bible [to erect] a totally un-Christian structure of the highest intellectual and religious quality and [win] over many Christians . . ." (*GL2*, 32). Cf. *GL2*, 41–42; *GL1*, 618.

42. "Faced with man's ambivalence and all the suffering in the world, they [Gnostics] try by means of speculation to 'get behind' the Christian mystery of the God-man who, in pure freedom and love, was crucified for us; they apprehend the abyss which the Cross opens up between sheer divine love and sheer God-forsaken-ness, but they attempt to trace it back to a source in the Absolute, so rendering it accessible to reason. This suppression of Christian faith by speculation begins as early as the second century in the grand manner of post-Christian Gnosticism . . ." (*TD2*, 419). For Irenaeus, von Balthasar writes, "it is the greatest possible slight to God to disparage the historical self-revelation of his immeasurable love and to look behind it for a non-existent access to the unknown God" (*GL2*, 61).

43. Cf. *GL4*, 38; *GL5*, 249; *GL7*, 7.

44. *SI*, 2; *GL2*, 34–35.

45. *SI*, 10.

46. In *TD2*, 111–12 von Balthasar identifies Origen as a proponent of *corpus triforme* Christology. For a brief discussion of the concept of the *corpus triforme* (sometimes also referred to in patristic writings as the *triplex modus corporis Christi*), see de Lubac's *Catholicism*, 100. It must also be noted here that von Balthasar also finds a version of this *corpus triforme* theology of the incarnation in the theology of Henri de Lubac. See von Balthasar's *THdL*, 35ff., and passim. Given his positive appraisal of his theology as a whole, it seems likely that de Lubac's understanding of patristic and mediaeval *corpus triforme* Christologies functions to some degree as a guide in von Balthasar's interpretation of the Alexandrian tradition.

47. *GL1* 528–30. *TD2*, 111–12.

48. *GL1*, 531. This point helps us understand why von Balthasar insists that the

theology of the medieval Byzantine iconoclasts was not entirely without merit. See *GL1*, 41.

49. Ibid.

50. Ibid., 529.

51. *GL2*, 68.

52. *GL2*, 44.

53. *TD2*, 140. Also, in the section immediately before this excursus on Irenaeus von Balthasar points out the presence of *corpus triforme* Christology in Origen. He mentions Origen's claim that there is an "enfleshing" of the Logos in the modes of Scripture, the physical body of Jesus, and in the eucharistic body of the church (ibid., 111–12).

54. Ibid., 146–48.

55. *GL2*, 79–81.

56. Ibid., 43, 51, 55–58, 60, 92–93.

57. Von Balthasar, *Origen: Spirit and Fire: A Thematic Anthology of His Writings*, trans. Robert J. Daly (Washington, D.C.: Catholic University of America, 1984), 17.

58. Ibid., 18.

59. In a taxonomic discussion of contemporary theologians, David Tracy incorrectly places von Balthasar in the category of modern speculative theologians who are committed to the Christian Neoplatonic tradition. See *Analogical Imagination* (New York: Crossroad, 1981), 380.

60. For Irenaeus, von Balthasar explains, humans have a *"capere et portare Deum"* (*GL2*, 57, 74–76).

61. *GL2*, 75–76.

62. Ibid., 77–80.

63. Ibid., 81.

64. Ibid., 85, 87–90. Even in the eschaton, von Balthasar points out, Irenaeus believes there will be a process of becoming "accustomed" to eternity. This process will take place in a thousand-year kingdom following the general resurrection (79).

65. Ibid., 32.

66. Ibid., 69.

67. *TD1*, 9. The church's general failure to grasp the connection between aesthetics and dramatics resulted in a long and, from von Balthasar's perspective, unfortunate tradition of ecclesial hostility and suspicion toward the theater (*TD1*, 89–112).

68. Cf. *TD1*, 74, 413–24.

69. *TD2*, 33–35.

70. *TD2*, 145. Von Balthasar draws an analogy between the ecclesial and theological situation in the late twentieth century with Irenaeus's second-century struggle against Gnosticism: "The situation is somewhat similar to Irenaeus' campaign against Gnosticism, but it is more acute insofar as the Gnostic sects that claim to have the correct interpretation are no longer outside the church: they are inside her, claiming to have the proper scientific tools and to be in authentic communication with all religions and world views. . . . A 'battle of the Logos' within the *Catholica* herself is today unavoidable" (*TD4*, 460).

71. *TD4*, 181.

72. Ibid., 430.

73. *TD2*, 411.

74. See *TD4*, 145, 411–12, 445, 452 for von Balthasar's explicit references to the "disincarnation" of religion. With regard to the refusal to accept the necessary connection between grace and freedom, von Balthasar explains that "this desire to exercise freedom on the basis of one's *own* source, is the sin that comes into full consciousness through the provocation offered by Jesus." *TD4*, 435.

75. *TD2*, 165. See also *TD4*, 439.

76. For discussions of this theme in *Theo-Drama*, see *TD2*, 417–28; *TD3*, 391–401; *TD4*, 20, 56ff., 64ff., 427–503. All of von Balthasar's exegetical work with the book of Revelation in *Theo-Drama* is intended to give scriptural support to his theological articulation of this theme. See *TD4*, 15–58.

77. *TD4*, 21, 463. It is important to note here that for von Balthasar this "theo-dramatic war" does not imply a destructive and violent holy war but instead a constructive and peaceful attempt to incarnate in the world a distinctively sacramental religious ethos. See *TD2*, 35.

78. *TD4*, 21.

79. Ibid., 428–31.

80. *TD2*, 9.

81. *TD1*, 131.

82. Cf. *TD2*, 39–51, 53–57. Cf. *TD4*, 62; cf. *TD2*, 77–89.

83. Ibid., 59.

84. *TD1*, 136.

85. The two main dangers are the deist notion of a spectator deity and a deterministic conception of human persons as merely puppets dancing on strings pulled by the gods (*TD1*, 69, 137, 255).

86. See *TD4*, 442–43, 445–46, 457–64.

87. Ibid., 66.

88. *SI*, 8.

V. B = gnosis is trying to find God — outside scripture, Eucharist, and church

- Faith, hope, and love has been replaced by knowledge → this is bad!
- must encounter God in tangible forms.

# PART TWO

## *CORPUS TRIFORME* COROLLARIES

*[handwritten margin note, top right: Corollary — a proposition inferred immediately from a proved proposition & little or no additional proof]*

In the following three chapters I will explore in detail von Balthasar's definition of the Christian protagonist in the theodramatic war for the *corpus triforme*. My goal is to show that his definition demonstrates the Irenaean logic guiding his theology. It is the doxa-logic of the mutual glorification of God and world. This logic is intertwined with a *corpus triforme* Christology. Von Balthasar follows Irenaeus's lead in asserting this Christology's three logical corollaries: the unity of the old and new covenants, the unity of creation and redemption, and the unity of the Spirit of the risen Christ and the institutional church.[1] Thus, the focus of the following three chapters will be on the presence of these three *corpus triforme* corollaries in von Balthasar's theology. *[handwritten margin note: 3 logical corollaries]*

I will focus on his interpretation of the Old and New Testaments, giving primary attention to *GL6* and *GL7*. My working assumption is that these two volumes most clearly represent von Balthasar's thinking about the Christian protagonist in the theodrama of history. In *GL7* von Balthasar presents his theological interpretation of the entire New Testament. It is clearly Irenaean. He credits St. Paul in 1 Cor. 2:6–16 with supplying the "fundamental thesis" guiding his hermeneutic approach to the New Testament. Yet in commenting on this passage Irenaeus's doxological theology actually seems to be his hermeneutic guide. He comments that, for Paul, God's plan for creation is neither that God will glorify God nor that humanity will possess an absolute knowledge of God. Rather, God will glorify human persons by giving them the gifts of freedom and spiritual understanding, thereby allowing them to become

*[handwritten note at bottom: GL6+7: The Glory of the Lord vol. 6 (OT) + 7 (NT)]*

wholly radiant in divine light without thereby ceasing to be personal and finite.[2] This is a fascinating claim because von Balthasar is obviously reading this Pauline passage—and thus all of the New Testament, and hence all of the Old Testament because he interprets it in light of the New Testament—through an Irenaean lens. He suggests the Irenaean connection himself in the way he highlights Paul's use of the phrase "our glory" (1 Cor. 2:7), interpreting it in terms of "the glorification of man in God."[3]

Whether or not von Balthasar reads Scripture "correctly," however that may be defined, does not concern me here. I understand that many readers may be shocked and horrified by what seems to be an uncritical handling of biblical texts. My aim, however, is neither to defend nor to criticize von Balthasar's exegetical and hermeneutic methods. My aim is simply to present his claims and expose for scholarly reflection their internal logic.

### Notes

1. *TD2*, 146–48.

2. *GL7*, 524–25.

3. Ibid., 526. See also *AH* 4.17.6; 4.14.1; 4.20.7. The implicit connection here becomes explicit in *Theo-Drama* when he cites Irenaeus quoting Paul in 1 Cor. 2:15. In his excursus on *Against Heresies*, von Balthasar writes, "It sounds like a victory chant when, in a masterful passage, Irenaeus applies Paul's dictum [in 1 Cor. 2:15], 'The spiritual man judges all things but is himself judged by no one' to the Catholic position vis-à-vis all forms of heresy . . ." (*TD2*, 140).

# Chapter II

# Creation and Redemption

Von Balthasar thinks that the first corollary of the Irenaean version of *corpus triforme* Christology is that creation and redemption are united. This unity implies a highly sacramental interpretation of creation's natural potential in general and of human potential in particular. Operating doxologically, grace perfects the created order by actualizing its potential for receiving and sacramentally expressing the divine Word. Insofar as redemption is the fulfillment of creation's sacramental potential by uncreated grace, the unity of creation and redemption remains a unity-in-difference. For von Balthasar, therefore, the first corollary of the *corpus triforme* is analogically related to the paradoxes expressed by the Councils of Chalcedon (451) and Third Constantinople (681) in their teachings that Jesus has fully human and fully divine natures and wills that are united without confusion, separation, division, or change.

### Against Neoscholasticism's Rationalist Theory of Grace

It would be difficult to overestimate the influence of de Lubac's *ressourcement* vision on von Balthasar's theology, particularly on his interpretation of and efforts to retrieve Irenaeus. For von Balthasar, the specific issues in the *nouvelle théologie* debate symbolized a fundamental disagreement between Catholic intellectuals about the proper relationship between concept (*Begriff*) and symbol (*Vorstellung*) in theology. In other words, he viewed the underlying issue in the *nouvelle théologie* controversy as follows: what would be the primary source and guide for theological reflection: (a) an abstract and purely theoretical rationalism that privileged neutral concepts; or (b) a faithful life directly imbued by grace through active personal engagement with the symbolic narrative of the Bible and the church's sacramental rituals? For von Balthasar, (a) corresponds to the illegitimate attempt to explain concrete revelation to neutral outsiders in universal terms, whereas (b) corresponds to the legitimate attempt to demonstrate the universal truth of Christianity through concrete gestures and lived example. Given his reading of Irenaeus, it seems fair to assume that he generally interpreted neoscholasticism as a revival, in form but not content, of ancient Gnosticism. In neoscholasticism he saw theologians who simply refused to *see* the image of God in Christ, who insisted on thinking outside the context of sacramental and liturgical experience. These theologians, he believed, were engaged in a misguided quest for maximal intellectual precision, and hence they gave primacy in their thinking to abstract rationalistic theories formulated in neutral concepts isolated from biblical and sacramental-liturgical symbols. Recall how starkly he framed the issue in the *nouvelle théologie* controversy: "With *Surnaturel* . . . a young David comes onto the field against the Goliath of modern rationalization and reduction to logic of the Christian mystery."[1] The following highly polemical passage from *Theo-Drama* about the origins and dangers of modern theological "rationalism" frames the issue in a similarly Manichean way:

> . . . the Reformation and the religious disputes that followed it brought about the final victory of rationalism [in Christianity]: now man and his reason were exalted as the measuring rod of a sustainable religion—even of one calling itself Christian—with the result that mystery and dogma, along with the authority that took responsibility for them, were evacuated from the Christian faith. This rational faith, which is the product of the religious wars, then mingles with another movement that comes straight from a scholasticism that is undergoing progressive collapse. Whereas High Scholasticism had made the mistake of thinking that it had to give an appropriate answer to every inquisitive question, however untheological,[2] *now, in the theology of its imitators,* [emphasis added] such questions are multiplied beyond all bounds; the answers become more and more hair-splitting as the legitimate rational method of a Thomas is increasingly distorted into an unbearable rationalism by the overweening deduction of a "theology of conclusions." G. Siewerth, in his presentation of this process, spoke of it "advancing into the divine ground," because the ratio, abandoning all restraint, thinks itself empowered and authorized to plumb the ultimate mysteries of God. In the end, this leads to Hegel's God, who is without all mystery: behold the door to atheism.[3]

Von Balthasar's point here is not that neoscholasticism denied the existence or mysteriousness of God. On the contrary, its attempt to construct an a priori explanatory system that denied regulative primacy to nonexplanatory symbols perverted Catholic theology with rationalism. The neoscholastics, he believed, were overly fond of pure doctrinal propositions and insufficiently aware of the origins of all doctrine in sacramental and liturgical life. Von Balthasar believes this "rationalist" grant of primacy to pure concepts over symbols inevitably leads to heterodox theological claims, and therefore is fatal to Catholicism.

In von Balthasar's telling of the story, official Catholic theology in the modern period gradually succumbs to depravity.[4] Under the warping influence of neoscholasticism, official Catholic theology in the nineteenth and first half of the twentieth century (which ironically prided itself on being "anti-Modernist"), almost succeeded in eliminating from theological discussions of grace any reference to God's glory. This trend in modern Catholic theology greatly alarmed von Balthasar, given that, as he notes in *The Glory of the Lord*, the New Testament uses the word "glory" 116 times and the phrase "to glorify" over 60 times.[5] Following St. Paul's theology, von Balthasar identifies "glory" in the New Testament with the "mystery" of God's glory revealed by the incarnate Word (Eph. 1:3-10). Paul's use of the word "mystery" as a synonym for "glory" indicates that his understanding of it differs greatly from neoscholasticism's definition of mystery as that which must simply be believed because it is unexplainable. Von Balthasar agrees that divine glory is a "cipher" that cannot be explained in a theory.[6] Hence, he argues, the glory of God cannot be mastered by theoretical systems.[7] Although these claims have a fideistic ring, von Balthasar's intentions are quite contrary to fideism. Fideism is a product of rationalism because it values propositional truth claims whose meaning is accessible to any rational person irrespective of ritual initiation and spiritual commitment.[8] In other words, fideism's allegiance to abstract truth claims breaks the cardinal rule of orthodox Christology in that it does not allow Christ to be the flesh and blood "image" of God for humans who are biased enough to look at it seriously. For von Balthasar, God's glory is fully revealed in Christ, who is the "image" or symbol (*Vorstellung*) not the abstract concept (*Begriff*) of the invisible God (see Col. 1:15). In a sarcastic swipe at neoscholastic notions of mystery, he observes, "A surprising thing: nowhere does Jesus demand of his disciples that they believe things which are simply inaccessible to their understanding."[9] Jesus does demand, however, that his disciples overcome their blindness and see his glory.[10] This blindness is in most cases self-inflicted. It is the result of "pure prejudices" against the "scandal" of the incarnation: various types of false gnosis assume that the glory of Christ "*cannot* be what it claims to be" and hence "cannot withstand looking at the form of Christ."[11] It is the essence of heresy to filter and "screen" the image of Christ so as more easily to accept that which is "reasonable" and to reject what is not.[12] God's glory in Christ, however, is paradoxical and disruptive of the prejudices of a priori reason. Von Balthasar writes, ". . . it is not our concern to get a secure place to stand, but rather to get sight of what cannot be securely grasped, and this must remain the event of Jesus Christ; woe to the Christian who would not stand daily speechless before this event! If this event truly is what the church believes, then it can be mastered through no methodology. . . ."[13] Standing "speechless" before the image of God in Christ allows its glory to speak. When humans see and listen (von Balthasar is generally careless in switching back and forth between visual and auditory metaphors) it tells us that God is beyond human explanations.

Von Balthasar finds traditional warrant for this christological assertion in the Fourth Lateran Council's teaching that however great the similarity between God and creatures, there is always an ever-greater dissimilarity.[14] He interprets this doctrine as mandating that theology always situate "negative theology" within the wider frame of a "theology of revelation, in which God 'appears' unreservedly . . . in his ever-greater incomprehensibility."[15] This is essentially a sacramental injunction: only the sacramental image of Christ reveals the mysterious depths of God. Von Balthasar thinks neoscholastic theology never understood this point because it did not understand the principle of sacramentality latent in the Christian doctrine of the incarnation. Similar to Irenaeus's interpretation of the ancient Gnostics who "refuse to see,"[16] von Balthasar faults the neoscholastic theologians and all their theological descendants for constantly substituting human theories for the "phenomenon" of Christ's sacramental glory.

> Our choice to begin with "glory" is comparable to what was once called apologetics or, if you will, fundamental theology. Our idea was that today's positivistic, atheistic man, who has become blind not only to theology but even to philosophy, needed to be confronted with the phenomenon of Christ and, therein, to learn to "see" again—which is to say, to experience the unclassifiable, total otherness of Christ as the outshining of God's sublimity and glory. . . . This option seemed even more needful given its underdeveloped role in contemporary, postconciliar attempts to reform Catholic theology, where it tends to get resubmerged under the rationalism with which many exegetical accounts of the phenomenon of Christ simply replace the older rationalism of the Neoscholastics.[17]

In the case of the neoscholastics, this "rationalism" expressed itself in the assumption that positive revelation and mystery are mutually exclusive. Von Balthasar rejects this assumption.

> . . . the first and pre-eminent intention of the self-revealing God is, precisely, really to reveal himself, really to become comprehensible to the world as far as is possible. If his first intention were to make those who believe in him assent to a number of impenetrable truths, this would surely be unworthy of God and it would contradict the very concept of revelation. To be sure, if God is to become manifest in his nature as God, then a necessary part of this manifestation is his eternal incomprehensi-

bility: *si comprehendis, non est Deus.* But here "incomprehensibility" does not mean a negative determination of what one does not know, but rather a positive and almost "seen" and understood property of him whom one knows.[18]

In making this claim, von Balthasar is insisting that any theology of mystery must be governed by a theology of revelation based on "seeing" the sacramental image of Christ, not merely believing fideistic propositions about him.[19]

### The Revelation of God's Plan:
### The Mystery of Glory

What then does von Balthasar mean by seeing the glory of God in the image of Christ? In the passage from Ephesians cited earlier, Paul identifies the "mystery" of God with "the plan he was pleased to decree in Christ, to be carried out in the fullness of time: namely, to bring all things in the heavens and on earth into unity under Christ's headship" (1:10). All of von Balthasar's teachings on the mystery of God's glory should be read in light of Paul's doctrine of mystery (cf. Rom. 8:28-39). Von Balthasar argues that God's plan can be narrated as a trinitarian metanarrative of history, but it cannot be explained conceptually. In Christ, God reveals the glory of his inner-trinitarian life, which means God reveals his own internal unity-in-difference as three persons in one Godhead. In revealing this "*doxa*" God reveals the meaning of history as the opening of this trinitarian life for participation by humanity.[20] This participation involves incarnating the trinitarian unity-in-difference in creation. This incarnation involves unifying in love different persons, genders, races, ethnicities, nations, species, and so on. The world becomes a polyphony of difference. Christ remains the *cantus firmus* of the polyphony. As the revelation of trinitarian openness to creation, von Balthasar argues, Christ is "the unchangeably valid blueprint in every situation in the world and in history."[21] Hence in Christ Christians see God's plan from before the creation of the world and the early outlines of what the fulfilled plan will entail. This plan, von Balthasar explains, is summarized in Paul's reflections in 1 Cor. 2:6-16 on the "wisdom" of the "spiritually mature" who have "the mind of Christ": the wise know that God's plan from before the creation of the world is to glorify the creation, to clothe humanity in the mantle of divinity, thereby permitting human persons to penetrate into God to such an extent that they become wholly radiant in divine light.[22]

It is at this point that von Balthasar's theology seems on the way to becoming a speculative metaphysics of providence. A closer reading of this passage, however, indicates that he explicitly denies that knowing God's plan for creation with the "mind of Christ" means having "absolute knowledge" in a Gnostic sense.[23] He strongly believes it is possible for God to "reveal himself to man *as God* without losing his divinity, without falling victim to a . . . dialectic between God and world . . . without . . . giving man an excuse to fashion an idolatrous concept of him."[24] It is important to notice the uniqueness of von Balthasar's position: he makes his case by arguing that the doctrine of trinitarian providence has its origin in a contemplative and sacramental rather than in a theoretical and speculative theological disposition. For example, he maintains that a theology of trinitarian mystery must originate in and refer back to the incarnation, cross, and resurrection of Christ.

> . . . it is only on the basis of Jesus Christ's own behavior and attitude that we can distinguish such a plurality in God. Only in him is the Trinity opened up and made accessible. . . . We know about the Father, Son and Spirit as divine 'Persons' only through the figure and disposition of Jesus Christ. Thus we can agree with the principle, often enunciated today, that it is only on the basis of the economic Trinity that we can have knowledge of the immanent Trinity and dare to make statements about it.[25]

He is very careful to qualify this point. Catholic theologians must say that the economic Trinity interprets itself as the *epistemological* source of the immanent Trinity, but not that the immanent Trinity is the *ontological* source of the economic Trinity.[26] To assert the latter, von Balthasar contends, would be to leave trinitarian theology open to a speculative "process theology" that fails to maintain the ontological difference between God and creation.[27] Von Balthasar believes that maintaining this distinction is necessary for preserving the dramatic seriousness and spiritual ultimacy of salvation history—if God is the world and the world is God, either tragedy is not real or God is tragic. Neither option is Christian, von Balthasar thinks. This is why he frequently attacks as epic "mythology" the assertion that the Trinity needs creation to avoid being "static," "abstract, "self-enclosed," and isolated from the seriousness of love.[28] Any trinitarian theology that deviates from a christocentric and historical norm risks either treating the mystery of the Trinity as an inscrutable philosophical proposition that is totally beyond all comprehension and thus without any direct relevance to the life of faith, or lapsing into Gnosticism's "pseudo-logical speculations" about the God-world relationship that reduce both poles to a monist whole.[29] In both cases, theology surrenders the soteriological meaning of the Trinity to speculative reinterpretation. It is an act of resistance, therefore, when von Balthasar insists that "there is only one way to approach the trinitarian life in God: on the basis of what is manifest in God's kenosis in the theology of the covenant—and hence in the theology of the Cross—we must feel our way back into the mystery of the absolute. . . ."[30]

What is involved in "feeling" the way back to the mystery of God? The short answer is that Christians need to retrieve an Irenaean understanding of faith as "true gnosis." Recall von Balthasar's claim that Christ is the "blueprint in every situation in the world and in history." Seeing this "blueprint" means for him participating in the plan of action it outlines. To "see" the glory of God in Christ, therefore, is to actively live out—not simply to think through in abstract concepts—one's unique role in God's plan. With Irenaeus, von Balthasar assumes that this participation first of all requires receptivity to being educated by God, the great pedagogue.[31] What is the curriculum of this pedagogy? As mentioned earlier, it is incarnating trinitarian unity-in-difference. More specifically, this incarnation involves embodying the glory of the creator's joyful love for life into a creation plagued by sin and death.[32] Von Balthasar writes, the goal of faith is "an increasing mutual integration of joy and suffering, indeed of joy and the Cross."[33] In other words, the trinitarian metanarrative of history is the story of divine pedagogy training humanity in the spiritual skill of incarnating ever-greater joy into a world of suffering. Just as the Word entered into the reality of suffering to save humanity, so too those who see the Word and take part in the plan he reveals will enter the reality of suffering to transform it from within. Von Balthasar holds that "suffering is not entry into alienation, but an exit from it. On a deeper level, suffering is a participation in the suffering of the one who leads us out of alienation."[34] Without this pedagogical lesson in sharing in the "paschal mystery," the reality of suffering and tragedy Christians encounter in their mission would lead them into either despair or stoic fatalism. The pedagogy of the paschal mystery is designed to prevent this. In the paschal mystery, von Balthasar explains, the triune God is at work "seizing fate and destiny . . . wrenching them out of their axes. . . . It is by this [the paschal mystery] that principalities and powers of fate, which keep man subordinate, are absorbed into the realm of grace and freedom, and 'made ineffective' (1 Cor 2.6; 15.24ff.; Heb 2.14)."[35] Von Balthasar maintains that participation in the paschal mystery, therefore, liberates humanity from despair and/or fatalism, thereby enabling it defiantly to reject all human-made utopias in the name of an alternative "utopian hope" based in the memory of Christ's death and resurrection.[36] In living out their memory of the paschal mystery, Christians *sacramentalize providence* by incarnating Christ's victory over the principalities and powers of fate. If only humans would "see" the glory of Christ, von Balthasar assumes, then all their shields against grace, all their reasons for not taking seriously God's utopian plan for the creation, would dissolve. Grace would then permeate nature, thereby transforming the world into the image of trinitarian unity-in-difference.

## Grace Perfects Nature:
### Reuniting Beauty, Goodness, and Truth

All of this presupposes that creation has the potential to be redeemed. If the neoscholastics contradicted Scripture and tradition, they did so because they also failed to understand the potential of human nature for the divine. Von Balthasar's discussion of the mystery of God's glory throughout all the volumes of his trilogy is in large part determined precisely by this point of consensus with de Lubac's theology of grace. A careful reading of these texts makes it obvious that von Balthasar presupposes a sacramental conception of mystery along the lines of de Lubac's supernatural. One year after de Lubac's *Surnaturel* was published, von Balthasar published *Truth of the World*.[37] Fourteen years later, in the first volume of *The Glory of the Lord, Seeing the Form*, von Balthasar developed his theology of truth into a theological aesthetics. In these books he argues for a retrieval of patristic theology's sacramental view of creation as wonderous because it is a vehicle of the divine.[38] He argues that "the supernatural takes root in the deepest structures of being, leavens them through and through, and permeates them like a breath or an omnipresent fragrance. . . . [T]he supernatural has impregnated nature so deeply that there is simply no way to reconstruct it in its pure state (*natura pura*)."[39] The truth about the world is therefore analogous to the truth of God—both are vast and inexhaustible, and hence cannot be explained comprehensively in tidy theories.[40] For this reason he asserts, following St. Paul in Rom. 1:19ff., that creation itself is a permanent and inalienable "manifestation of God."[41] The revelation of God in creation does not contradict the revelation of God in Christ, but rather, when considered from within the perspective provided by Chalcedonian Christology, "the revelation in the creation is seen to have occurred for the sake of the revelation in Christ, serving as the preparation that made it possible."[42] Just as in Christ the divine and the human coexist in a paradoxical unity-in-difference, so too in all aspects of the visible world there is an "invisible" element that indicates for us the revelation of the "mystery of Being."[43] The mystery of spirit-in-matter analogically indicates the same sacramental "paradox" revealed by Christ, namely, "the paradox that unveiling is perfectly compatible with veiling and mystery."[44]

Von Balthasar believes that he is affirming the "the venerable principle that grace builds on nature," an affirmation that leads him to retrieve from the patristic era a notion of "the vital interlocking of truth, goodness, and beauty."[45] He recognizes that this is a risky retrieval because, citing Nietzsche's complaint, realism compels us to admit that "truth is ugly" and goodness requires lying; in a world dominated by the will to power, it is simply naïve to think otherwise.[46] Von Balthasar respects the rhetorical appeal of Nietzsche's complaint but believes Christians cannot agree with it. If creation is redeemed, then grace, and not the will to power, dominates the world. But as Nietzsche wryly observed, the world seems quite unredeemed. Von Balthasar's entire theological project is an attempt to answer this point. He grants it but adds that this is because Christians have failed to sacramentalize the Word's redemptive presence. He is convinced that the revelation of divine glory in Christ redeems worldly beauty and makes possible its realistic unity with goodness and truth. It could not be otherwise because God redeems creation *qua* creation, and hence sacramentally infuses and unites worldly beauty, goodness, and truth with supernatural grace. His desire to articulate this sacramental ontology in the face of Nietzschean objections explains why von Balthasar felt not only justified but required to write a theological aesthetics.

Understanding the place of aesthetics in von Balthasar's theology requires beginning with the rhetorically tendentious contrast he draws between a classical and a Romantic understanding of beauty.[47] This contrast is designed to underwrite an Irenaean distinction between true and false gnosis. The contrast, he explains, is that classical aesthetics has a much more objective standard than Kantian-Romantic aesthetics. Von Balthasar considers the former as cosmocentric and the latter as anthropocentric.[48] Neither are christologically theocentric, as is an Irenaean conception of faith. The cosmocentric view of classical aesthetics, however, is open to becoming christologically theocentric, but the anthropocentric view of Kantian-Romantic aesthetics is closed to this possibility.[49] Indeed, he sees the anthropocentric epistemology of Kantian-Romantic aesthetics as analogous to the way of thinking the serpent in the Garden of Eden used to lead Adam and Eve away from God.[50] Classical aesthetics, on the contrary, is on the side of the angels. It focuses attention on the power of beautiful objects to captivate the self with spiritual light and hence cause one to become forgetful of the self. Kantian-Romantic aesthetics focuses attention on the private, interior sense one feels when perceiving a work of art or the sublime power of nature, and hence causes one to stray from the objective into the abstractions of the subjective. Moreover, classical aesthetics emphasizes the divine power of a god or the gods to transform nature and the self, but Kantian-Romantic aesthetics emphasizes the power of human imagination to create gods and transform nature.[51] Aesthetics in the classical sense, therefore, leads to the veneration and worship of some specific object that is other than the self, but Kantian-Romantic aesthetics leads to veneration and worship of the creative self; classical aesthetics celebrates nature and the gods, but Kantian-Romantic aesthetics celebrates the self who is capable of celebrating nature and the gods. Therefore in his effort to construct a theological aesthetics he takes classical aesthetics as his primary dialogue partner. For von Balthasar the religiosity of pagan devotion to a particular god is analogically related to Christianity's devotion to the image of God's glory in Christ. The religiosity of Kantian-Romantic aesthetics is analogically related to Gnosticism. He thinks this because although Kantian-Romantic aesthetics uses the rhetoric of the "beautiful" and the "symbolic" it is ultimately more interested in abstract anthropological theories about the human spirit than in concrete objects of beauty. Von Balthasar argues that Kantian-Romantic aesthetics assumes "that the material is the dispensable shell, and can be left behind by those with advanced spiritual vision once they have penetrated to the pure spiritual core."[52] For Kantian-Romantic aesthetics this "spiritual core" is always the human "subject" and never the transcendent God of biblical monotheism. Hence it epitomizes humanity's "original sin" against God.[53]

According to von Balthasar, the two terms "form" (*species, Gestalt*) and "splendor" (*lumen, Glanz*) define the basic content of classical aesthetics.[54] Classical aesthetics always holds together both of these elements: the beautiful is simultaneously an invisible spiritual light and a particular sensory pattern. His understanding of classical aesthetics is analogically related to the traditional Catholic notion of a sacrament as a sensory symbol that communicates grace. The supernatural permeates nature, and therefore all truly beautiful forms are sacramental expressions of God. For example, von Balthasar's description of aesthetic "form" is very similar to the Catholic understanding of a sacramental species. He describes form as "a totality of parts and elements, grasped as such, existing and defined as such, which for its existence requires not only a 'surrounding world' but ultimately being as a whole: in this need it is (as Nicholas of Cusa says) a 'contracted' representation of the 'absolute,' in so far as it transcends its parts as members and controls them in its own confined territory."[55] Therefore every particular finite reality can be a communication of spirit and the absolute truth of being.[56] This claim for access to "absolute" truth is carefully qualified to prevent it from drifting into Gnostic abstraction. Humans cannot think truth in pure reason, nor can they abstract truth from its "confined territory" in sensory form. Again this is analogically related to Catholic sacramental theology. Von Balthasar writes, "God is not immediately disclosed in himself, but only indirectly, on the basis of the disclosedness of being as a whole. The finite intellect has no means, either inside or outside itself, to get an immediate glimpse of God; it remains dependent upon the sign language of the things through which God speaks it."[57]

Von Balthasar believes that some of these signs or forms are purer and more transparent to the "ground of being" than others, and hence allow more of the light of beauty to radiate from their depths. The most sacramentally powerful images are the ones that reveal the truth of the world because they "overflow" with grace:

> . . . if God appears in the signs of his creation, he can do so only within the tension that . . . marks the appearance of the ground in the image. On the one hand, this appearance can look like the uttermost manifestation of the ground in the image, so that the image could almost be mistaken for the ground itself. . . . The image, then, is filled to the brim with the whole significance of the ground—so much so that the vessel appears almost to overflow, that, what the vessel contains seems better than the vessel itself. By the same token, worldly truth, but God's gift, often appears to contain an intrinsic infinity, an inexhaustible truth, beauty, and goodness, and immediate gleam of God's eternity and infinity, an irradiation of something more than it could contain simply on account of its own creaturely truth. This mysterious "more" . . . is the uttermost filling of the vessel of the worldly symbol with the divine content. This explains how a kind of plenitude can invade a moment of time, making it seem to be an immediate appearance of eternity, or how a work of art can be so perfect that it seems to have the quality, no longer of an earthly, but of an immediately divine idea.[58]

Von Balthasar's theological aesthetics, therefore, leads him to discuss the "subjectivity" of faith very differently than most modern theologians.[59] In particular, he maintains that subjectivity correlates personal, interior religious experience with the objective revelation of God's glory in Christ. This explains why positive revelation is not simply a supplement to the human self's inner religious experience of mystery. God's historical revelation in Christ is the origin of this inner experience. Christ possesses what von Balthasar terms "objective evidence." The "objectivity" of this evidence is aesthetic and contemplative not scientific and analytical. "It is the kind of evidence that emerges and sheds light from the phenomenon itself," and therefore "we can say that . . . a revelation of [God's] glory needs no justification but itself."[60] In other words, the revelation of glory reveals the truth of the world as the creaturely capacity to incarnate the supernatural in beautiful sacramental images, which in turn reveals the moral imperative to facilitate this incarnational process. In this sense there is an "aesthetic analogy" between a great work of art and/or natural beauty and God's self-communication in the incarnation.[61] It is precisely this analogical relationship between worldly beauty and the glory of God revealed in the incarnation that leads von Balthasar to insist on the unique meaning of Christ as the aesthetic "image" of God.[62] For him, Christ has the status of an aesthetic archetype that includes but surpasses mythic religion because it most clearly reveals God's will to redeem creation by assuming it in an incarnational process.[63] Whereas pagan piety is always to one degree or another naturalistic, Christian piety is focused on the redemption of nature by the transcendent Jewish God who created the cosmos and hence rules over it. As such, grace communicated by Christ interprets itself as a sovereign, lordly freedom that escapes any determination by impersonal cosmic laws. Moreover, as fully human Christ interprets himself as the archetype of human freedom and autonomy.

> [Christ reveals that God] is present in his creatures and gifts in such a way that he distances himself from them in order to leave them a space of freedom. . . . It is precisely this interplay of the immanence of God's power and wisdom in all that exists in the world, and his transcendence over the creatures (as the free creator who remains free), who thereby receive a space for their own existence and freedom, that is the foundation of the biblical doxa; and precisely this free elevation above what is not God gives God again the freedom to reveal himself in his free divinity personally—in the "Word"—to what is not God.[64]

This revelation makes possible an intimacy with the divine that goes beyond mythic religion because it preserves the personal identity of both the divine and human participant in mystical union.[65] Although forms of worldly beauty and the Christ-form both call forth a response of extreme "interior self-transcendence," the latter demands a response far surpassing any mythical standard because it emphasizes so strongly God's desire to enter into a relationship of personal, mutually self-giving love with his free human creatures.[66] Von Balthasar maintains that the objective meaning communicated by the image of God in Christ is that the creator, in an act of divine Eros, "goes out from itself in order to become man and die on the Cross for the world."[67] When this "image" captivates those who see it and understand it, they are drawn out of themselves to make "an act of serious love which corresponds to God's own act of taking love seriously." I will return to this point below. For the moment the point is that the corresponding response to God's love in Christ is one in which the creature *qua* creature receives grace and is transformed into a Christ-like radiant image of God by it.[68] In the process the human self undergoes a paradoxical rebirth-through-death in which its true personal identity emerges through becoming transparent and being irrradiated by God.

> When God shines through, the creature has to become more transparent. When God lovingly elevates the creature to the loftiest heights, the creature must humble itself in the deepest reverence before him, acknowledging itself to be only a servant and handmaid of the Lord. Thus, the creature cooperates most with God and his revelation when it lets God use it as an instrument for his purposes. The creature is most alive when, by God's life indwelling in it, it submits in the most deathlike way to the hand of the divine potter. Insofar as the creature's own truth stands over against God's it can seek this truth only by entering into the pure distance of an instrument that, far from considering itself to be of any importance in its own right, sees itself as a kind of appendage. The objectivity of the creature's attitude consists in this withdrawal before God. Retreating to the point of a thinglike transparency, the creature is no longer noticed, because the onlooker's attention glides immediately (*immediate*) to the archetype who expresses himself in it: such is the correct attitude demanded by the relationship of analogy.[69]

In this process, the self is not annihilated and replaced by God, as in pantheistic religions.[70] Von Balthasar's point about analogy here is meant to forestall any misreading of his claims about sacramental transparency as a doctrine of "no self." His point is that in becoming an instrument of God one becomes a new self with a distinct ethical mission; one becomes the person God the "potter" intended. Moreover, as suggested by the point about the onlooker's attention on the servant identity of the creature transformed by grace, the most sacramentally powerful images are the ones that carry an ethical imperative. In his understanding of classical aesthetics, a contemplative orientation is only the precondition for the practical and ethical dynamic latent in all genuine encounters with beauty. According to von Balthasar, there is a call to action latent in aesthetic receptivity. He asserts that the ethical is

> beauty's inner coordinate axis, which allows beauty to unfold to its full dimensionality as transcendental attribute of Being. . . . [F]or Origen, the moral meaning of revelation is not to be found *alongside* its mystical meaning: the spiritual light proceeding from revelation's depths. For Origen the "moral meaning" refers to the urgency with which such light penetrates the beholder's very heart, in a manner described by Rilke in his "The Archaic Torso of Apollo": "There is no place in it which does not see you. You must change your life."[71]

He explains later that "what is beautiful in this world—being spirit as it makes its appearance—possesses a total dimension that also calls for moral decision."[72] Von Balthasar returns to this point in *TheoDrama*, where he insists that "God only shows himself to someone, only enraptures him, in order to commission him. Where this is not taken seriously, where the aesthetic fails to reveal the ethical that lies within it, such rapture is degraded to a prettifying excuse (*"ravissant"*). Where a thing of beauty is really and radically beheld, freedom too is radically opened up, and decision can take place."[73] It is the clear ethical dimension of the mystery in classical aesthetics that allows it to be "the foundation and foreshadowing of what in the realm of revelation and grace will be the attitude of faith."[74] The moral response inevitably provoked by the beautiful involves the self in a process of transformation in which it remakes itself according to the likeness of the beautiful form that inspires it. For von Balthasar, therefore, when an aesthetic discourse of beauty fails to deal with moral decision, it becomes a type of "aestheticism" that deserves to be rejected.[75]

Von Balthasar's point is that "the beauty of Jesus Christ" embraces life and death, joy and fear, the beautiful and the ugly. Quoting Karl Barth, von Balthasar writes, "'The beauty of God' in the 'beauty of Jesus Christ' appears therefore precisely in the crucified, but the crucified, precisely as such, is the one risen: 'in this self-disclosure, God's beauty embraces death as well as life, fear as well as joy, that which we would call ugly, as well as that which we would call beautiful.'"[76] Von Balthasar comments that Barth's point here "agrees with [my] own overall plan" in formulating a theological aesthetics. Hence a theological aesthetics cannot allow itself to become an "aesthetic theology." The difference is that "aesthetic theology" is ultimately a Gnostic project, and "theological aesthetics" is an expression of Irenaean true gnosis. Von Balthasar believes Irenaean true gnosis is committed above all to historical realism and therefore includes the imperative to respond to the realities of tragedy, ugliness, and death in its reflections. Gnosticism's "epic" view of history is also interested in suffering and tragedy but only to argue for their teleological necessity. Von Balthasar, on the other hand, is convinced that teleological explanations of suffering and tragedy are a type of aesthetic theology; aesthetic theology includes tragedy, sin, and death into its reflections only in order to explain away their concrete existential seriousness with abstract theories that conceptually synthesize light and shadow, harmony and dissonance, good and evil. The issue for von Balthasar is whether the dark elements of life will be accepted as ultimately real and lived with existential seriousness, or whether they will be rendered merely illusory by speculative theories constructed by armchair theologians who are trying to evade sharing in the world's suffering? More specifically, he refuses any attempt by Gnostic rationalism to explain away, and thereby avoid dealing with, the incomprehensibility of tragedy and suffering. Von Balthasar firmly insists that, contrary to aesthetic theology, theological aesthetics cannot allow itself to "exclude the element of the ugly, of the tragically fragmented, of the demonic, but must come to terms with these. Every aesthetic which simply seeks to ignore these nocturnal sides of existence can itself from the outset be ignored as a sort of aestheticism."[77] Such "aestheticism" operates according to a purely human standard derived from the realm of artistic creativity, not from a christocentric focus. Because it lacks this focus, aesthetic theology is simply yet another form of intellectual idolatry that is guilty of evading the seriousness of our existential situation.

This brings us to the second difference between theological aesthetics and aesthetic theology. In theological aesthetics the goal is not to explain (so as to explain away) the "nocturnal sides of existence" but rather to come to terms with them by living them. This process begins by contemplating "the beauty of Christ," which means, for von Balthasar, contemplating the crucified and risen Lamb of God who "takes away the sins of the world." By contemplation he does not mean detached philosophical speculation. Contemplation means for him joining with the liturgical, eucharistic community of the church in remembering Christ's cross, descent into hell, and resurrection, and then entering personally into this paschal mystery to share in Christ's journey from death to life.[78] Von Balthasar believes it is legitimate to refer to the paschal mystery of Christ as "beauty" because its effect on human souls is analogous to the effect worldly forms of beauty have on souls. Just as worldly beauty allures, obsesses, and captivates people, drawing them into a world of meaning with its own moral norms and internal logic, so too the paschal mystery is an alluring mystery that captivates those who contemplate it, drawing them into a world of meaning with its own proper morality and logic. The world of meaning proper to the beauty of the paschal mystery, von Balthasar believes, is communal and ecclesial. Sharing in Christ's paschal mystery occurs through committed, responsible involvement with the church as it lives through and comes to spiritual, existential terms with the tragic situations of life. Human fulfillment takes place, von Balthasar argues, "not in glory of paradise, but in the crucifying encounter of the crucified Lord in the sin-distorted face of one's fellow man. And it is in terms of this encounter that we shall be judged."[79] Therefore, theological aesthetics is for von Balthasar a means of expressing the primacy of eucharistic sacramentalism over abstract theoretical speculation in Catholic theology.

It is precisely the sacramental unification of contemplation, moral action, and intellectual reflection that prevents von Balthasar's approach from falling into fideism, as some who have misunderstood his critique of neoscholasticism have charged.[80] To understand why, we need not return to this critique. It will suffice to return for a moment to his critique of aesthetic theology. For von Balthasar aesthetic theology is the product of a purely theoretical mode of reflection, not a sacramental mode of reflection. In theology, any purely theoretical mode of reflection will inevitably breed fideism because it asks people to make a purely cognitive act of intellectual assent to a speculative proposition; in fideism, only the intellect is involved, and the will is marginalized. In the case of an aesthetic theology of providence, the fideistic proposition to be believed is "divine providence is real and therefore evil and suffering are merely temporary illusions." As with all forms of fideistic proposition, this claim only inspires philosophers to abstraction and more abstraction. Fideism encourages an apostasy from reality because it suggests that having the right opinions is a license to remain detached and uninvolved. But Christian contemplative thought—reflection grounded in participation in the sacramental life of the church—engages the will and inspires action. Indeed, a "crucifying encounter [with] the crucified Lord in the sin-distorted face of one's fellow man" is, for von Balthasar, the condition for the possibility of sustained, zealous moral action that honestly faces the reality of evil and suffering. Hence, for von Balthasar, theological truth claims have nothing to do with abstract propositions written up in a catechism. Theological truth claims follow organically as a consequence of aesthetic contemplation and moral action. Thus only through involvement in eucharistic christocentrism, he believes, will it be possible for theology to nonreductively assimilate "what is crude, what is explicitly ugly, what is painful to the point of meaninglessness, the experience of being handed over to what is vulgar and humiliating . . . into a totality which can and must be accepted positively—without artificial sweetening, just as it is."[81] As I discussed above, this totality is for von Balthasar a trinitarian metanarrative of history.

The premodern Christian tradition recognized these connections between sacramental grace, ethical action, and metaphysical thought. It shrewdly used aesthetic discourse to present to the pagan world an intellectually coherent and morally compelling theology of divine truth in sacramental forms.[82] In deploying the aesthetic categories of form and splendor to unify theologically beauty, goodness, and truth, therefore, von Balthasar understands himself as retrieving the normative theological practice of the premodern Christian tradition. Specifically, he thinks classical aesthetics provided the background assumptions for the conceptual arguments on behalf of what became christological orthodoxy. For him, it ought to be axiomatic in Christian theology that Jesus Christ is the fullest expression of the divine mystery of God, or, as he puts it, "the central form of revelation."[83] He argues that the "Christ-form" is the "perfection of the form of the world" and the "super-form" of biblical religion because it is the most transparent of all worldly forms, radiating both the "the light of absolute being" and the light of God's trinitarian mystery.[84] All the "mysteries" of Christianity as an ecclesial religion are mysteries only insofar as they receive their light from and cast light back onto Christ's total form.[85] Therefore Christianity is "*the* aesthetic religion *par excellence.*"[86] In making this claim he asserts that the meaning of worldly beauty was radically changed by Christ. In the Christ, von Balthasar asserts, all earthly aesthetics are "superabundantly fulfilled" so that in their theological deployment it becomes proper to speak no longer of mythic beauty, but of biblical glory.[87] For him, therefore, the incarnation does not merely supplement natural worldly aesthetics, nor does it transform the once luminous pagan gods of mythological religions into dark idols. Rather, he explains, "God's Incarnation perfects the whole ontology and aesthetics of created Being. The incarnation uses created Being at a new depth as a language and a means of expression for the divine Being and essence."[88] Christological orthodoxy's teaching on the two natures and two wills in Christ is never far from von Balthasar's mind. He is never interested in aesthetics for its own sake. He is interested in it only because it sheds light on the profundity of orthodox Christology. Recovering this profundity will allow theology to affirm the unity of creation and redemption in Christ, and hence sacramentally reconnect contemplation, action, and metaphysics, or beauty, goodness, and truth.

## Notes

1. *THdL*, 63. Later in this same text he writes that the issue in *Surnaturel* was not "merely . . . overcoming theologically the poison of Jansenism that had smoldered for centuries in French intellectual life but rather with the poison (intended as an antidote) of a rationalism become worldwide, which treated man (and the angels), as if (following Aristotle) it was true that 'the natural desire does not extend beyond what lies in the natural capacities.' What was devised by theologians to protect the order of grace turns, according to an inner logic, into a closed order of nature for which the 'supernatural' can only be something 'superadded' exteriorly and thus can be dispensed with" (ibid., 66).

2. Here von Balthasar inserts a footnote to the following passage from Louis Bouyer: "One of the greatest weaknesses of Scholasticism, even in its full flowering in Thomas Aquinas or Duns Scotus, was the way it felt it necessary to answer all the questions put to it, and that on the basis of the word of God. . . . Even Thomas showed this weakness by uncritically accepting a mode of questioning that was due

in part to the under-rationality of a particular cultural-epoch; he should rather have said openly that such a way of proceeding is illegitimate and that the questions a man puts . . . are always more or less incorrectly put, because of his fallen state. Before God can grant an answer, he must put the question straight. And that is the first thing that God's word enables us to do" (Louis Bouyer, *Das Handwerk des Theologen* [Einsiedeln: Johannes Verlag, 1980], 170–71).

3. *TD4*, 458–59.

4. See *GL1*, 70–79. Von Balthasar believes that modern neoscholastic theology unwittingly conspired with Enlightenment rationalism to produce a Catholic form of deism. In opposition to this neoscholastic project, von Balthasar asserts that theology can no longer acquiesce to "the modern world's blindness to the glory of God" as if modernity's "de-deification of the cosmos" has nothing to do with Christian faith and life, nor can it accept modern materialism's antimetaphysical attempts to reduce Christianity to true propositions or good actions (*GL4*, 17, 38).

5. *GL7*, 239.

6. See *GL7*, 242.

7. "The subject of theology is not to be 'mastered' gradually by the understanding through a series of approximations that circle round the subject: rather, every approach in thought is continually 'judged' anew by the absolute superiority of the subject. For this subject is the absolute trinitarian love of God, which discloses itself and offers itself in Jesus Christ, which disarms by its humility and simplicity every 'stronghold' of would-be mastering thought that 'rises up' (2 Cor. 10.5)" (*GL7*, 15).

8. Von Balthasar defines "fideist" theology as "the self-righteousness of rationalism" (*TD2*, 127–28).

9. *GL1*, 187.

10. Ibid, 509–25.

11. Ibid, 515, 511, 513.

12. Ibid, 513. Kierkegaard's name comes up in this discussion, but de Lubac's argument that the paradox of grace is offensive to human reason is likely also not far from von Balthasar's mind.

13. *GL7*, 10.

14. *GL1*, 461; *TL1*, 18. See DZ 432: "*in tanta similitudine major dissimilitudo.*"

15. *GL1*, 461.

16. *GL2*, 45 n. 52.

17. *TL1*, 20. Regarding his assertion about the "postconciliar attempt to reform Catholic theology" it is very likely that von Balthasar has in mind some forms of Catholic transcendental Thomism and some of the uses of historical-critical method in Catholic biblical scholarship. I will briefly deal with the question of historical-critical method in chapter 4. Examining the complex details of von Balthasar's thinking about transcendental Thomism, however, is beyond the scope of the present work. For readers interested in his critique I suggest beginning with *LA*, 25–42. For a useful secondary source that focuses on von Balthasar's criticisms of Karl Rahner, see Eamonn Conway, *The Anonymous Christian—A Relativized Christianity?* (Frankfurt: Peter Lang, 1993).

18. *GL1*, 186; cf. 147–48 and 461–62.

19. Von Balthasar holds that "God's incomprehensibility is now no longer a mere deficiency in knowledge, but the positive manner in which God determines the knowledge of faith: this is the overpowering and overwhelming inconceivability of the fact that God has loved us so much that he surrendered his only Son for us, the fact that the God of plenitude has poured himself out, not only into creation, but emptied himself into the modalities of an existence determined by sin, corrupted by

death and alienated from God" (*GL1*, 461). Von Balthasar contrasts his holistic understanding of revelation in Christ with "a mere 'fundamentalism' of facts of salvation, strung together 'to be believed' . . ." (*GL7*, 113–14).

20. *GL7*, 308–9, 314, 376.

21. *TD2*, 277.

22. *GL7*, 524.

23. Ibid. The reference here is to Hegel. As I will argue later in chapter 6, he considers Hegel a quintessentially Gnostic thinker.

24. *TL1*, 17.

25. *TD3*, 508. Hence von Balthasar affirms Karl Rahner's axiom, "'The economic Trinity is the immanent Trinity and vice versa." See *TD4*, 320; *TD5*, 224–25. He contends that the starting point in the economic Trinity necessarily implies that "only with great caution should we adduce analogies from the Trinity from outside Christianity. Such analogies lack the 'economic' basis and can easily appear as a mere collection of cosmological principles . . . that does not get any farther than tritheism, or else they stay at the level of modalism, speaking of three aspect of the One . . ." (*TD3*, 508).

26. *TD3*, 157, 508; *TD4*, 320–23. See also von Balthasar's essay, "Creation and Trinity," *Communio: International Catholic Review* (Fall 1988): 285–93.

27. *TD4*, 325; see also *TD3*, 508; *TD1*, 319.

28. The reference here is to Hegelian theology. See *TD4*, 325–27; see also *TD5*, 245, 508–9.

29. *TD5*, 14.

30. *TD4*, 324.

31. *GL7*, 534–35. See also his positive discussion of Irenaeus on this point in *GL2*, 79–81.

32. Von Balthasar writes, ". . . *doxa* can encircle God's self-revelation and make its voice heard in very many different ways, for it would not be a statement about God unless it were the expression of his hiddenness just as much as the expression of his manifestation, possessing dimension enough to make itself known in Cross and death just as much as in Resurrection and 'return in glory.' The message of the New Testament, transcending all the statements about glory in the Old Testament, is precisely that God's glory can embrace 'transcendentally' even these uttermost contradictions, and so need not be brought to a halt before Sheol" (*GL7*, 242).

33. *GL7*, 534

34. Ibid., 536.

35. Ibid., 234.

36. Ibid., 526–31.

37. This book was republished as the first volume of *Theologik*, *TL1*. It has recently been translated into English as *Theo-logic: Theological Logical Theory: Volume I: Truth of the World*, trans. Adrian J. Walker (San Francisco: Ignatius Press, 2000).

38. *GL1*, 34–45; *TL1*, 11, 28.

39. *TL1*, 31.

40. *TL1*, 26–27. Von Balthasar observes that the truth about the world is so rich that "it would be strange if [it] could be defined, classified, skimmed over, and finished off in in a few dry propositions." Every great philosopher knows this, he contends, especially Aquinas. His neoscholastic disciples lack his greatness. Their "ideal of truth is certitude of truth's existence, or, at the very least, a kind of scientific clarity and unassailable certainty that can only be purchased by selling off huge acreages of truth" (ibid., 28, 32).

41. *GL1*, 430.

42. Ibid., 431. Elsewhere von Balthasar explains that God "has revealed himself to us on the basis of our creaturely existence" (*TL1, 256*).

43. Ibid., 444; cf. 446–47.

44. Ibid., 9; cf. 206–16.

45. Ibid., 32.

46. Ibid., 16.

47. See *GL4*, 11–313 and *GL5*, 247–610.

48. *GL1*, 33–34; *GL4*, 166–216.

49. For this reason von Balthasar affirms the early Christian belief that Christ "inherits" rather than abolishes the gods of paganism. He writes, "The gods cannot be interpreted as the personifications of human and cosmic forces which could just as well be given abstract names. As concrete forms, they are radiant, unique images and unveilings of Being, of human existence within experienced Being, of 'regions' of Being which cannot be divided by arbitrary borderlines. Within finite contours, these images validly encompass and embody the fullness of the universe. A Michelangelo, a Goethe, a Keats must still have seen such gods with their inner eye; many of their figures presuppose such encounters. And we must ask ourselves whether the inability of the modern heart to encounter gods—with the resultant withering up of human religions—is altogether to Christianity's advantage. The derision of the gods by Christian apologists, even by the great Augustine, is not indeed in every respect a glorious chapter of the Church's history" (*GL1, 500*). Von Balthasar therefore can affirm poets like Holderlin, the late Schelling, and Hopkins in their notion that Christ "inherits" the gods of paganism. "In what concerns Christ's heritage, Greek and Russian theology as a rule has a far better understanding than the West" (*GL1, 501–2*).

50. *TL1*, 262.

51. *GL4*, 19

52. Ibid., 437; cf. 124–26, 215–16. See also *OPSC*, 121.

53. Von Balthasar writes, ". . . it is no accident that the first sin consists precisely in a desire to know more than is allowed. . . . The error we thereby commit, which is the primal and archetypal sin, is that man makes himself the criterion and so concludes that where *he* sees no barrier none can in fact exist. Now, it is not so much the yearning for truth as a whole that is to be considered disobedience, but rather the way in which it is sought—as a mere knowing without receptive faith" (*TL1, 262–63*).

54. *GL1*, 118.

55. *GL4*, 29.

56. *TL1*, 131ff.

57. Ibid., 234.

58. Ibid., 235–36.

59. See *GL1*, 418, 465.

60. *GL1*, 464 and 140.

61. Ibid., 488. He writes that the figure which Christ forms has in itself an interior rightness and evidential power such as we find—in another, wholly worldly realm—in a work of art or in a mathematical principle" (465–66) Seeing the Christ-form requires "an 'eye for quality' . . . analogous to the eye of the connoisseur which can infallibly distinguish art from kitsch, excellent quality from average or merely good quality"(481). Nevertheless, von Balthasar adds, the analogy is imperfect because worldly beauty and the biblical revelation of divine glory are "qualitatively different" and thus cannot be said to carry their own evidential power in the same sense (618).

62. "Now, the evidential power (which is, admittedly, of a very special kind) lies in the phenomenon itself and demands a theological act of seeing the form" (ibid., 466).

63. "The interior attunement, proportion, and harmony between God and man in Christ-form raises it to the level of an archetype, not only of all religious and ethical, contemplative and active behavior, but equally of the beautiful, regardless whether this is agreeable or not to the person with a creative aesthetic sensibility. . . . For this beautiful object *is* revelation: it is the beauty of God that appears in man and the beauty of man which is to be found in God and God alone" (ibid., 477).

64. *GL7*, 268.

65. *GL1*, 216.

66. Ibid., 464

67. Ibid., 216–17; cf. 473.

68. Von Balthasar explains that the Word of God in Christ "no longer stands before us and alongside us, but has truly been implanted into us (Jer 31.31f.; Ez 36.26f.). And we ought not to understand this in the way the likewise 'naive realism' of Catholic theologians would have it, that is, that this implantation of the Word of God in us occurs only in a 'second movement,' after God's objective deeds of salvation in Christ had occurred 'in a first movement' (*in actu primo*), 'in themselves' and 'for us,' but had not yet been wrought 'in us.' Such a conception contradicts precisely the principle of the Incarnation as understood especially by the Greek Fathers" (*GL1*, 537–38).

69. *TL1*, 237.

70. "If God did not in himself possess form, no form could ever arise between him and man. . . . What would occur, rather, is what *must* occur in all non-Christian mysticism: the finite is absorbed by the infinite and the non-identical is crushed by identity" (*GL1*, 480). See also *TL1*, 244ff.

71. *GL1*, 23; see also *TD2*, 24.

72. *GL1*, 34

73. *TD2*, 31.

74. *GL1*, 153.

75. Ibid., 22.

76. Ibid.

77. *GL1*, 460. Breandán Leahy rightly highlights this point in his discussion of von Balthasar's distinction between theological aesthetics and aesthetic theology. He notes the often overlooked point that von Balthasar's intention is to focus our attention on the cross, not "to make theology or the Christian life more appealing." See Leahy's "Theological Aesthetics," in *The Beauty of Christ*, 25, 28–29.

78. *GL1*, 556ff.

79. Ibid., 470.

80. See Richard Viladesau, *Theological Aesthetics: God in Imagination, Beauty, and Art* (New York: Oxford University Press, 1999), 35–38.

81. *GL4*, 28–29.

82. See *GL1*, 38–40.

83. Ibid., 153–54; 463.

84. See ibid., 141, 432, 602; *GL4*, 31; *GL7*, 14.

85. *GL1*, 202–3.

86. Ibid., 216.

87. Ibid., 457

88. Ibid., 29; see also *GL5*, 249.

# Chapter III

# The Old and New Covenants

According to von Balthasar's Irenaean version of *corpus triforme* Christology, the redemptive operation of the Word's incarnations in Jesus Christ and in the church follows the incarnational pattern set in the old covenant. Von Balthasar assumes, therefore, that understanding all the dimensions of God's incarnate image in Christ requires a theological analysis of Judaic monotheism. Specifically, he thinks that the doxological view of the God-world relationship in Judaism's prophetic tradition inchoately expresses the essence of the patristic consensus on the unity of the divine and human in Christ. For the old covenant prophets, ethical activity is the quintessentially incarnational activity because it mirrors God's holiness in creation.

### The Unity of the Covenants: Monotheism versus Marcionism

Von Balthasar follows Irenaeus's precedent in seeing the biblical canon's unification of the Hebrew and Christian Scriptures as expressing the *corpus triforme* corollary of the unity of the old and new covenants.[1] A careful reading of his theology in *GL6* and *GL7*, as well as his discussion of the relationship of synagogue and church in *TD3*, also shows that he follows Irenaeus's lead in interpreting the unity of salvation history as a process of divine pedagogy into the true gnosis of the paradoxical union of divine and human, creator and creation. The canon is unified because it narrates the three asymmetrical phases of one educational process embodying eternal love in time. That is to say, the true gnosis of faith sees the canon as revealing God working as the providential Lord of history to educate the human race into a unity of love that mirrors the eternal love in the Trinity between the Word (Son), Father, and Spirit. Faith sees this because it is by definition a participation in the third phase of the incarnational process. Failure to look at the canon with the eyes of faith, von Balthasar believes, leads to a host of mistaken interpretations of it. Worse, it leads to Gnostic reinterpretations of it. Like Irenaeus, he considers Marcionism one of the most dangerous forms of Gnostic reinterpretation.

The biblical canon was formed in large part to oppose Marcionism. Marcion (84-160 C.E.) was the son of the bishop of Sinope in Pontus. Most of what is known about his life and teachings comes from the writings of his opponents, primarily Justin Martyr, Irenaeus, Tertullian, and Hippolytus.[2] It is possible that he was himself a consecrated bishop, although this is unclear. It is known that he was a wealthy shipowner and merchant. He moved to Rome around the late 130s or early 140s and made a name for himself among Christians there by donating a large sum of money to the Roman church. However, his insistence that the Roman church accept and teach his doctrinal system quickly alienated its leaders. They returned his donation and excommunicated him in 144 C.E. His doctrinal system proved intolerable because of its quasi-Manichean assumption that there were two Gods: the creator God of Jewish monotheism and the redeemer God of Christianity.[3] According to Marcion, these two gods, and hence the Jewish and Christian religions, were fundamentally incompatible. He rejected all of the Hebrew Scriptures, and even most Christian Scriptures, because he considered them contaminated by Jewish ideas; he accepted as valid revelation only ten letters attributed to St. Paul and parts of the Gospel of Luke. The God of Christianity, whom Marcion identified as God the Father, sent Christ to save humanity from the materiality of the world created and ruled by the Jewish God. For Marcion redemption meant "the salvation of the soul" and its escape from the natural world.[4] To make this case Marcion drew a sharp contrast between Judaism as a religion of Law and Christianity as a religion of grace and love. The former involved slavery to the "judicial" God of Judaism, whereas the latter involved the gift of freedom and mercy from the "good God" of Christianity.[5] Moreover, for Marcion, Christ was separated from the "political Messiah of the Jews" by an "absolute difference" because he was not a human being, did not have a human body, and was entirely uninterested in anything the Old Testament prophets had to say about earthly justice.[6] As Jaroslav Pelikan explains, Marcion's insistence on the "discontinuity" between Old and New Testaments was logically accompanied by dichotomies between creation and salvation, the law and the gospel, the creator and the Father, and humanity and Christ.[7]

Von Balthasar also reads Marcion in this way, and he brands his set of theological dichotomies a "demonic contrivance" and "the first systematic form of theological anti-Semitism."[8] For von Balthasar, Marcion's theology was "mythical" but closely resembled the biblical narrative, and hence among Gnostic systems it seemed "closest to Christianity and the least burdened by fantasy."[9] Marcionism's similarity to Christianity, however, and its ability to parody convincingly Christian theology through the use of scriptural exegesis and an apparent interest in salvation history, qualify it as a paradigmatic instance of the Gnostic subversion of the *corpus triforme*. Von Balthasar thinks that Marcionism never died in Christianity.[10] Moreover, he believes that much of what happens in the contemporary theological academy under the heading of "biblical criticism" is riddled with Marcionist assumptions. Some modern biblical scholars disconnect the canon by affirming the real incarnate presence of the Word in Jesus and the church, but denying its presence among the Jews. Other modern biblical scholars deny the incarnation of the Word altogether; either they simply do not believe in the possibility of a supernatural presence in history or they doubt Jewish and Christian claims to have privileged access to this presence. Von Balthasar sees his theological task as twofold: expose the Marcionist assumptions in modern biblical criticism and challenge them with a patristic biblical hermeneutic based on *corpus triforme* Christology. I will discuss his efforts to expose the Gnostic assumptions in modern biblical criticism in chapter 4. In this chapter I will focus on examining his use of *corpus triforme* Christology as a biblical hermeneutic.

At the beginning of his studies of the theology of the old and new covenants von Balthasar does not openly declare that he is following a *corpus triforme* patristic hermeneutic. Yet, his assertion that the canon narrates an overall pattern of divine activity in creation strongly suggests this as his hermeneutic model. According to this hermeneutic model, the canonical Scriptures present a trinitarian and christocentric metanarrative that interprets history according to a unified narrative of the redemption through the Word's incarnation in creation.[11] There are three major leitmotifs in this narrative. The first is humanity's creation by the Father through the Son and Holy Spirit. The second is the Trinity's pedagogical work to prepare humanity for the coming of Christ. The third is the coming of Christ as the full sacrament of divine presence in creation and the archetype of human perfection.[12] Von Balthasar follows this interpretive model in *GL6* and *GL7*, where he reads the Old and New Testaments together by interpreting the Old Covenant's monotheistic theology of glory through the prism of the New Testament's christocentric and trinitarian reconfiguration of this theology. He concisely restates this position in a section in *TD3* entitled "The Church of Jews and Gentiles."[13]

There are many supersessionist implications of this hermeneutic practice, but von Balthasar believes he can avoid them. Contrary to many of the church fathers, he does not think it necessary to consider Judaism an anachronistic or defunct religion.[14] Indeed, his primary intention in reviving the patristic model is to affirm Irenaeus's rejection of Marcionism. He thinks this model can show why the Old and New Testaments belong together as a unified testimony to divine revelation in history, and thereby demonstrate that both covenants are part of a broader, more inclusive incarnational process. Marcion's theological error, he argues, lay not in prioritizing Christianity over Judaism but in failing to see that the new covenant fulfills the old covenant because it brings to ultimate completion God's process of becoming incarnate in the temporal order. Irenaeus understood this, and hence his theology of canonical unity does not assume that the new covenant inaugurates an abstract, ahistorical, and generally universal divine presence that supercedes Israel's religion.[15] On the contrary, the new covenant deepens it by creating a historical community whose historical concreteness surpasses the already radical concreteness of Israelite religion. In locating the maximal site of divine disclosure in the new covenant, Irenaeus was not drawing an exclusionary line between the two covenants. Instead, he was asserting the continuity and inseparability of the two covenants as traditions of divine pedagogy and divine incarnation in concrete human communities. This is precisely what von Balthasar means when he asserts that the modern historical-critical method does not undermine in any way the validity of Irenaeus's overall theology but in fact works to enrich it by confirming its best intentions.[16]

### Divine Pedagogy and Salvation History

Von Balthasar bases his understanding of the unity of the old and new covenants on Irenaeus's doctrine that the economy of salvation history "is the training of man by God to encounter the God-man: the Old Covenant is *paidagōgos eis Christon*."[17] This pedagogic model implies the importance of patience and the right timing of lessons to achieve maximal educational effect, and hence presupposes a *kairos* in which all previous learning crystallizes into an unforeseen clarity around a central organizing principle or idea.[18] This explains in part why von Balthasar rejects both dualist and monistic interpretations of the relationship between the two covenants as too static. He advocates instead a dynamic teleological reading in which the salvation-history narrative unfolds according to God's pedagogical design.[19] It is interesting, however, that von Balthasar feels compelled to offer an internal critique of Irenaeus on this point. He questions Irenaeus's literal reading of Old Testament prophecy because it is doubtful that the prophets could have known as much as Irenaeus attributes to them before the *kairos* of

Christ crystallized all Gods' lessons to Israel into a coherent whole.[20] Nevertheless, von Balthasar still argues that the Word, with the aid of the Spirit, was gradually incarnating himself in Israel to prepare it for the next phases of incarnation in Jesus and the church.[21]

In this early phase of the incarnation, von Balthasar argues, the Trinity taught elemental doxology to the Jews as a prerequisite for the sophisticated doxology of the next phases. He explains that the movement from the old to the new covenant is marked by a pedagogical "integration" and "concentration" of the "abstract" glory of God in the beginning of the old covenant into the "concrete-personal" glory of God in the later covenant theology of Israel, and finally into the fully incarnate trinitarian glory of God in the new covenant.[22] In each instance, God's revelation of glory—or in Hebrew, *kabod*—has a sensory form. These sensory revelations of glory have a sacramental form in that they interrupt one's life, shock one into attention, and compel a doxological response of praise and thanksgiving.[23] In marked contrast to impersonal and terrifying inner-worldly epiphanies of beauty, however, von Balthasar believes that Hebrew religion gradually came to understand the *kabod* of God's revelation as a self-communication of personal holiness.[24] This revelation of God's personal holiness exposed the personal unholiness of the humans who encountered it and compelled them to reform their lives according to a divine standard. Von Balthasar uses analogies drawn from a phenomenology of interpersonal communication to describe this Hebrew experience of God's *kabod*:

> In the human realm *kabod* means the "resplendent and thus appearing 'weightiness' or might of a being." The root *kbd* initially connotes what is physically heavy or weighty, but then it can refer to everything which gives any living being, especially man, an external force or impetus (*gravitas*) that makes it appear imposing: . . . it is not only the mysterious external radiance that is designated as *kabod* but also the "radiant centre" of the person himself, his "I" or "self" in its stateliness for himself and for others. . . .[25]

God's personal *kabod* communicated to the Hebrews a seriousness of purpose and intensity of care that challenged the pettiness, vanity, self-centeredness, and triviality of human life. God's *kabod* judged its recipients and inspired them to reshape their lives in accordance with God's *gravitas*. The holiness of God's *kabod*, therefore, is not simply mysterious power, but rather the light and goodness of a personal God who offers a name, a face, and an identity: Yahweh is the one whose personal holiness trains the recipients of his presence in holiness.[26] Yahweh's holiness demands homage and adoration as transcendent and wholly-other, and yet paradoxically by its very otherness it challenges people to share in it through righteousness. Thus, for von Balthasar, in the biblical understanding of divine glory, it is God's distance from creation that makes possible intimacy with God, which in turn makes possible God's pedagogical training of human freedom in holiness.[27] The Sinai appearances of God's "beauty" to Moses (Exod. 33:11, 19, 23; Deut. 34:10; Num. 12:18) are paradigmatic instances of this paradoxical dynamic; God, in giving the law, shows his "face" to Moses while remaining wholly unknown and beyond human control in complete transcendence.[28] Clearly then, on von Balthasar's interpretation, the *kabod* teaches a concrete lesson in human freedom and moral responsibility, not an abstract lesson about an anonymous mythical god.[29] The content of the laws in the covenant between God and Israel make explicit the ethical-personal implications of *kabod*. Commenting on God's commandment to be holy as God is holy in Lev. 19:2 and 11:44, von Balthasar says that when God turns his face and gives his name to Israel this constitutes a sacramental "pledge" of divine presence, an open invitation to "rapture" into God's own "divine space (*temenos*)" of personal holiness.[30] The curriculum of divine pedagogy in the old covenant, therefore, was to train the Jews in an incarnational religiosity: God was teaching the Jews concretely to embody his divine holiness in human society and culture.

Von Balthasar thinks that the Old Testament's prophetic writings present this incarnational curriculum very clearly.[31] In particular, he believes the theology presented in the book of Hosea is an Old Testament prefiguring of a Johannine conception of divine holiness as divine love. Of the book of Hosea, he writes,

> God's relationship to the people is disclosed—for the first time in the history of Israel—as love, burning and tender love, because this love appears in the deepest humiliation. Through this, with disconcerting suddenness, we are given a proleptic view of the final act of the drama: that which is divine in God, his glory, becomes understandable as love, so that everything that God (in the image of the prophet) will undertake *vis-à-vis* his people—including the most terrible measures—is necessarily set under the sign of love.[32]

Hosea's portrayal of a God who is willing to take back an adulterous Israel demonstrates that the Hebrew understanding of *kabod* had progressed to "a new incomprehensible depth as the love that lies beyond wrath and has to do with God's being God, with his absoluteness."[33] Moreover, not only has God's pedagogy taught that God is faithful in loving Israel but also that God shows a level of commitment to it that is inexplicable by human standards. This lesson that divine holiness is pure, undeterred love completely contradicts the impersonal, aloof, and potentially terrifying nature of the gods adored in pagan aesthetics.

This reading of Hosea itself draws upon von Balthasar's interpretation of Deuteronomy. In von Balthasar's exposition of Deuteronomy he highlights the theme that God trains the people of Israel by electing them into a covenant (*berith*) whose sole purpose is to teach them the meaning of divine love.[34] The covenant begins with God's unilateral offer of love to the people. God's only expectation from the Hebrews is that they respect his transcendent difference and glorify him as their creator by being the worshipful and ethical creatures he intended them to be. All other cultic, liturgical, and moral laws are meant to teach this doxological lesson.[35] Von Balthasar explains that in Deuteronomy the encounter with God's *kabod* always inspires a concrete ethical response. Deuteronomy often refers to this response as "giving back" God's glory in praise and glorification.[36] This "giving back" is not purely interior but rather involves going out of one's self in service to others. In Deuteronomy's theology, von Balthasar believes, ethical activity is the quintessentially incarnational activity because it mirrors God's holiness.[37]

On von Balthasar's reading of the Old Testament, God intended to train the Jews for a preliminary incarnation of the divine Word in Israel which would transform their covenant community into a sacrament of the supernatural in history. As the Old Testament's prophetic literature makes clear, however, the Hebrew people substantially—but not totally—failed to receive the Word and sacramentally mirror Yahweh's holiness to the world.[38] God worked with this failure by training the Jews in the prerequisite paradoxes of glory in ignominy, dignity in debasement, spiritual fullness through spiritual emptiness, and faithfulness through abandonment.[39] Von Balthasar sees this training process at work in the Old Testament's exilic and postexilic literature. For example, he argues that God turns away from Israel after the exile, in effect suspending the history of salvation, to test the Jews and teach them faithfulness.[40] The Jews responded poorly to the lesson, however, and, in a variety of ways, forfeited their monotheistic identity and forgot their incarnational mission. Postexilic Jewish religion became plagued with historical pessimism, sectarian isolationism, other-worldly escapism, existential fatalism, and myopic ritualism.[41] In short, Judaism after the exile was deeply contaminated by Gnostic religiosity.

## God's Incarnational Curriculum:
## The Old Covenant's Prophetic Ethos

Von Balthasar believes that Western Christianity is haunted by Marcionism and thus always needs to be reminded that the fundamental theological assumptions of both the old and new covenants are monotheistic. In revealing himself, God first and foremost reveals he is ontologically different from all created reality. God's radical transcendence is clearly evident in the Old Testament's frequent assertions that Israel's God is the creator, Lord of history, and superior to all pagan gods. Moreover, God reveals that creatures cannot approach him across the ontological gap—they only know God as God when he enters the creation and shows himself to creatures in a manner they can recognize and accept.[42] Von Balthasar believes that it is nevertheless axiomatic for biblical monotheism that when God reveals and incarnates his Word he confronts the finite human mind with a reality it cannot conceptually master or speculatively manipulate.[43]

In the Bible's unique anthropology, human beings are created in the image and likeness of God. Von Balthasar draws the conclusion that humans are a mystery to themselves in a fashion analogous to the mystery of God. Humans can truly understand themselves only in light of divine revelation. Revelation teaches human beings that they are neither purely spiritual—and hence not innately divine—nor purely material, but instead a "psychosomatic unity" existing in a fundamentally mysterious state of "suspension" between nature and grace.[44] This suspension creates a fundamental tension within human existence because, although finite and created, humans nevertheless possesses an intrinsic orientation toward God. In an idea drawn from an Irenaean theology of divine pedagogy, von Balthasar maintains that this tension is a necessary consequence of God's decision to bestow free will on human beings, and to save them by redeeming rather than overriding their freedom. According to von Balthasar, Irenaeus thought that God trained human creatures to receive the Word by giving them "hints" instead of forcing the Word on them because he desired that their unity with him be based on love and not coercion.[45] Indeed, von Balthasar is in agreement with Irenaeus that the capacity to freely receive grace is precisely what constitutes human creatures as the "image" of God.[46]

This monotheistic interpretation of human nature stands in opposition to what von Balthasar refers to as "the determinism and fatalism of the ancient world."[47] He sets the biblical assumption of an ontological gap between God and world against ancient pagan mythology, which he broadly characterizes as either denying the visible world in favor of the divine or assuming that the natural laws of the world are divine.[48] In either case, pagan religions are inherently magical and cultic, their notion of time is cyclical, and their highest ideals are centered on human self-apotheosis into spirit.[49] He contends that the internal logic of all types of paganism negates creation because it presupposes an antagonistic relationship between matter and spirit, time and eternity. When pure spirit is the only ontological reality, it is inevitably the case that affirming spirit must mean negating matter. Therefore, contrary to surface appearances, paganism is not positive about the material world. Von Balthasar believes that, because neither humans nor the earth are in fact pure spirit, eventually every pagan religion becomes disappointed in humanity and the earth, and either begins to advocate escape from this world or counsels a fatalistic resignation to suffering. Von Balthasar believes that the view of human beings found in nonbiblical religions is irreconcilable with biblical monotheism's conception of autonomous and free human creatures existing across an ontological divide from a personal God.[50]

Von Balthasar believes, however, that simply asserting the difference between biblical monotheism and paganism is insufficient for understanding monotheism. He sees Israel's theology developing according to an internal logic that cannot be understood simply by contrasting it with paganism. For monotheists, God's radical transcendence does not mean, as in paganism, that God is distant from the world. Rather, God is the immanent non-other (*non-aliud*) to the world, the Other who is fully present in self-giving to human creatures but yet who always eludes the grasp of explanatory theories that pretend to see God and world together in one inclusive perspective.[51] Von Balthasar holds that the "wholly other" God of Israel's monotheism is so absolutely transcendent that even contradictions such as inner-outer, present-absent, and beautiful-ugly do not apply. In biblical monotheism, divine immanence in creation is neither a necessity for nor a contradiction of divine transcendence. This paradox is not possible in extrabiblical thought because here ontological dualism and ontological monism tend to be extremes that eventually meet. In ontological dualism the fundamental "contradiction between God and the world" can only be overcome "by a negative interpretation of the reality of the world and by its absorption into the fullness of God."[52]

Von Balthasar argues that biblical monotheists therefore have a unique understanding of redemption that cannot be reinterpreted as "enlightenment" about the illusory nature of the material world or as escape from it. On the contrary, redemption means the affirmation of the created order by its increasingly free integration—not absorption—into the divine life. In a relationship that is asymmetrical but nonetheless reciprocal, God opens the personal sphere of divine holiness for human participation and draws humans into it.[53] Directly corresponding to this ascent into God's opened space, there is a descent and incarnation of God's holiness and divine presence into human hearts that have made themselves malleable and receptive.[54] Von Balthasar insists that God's grace is glorious because it incarnates itself in and changes the lives of human creatures.[55] This incarnational dynamic constitutes the core meaning of religion in the old covenant, and thus it provides the basis for understanding the Christian doctrine of redemption.

The incarnational dynamic is prefigured most clearly in the Old Testament's prophetic tradition. Hence the prophetic tradition can be read christologically as the site of an ever-increasing incarnation of God in human hearts. Deutero-Isaiah is, for von Balthasar, the pinnacle of this christological, incarnational process in the old covenant. In Deutero-Isaiah, he writes, we see indications of "an intimacy with God that goes beyond everything known in the old covenant, a permanent initiation by God, going deeper and deeper, to which there corresponds on man's part pure 'non-resistance,' a state in which the only desire is to let oneself be drawn in."[56] This "non-resistance" in Deutero-Isaiah corresponds to the essence of created nature, which von Balthasar defines as "being-in-nothingness."[57] Outside of monotheism, the terms "non-resistance" and "being-in-nothingness" might imply that the created self is without substance or independent integrity, but in von Balthasar's thinking a doxological theology of mutual affirmation prevents this implication. When God becomes incarnate in human beings, he always respects the ontological difference between divine and human. In close conformity with Irenaeus, von Balthasar argues that God refuses to overcome human freedom by compulsion.[58] The grace that accompanies God's self-revelation in the old covenant refuses to do violence to the freedom and creaturely integrity of its recipient but instead is always an invitation in which "the infinite 'I' summons the finite 'I' to be fully itself."[59] This relationship between the infinite subject and the finite subject does not diminish the latter ontologically but instead brings it into its own proper created identity. In order to encounter the love of God in the covenant, however, it is necessary for the finite subject to open itself in obedience to God and then remain receptive to whatever God communicates.[60] "In its exact sense," von Balthasar explains, "prophetic existence is the existence of a person who in faith has been divested of any intent to give himself shape, who makes himself available as matter for divine action."[61] With Irenaeus, he argues that being a creature means existing in an unformed state so that, in pure obedience to God's will, it can undergo a perpetual training, shaping, and formation process by the hands of God.[62] Being a living form of God's glory leads one to become "detached from [one]self . . . [and] drawn into the emotions of the deity himself." This encounter is traumatic for the prophet because God gives him access to "the feelings in God's heart, wrath, love, sorrow, revulsion, and even doubt as to what to do or how to do it."[63]

All prophets, on von Balthasar's reading, experience this interiorizing of grace, but it never in any way disconnects them from society or ethical obligation. The practical implications of this understanding of grace become clear in von Balthasar's discussion of the prophets' encounters with divine truth (*emeth*). Contrary to Greek philosophy's visual term for truth, *aletheia* (unveiling), which implies a detached spectator, the Hebrew *emeth* indicates God's fundamental reliability and trustworthiness as one who makes dependable commitments and who keeps promises.[64] Dwelling in the space of God's truthfulness commits one to mirroring this truthfulness in one's life. Moreover, it requires that one mirror God's commitment to the goodness of creation.[65] In other words, dwelling in God's *emeth* means incarnating a religiosity that is unconditionally positive about life and the ultimate goodness of history. The conception of truth as *emeth* also demands an affirmative involvement with creation. The experience of God's love opens the prophets to the divine *chesed* and *rachamim*, which express the deeply ethical dimensions of the covenant. *Chesed* can be translated as benevolence, grace, and love, but also as favor, kindness, and graciousness. The word *rachamim* "is used of God as the one who has mercy on Israel and especially the poor, the widows and the orphans in Israel."[66] This meaning was developed by the prophets, who consistently preached that the gifts of God's *chesed* and *rachamim* required Israel to manifest benevolence and mercy for the poor in their midst.[67] The one who encounters God's glory is obligated to reciprocate it concretely.[68] For the prophets, interior grace becomes embodied in ethical action in conformity to the covenant law.[69] On von Balthasar's interpretation, the legal and ethical implications of *chesed* and *rachamim* as they are used in Old Testament literature are essentially rooted in a theology of Yahweh's glorious holiness (*kabod*).[70] Von Balthasar argues that this sharing in God's holiness means sharing in God's dispositions, especially mercy toward the poor.[71] The prophets rightly saw a close connection between idolatry and injustice toward the poor.[72]

Von Balthasar makes the concrete ethical content of the old covenant's monotheism even more explicit in his discussion of the prophetic conception of God's *sedaka*. The Hebrew word *sedaka* is usually translated as "righteousness," but its root (*sedek*) has the more general meaning of the most fundamental or highest value in life.[73] The words *sedek* and *sedaka* are therefore at the core of the old covenant's understanding of the continuity of grace and ethics. For example, *sedek* and *sedaka* indicate the close connection between one's acts and the world of consequences created by those acts. Von Balthasar defines the word *sedek* as "both correct behavior (as deed) and blessing. . . ."[74] In other words, *sedek* means God's fidelity to the covenant and its terms, and hence it implies living in the ethical-mystical space opened by God's holiness. Living according to God's revealed *sedaka*, von Balthasar argues, can be a "*sacramental form* by which one can place oneself, anew or more deeply, in God's mode of being right, thanks to the sphere of right which his grace has opened up."[75] This form of holiness is not the result of a "forensic" justification, von Balthasar explains, but rather is the predisposition to accept and carry out God's will in total obedience and thankful love. The grace of God's holiness makes an "unheard-of demand" on those who are encountered by it, lifting them out of themselves and into the *sedaka* of God. Von Balthasar writes, "Everything is now measured against the standard of divine rightness, of his ethical '*justice*' and his aesthetic '*justesse*'. In God's covenant, grace and demand are inseparably locked into one another."[76]

Another important element of God's holiness von Balthasar identifies in the prophetic ethos is the divine *mishpat*. It is perhaps the most concrete aspect of the mystery of divine glory in the prophetic tradition, yet it has a "spectrum of meanings" wider than any of the terms examined thus far.[77] He explains that in the old covenant *mishpat* means "what is ethically right (cf. Gen. 18.19), and this in turn emerges irrefutably in concrete terms in the claim of the poor to what is right." For the later prophets, *mishpat* means

> the just treatment of the poor, who are incapable of enforcing their own right and establishing it, in the very center of God's conventional requirements. In the face of the injustice done to him, the 'poor' becomes simply the one who is 'innocent' (Amos 5.12), and that which is 'right' becomes straightforwardly what is 'good' (5.14-15); once again, *mishpat* and *sedaka* appear jointly (5.7, 24; 6.12). In Isaiah, *mishpat* becomes the all-embracing concept for what is right, with an unconditional seriousness both in the area of ethics and in the area of law: *mishpat* is that which must be brought into force in all circumstances and is made clear again and again in the model of the poor and the oppressed, the widows and orphans.[78]

In both Isaiah and Deuteronomy, von Balthasar explains, *sedaka* and *mishpat* express God's fatherly concern about injustice toward the poor and the oppressed, as well as God's will that such injustice must not be allowed to exist on earth.[79] In Jeremiah and Ezekiel too this understanding of *mishpat* is dominant. Von Balthasar notes that for Jeremiah and Ezekiel the Babylonian Exile can be seen as a punishment for failing to enact God's *mishpat*. Von Balthasar also argues that in Second Isaiah *mishpat* comes to mean that "the raising-up of the poor involves the laying low of the rich and satiated, who are cited before the court of God's justice because of the injustice they have done."[80] Therefore, for von Balthasar, the incarnation of the Word in the old covenant's prophetic tradition always meant establishing a social order oriented toward justice for the weak, poor, and outcast.

## The Prophetic Ethos in the New Covenant

Von Balthasar thinks that the incarnational activity of the Word in the old covenant's prophetic tradition reaches its highest fulfillment in God's incarnation in Jesus Christ. At times, however, he seems to distinguish the old and new covenants in a way that undermines his *corpus triforme* assumptions about the on-going incarnation of the Word in history. He occasionally argues for a qualitative difference between the covenants, maintaining that the movement from the *kabod* to the trinitarian glory of Christ is not simply a quantitative development of Old Testament insights but a "qualitative leap" into a "wholly different order."[81] When encountering such claims, it is very important not to consider von Balthasar's point in isolation from the claims he makes throughout *GL6* about the embodying of the Word in Israel. Clearly he wants to assert that there is a substantial difference between God's incarnation in Israel and the prophets, on one hand, and God's incarnation in the church, on the other. Moreover, he asserts a radical difference between both of these and God's incarnation in Jesus.[82] "Theology cannot espouse a simple 'identity' between the People of God and the history of revelation," he explains, "for somehow this would make Christ merely one constituent element of the total process. Nor can it embrace a simple (Marcionite) opposition between Synagogue and Church, where the former is the *sarx* (*gramma*) and the latter is the *pneuma*."[83] Nonetheless, von Balthasar *does* think there is *one* incarnational process in history, even if Christ cannot be counted "merely" as one coequal element within it and the church's place in the process must be counted as superior to Israel's. All three phases, however profoundly asymmetrical they may be in themselves, testify to the one *corpus triforme*. Therefore it would be a mistake to think that the "qualitative leap" from the old to the new covenant is of the same type as the qualitative difference between paganism and biblical monotheism. In fact, if one interpreted von Balthasar as assuming this radical difference in kind, rather than a radical difference in degree, between God's incarnation in Israel, God's incarnation in Jesus, and God's incarnation in the church, it would completely undermine his anti-Marcionist case for the unity of the old and new covenants, as well as his generally Irenaean paradigm of salvation history as a form of divine pedagogy.[84]

The real issue for him is not a qualitative difference in the kind of grace in each covenant but rather a quantitative difference in the specificity of the form taken by grace, and, directly related to this, something like a sophisticated radical quantitative difference in the degree and efficacy of grace in each covenant. This sophisticated radical difference qualifies the relationship between the covenants as "dialectical" in a loose, almost rhetorical sense.[85] Israel's No to Christ and the church's Yes to Christ place the covenants in a permanent historical tension as rival forms, but, of course, the rivalry is contained and defined by a common participation in the single process of the Word's on-going incarnation. He expresses the nature of this rivalry in terms of a "primal rupture" in which the new covenant, due to the guidance of the risen Christ and Holy Spirit, is able to cross over a "threshold."[86] Yet the "discontinuity" of this rupture remains within a wider "continuity," as the metaphor of a threshold suggests.[87] He remarks that "we must agree with Karl Barth when he says that there is only one People of God, consisting of Synagogue and Church together."[88] Nevertheless, in the single process of salvation history the new covenant has a special status as an advanced form of monotheistic religion that has transfigured its preliminary preparation in Israel. It is an advanced form for three reasons. First, there is a radical deepening of the old covenant's incarnational dynamic in the new covenant due to the full recapitulation in the Christ-form of both Israel's history and universal human nature. This radical deepening of the incarnational dynamic in the Christ-form deepens what the Jewish prophets understood as Yahweh's *emeth, chesed, rachamim, sedaka,* and *mishpat* by revealing God's inner life as a Trinity of love opening itself for human participation. Second, the new covenant has transcended the ethnic "particularity" of the old covenant and opened the incarnational dynamic to all races and nations.[89] Third, both the radical deepening and the universalizing of the old covenant's incarnational dynamic are redemptive in a way the prophetic tradition was not and could not have been.[90] Again, von Balthasar's point here must be read as an assertion of a sophisticated kind of quantitative difference because all three phases of the incarnation count for him as (asymmetrically) redemptive. He maintains that "Israel and the Church represent two sides of the one redemptive mystery" of Christ.[91]

With regard to the first point that von Balthasar sees there a radical deepening of the old covenant's incarnational dynamic in the new covenant, both he and Irenaeus posit a recapitulation Christology. Both thinkers argue that when the Word takes on flesh in Christ this must mean that the Word becomes fully human and that he fulfills the inner telos of God's covenant with Israel.[92] Christ is thus both "a concentrated, transcending summary of the history of Israel" and the "wholly new image of man"; Christ is the "new Adam" who maintains an obedience to God beyond what Israel was capable of achieving.[93] Because Christ was fully divine as well as fully human, he could undergo the tragedies of death and hell, transform them from within, and establish solidarity among all creatures in the image of the "trinitarian solidarity of love in heaven."[94] Von Balthasar considers this interpretation of the incarnation essential if the new covenant is not to be seen, on one hand, as the negation of the old covenant's actual incarnational dynamic, or, on the other hand, as the negation of the created order's incarnational potential.[95] Interpreting the incarnation as recapitulation means, according to von Balthasar, that the new covenant collaborates in the redemption of the created order precisely in and through the perfection of the old covenant's prophetic ethos.

In Israel's incarnational dynamic, the covenant called upon the people to glorify God's revealed holiness through ethical lives of covenant obedience. Recall here von Balthasar's claim that the interior piety of the prophets gave no resistance to God's efforts to shape their lives into vessels of divine holiness. He contends that Jesus also educated his disciples into this prophetic attitude.[96] Often Jesus' pre-Easter teachings seem to be, von Balthasar explains,

> nothing else than the purified synthesis of the old covenant, as for example where he expresses its embodiment in the three words "justice" (*mishpat*, which derives from God and is to have its effect in men's deeds; Amos 5:24; cf. Mt 5:6; 6:33), "mercy" (*chesed, rachamim*, Mic 6:8; as embodiment of justice, Mt 12:7), and "loyalty and faith" (*emeth*), the fundamental attitude of the covenant God, which should pass over to man in his relationship to God and to his neighbor: Mt 23:23.[97]

Jesus, however, did not simply exhort his disciples to live an ethical norm. He also required that they leave all possessions behind and become completely poor so that they could learn "the essential *poverty* of human existence, its dependence on God (Mt. 6:25ff.)" and hence the connection between perfect poverty and the total readiness to accept whatever God commands in perfect obedience.[98] The maximalism of Jesus' requirement of total poverty, von Balthasar remarks, is "seemingly inhuman," but only if one lacks a holistic understanding of the Christ-form. First of all, in obedience to his Father, Jesus himself is "absolutely poor," and hence he realizes "archetypally, representatively and inclusively" the poverty and receptivity he demands as prerequisites for covenant obedience.[99] Indeed, Jesus actualizes this prophetic ethos to such an extreme extent that he is involved in an ever-increasing act of self-abandonment to the Father's love in every dimension of his human existence.[100] However, the inspirational power of the pre-Easter Jesus is only a prefiguring of the sacramental mystery of the cross and resurrection.

"[T]he formal *Leitmotiv* of all the Gospels," von Balthasar argues, is that Jesus went beyond what any prophet in the old covenant had taught by claiming for himself the divine authority to make a decision about the eschatological destiny of every person.[101] This claim of divine authority is directly connected to what the New Testament considers to be Jesus' post-Easter status as a new historical form of divine glory, a form that has unprecedented power to communicate grace and inspire faith. Von Balthasar does not think the "newness" of grace in Christ implies that grace in the old covenant is now defunct, nor does he believe Jews need to convert to Christianity to be saved.[102] Instead, the newness of grace refers to the degree, locus, and efficacy of grace. In Christ grace has a very specific form and an unprecedented symbolic power: the glory shining from the powerless, obedient Word of God in the crucified and resurrected rabbi, Jesus of Nazareth. In other words, the new covenant surpasses the old in the concreteness and specificity of grace, not in the incarnational dynamic of grace. Von Balthasar explains that although the prophets mediated God's presence to the people through their own participation in divine *kabod*, they were not themselves the *permanent* sources of divine grace in history. This is because the prophets were only "vessels for the Word, taken up and then allowed to go on their own way."[103] During his life a prophet could exemplify the incarnational dynamic and thereby inspire others to receptive obedience to the divine Word. After his death, however, a prophet no longer had even this exemplary power or mediator function.[104] But unlike the prophets, von Balthasar maintains, Jesus was not simply a temporary vessel for the Word—he was "the man in whose human existence God willed to proceed to his final act of self-utterance."[105] This is why, he argues, all Jesus' pre-Easter teachings on poverty and his claims to authority are "prima facie irreconcilable" and require the cross and resurrection to make them coherent.[106]

### Trinitarian Glory and the New Covenant

The discussion up to this point has already suggested what von Balthasar sees as the points of difference between the covenants. This section will focus and develop these suggestions. Von Balthasar believes that the Christian church formed after the death of Jesus represents the beginning of a new phase in God's pedagogical training of humanity in receptivity to the Word. The difference that constitutes the "newness" is that the new covenant community has an advantage the old covenant community lacked: the full and complete incarnation of the Word in Jesus. In other words, God gives educational assistance to the new covenant community that he withheld from the old covenant community. This assistance has two elements: (1) a perfect human model of incarnational religiosity that mirrors God's holiness on earth; and (2) a permanent supernatural presence in sacramental form to inspire and guide them when tragedy and sin threaten to render meaningless and ineffectual their efforts to incarnate divine holiness.

Recall von Balthasar's understanding of the analogy between classical aesthetics and sacramentality. He thinks that the most beautiful forms and the most grace-filled sacraments are the ones that are most transparent to the light of being and the light of God, respectively. He argues that the Christ-form sacramentalizes the light of the Father's holiness into human hearts because in his death and resurrection he becomes "fully transparent to God."[107] Von Balthasar asserts it is precisely this that makes Jesus the incarnate Word of God.[108] For this claim to be congruent with his overall position, however, it must be qualified with the terms "full and permanent." Jesus surpasses the prophets because in his resurrection he becomes the full and permanent vehicle for the Father's plan to continue the incarnational process in creation as a whole. The divine pedagogy always relied on the power of symbols to motivate, but after the resurrection the Father has the ultimate pedagogical symbol. The range of meaning in the Christ-form is so broad, von Balthasar believes, that the Father—the divine pedagogue—can use the risen Christ "like an alphabet or a keyboard" to express customized sacraments of divine love uniquely suited to the educational needs of all his human pupils.[109] This is, for von Balthasar, the core of the new covenant's distinctive theology of the mystery of grace, or, as it is traditionally termed, the paschal mystery.[110] In his last act of "self-giving" on the cross, Jesus holds up for his disciples an act of "incomparable self-abandonment" that finally makes clear for them the meaning of all the requirements he gave them "of hatred of self, of denial of self, of the abandoning of all things, of the daily bearing of the cross, and of the losing of one's soul in order to gain it."[111] It is not that the disciples simply imitate Christ's poverty and self-abandonment on the cross from an external perspective, but rather they contemplate its attractiveness and allow it to communicate the grace of the Holy Spirit to them, thereby drawing them into the third phase of the incarnational dynamic.[112]

Clearly then, von Balthasar's understanding of the incarnation of the Word in the "flesh"—and consequent communication of grace in the Holy Spirit—is a synthesis of classical aesthetics and a Johannine theology of the paschal mystery. This synthesis can be understood as a trans-figuration of the former by the latter when we see that for von Balthasar the Johannine theology of the paschal mystery is always contextualized within the parameters of a theology of divine *kenosis*. Von Balthasar constructs this synthesis because for him kenotic theology is the primary engine of the New Testament's trinitarian reinterpretation of the Old Testament's theology of Yahweh's glory. Commenting on Phil. 2:6-11, von Balthasar writes, "The one who was 'emptied out' received a share in the doxa of God the Father, through the bestowal of the divine title 'Kyrios'; it is not this doxa, however, which is of course presupposed, that the hymn wishes to glorify, but the thing that was inconceivable in the Old Testament, the reason for his exaltation—his opening-up of the empty space through which the doxa can send its rays."[113] This New Testament understanding of glory brings to fulfillment the Old Testament's various, and sometimes competing, conceptions of the *kabod* as divine power, freedom, sovereignty, holiness, justice, mercy, loyalty, truthfulness, and love by reconciling them all into the new covenant's theology of glory as the power of divine love in utter powerlessness.[114] In other words, by reinterpreting revelation in light of the cross and resurrection, the new covenant fulfills the old covenant's understanding of divine love by making it explicitly trinitarian. Having said this, we must remember that von Balthasar does not believe the wholly-other God becomes deeply present in creation as the non-other (*non-aliud*) for the first time in Jesus Christ. He does think, however, that Christ permanently and unsurpassably bridges the eternal and temporal realms. Only a trinitarian theology of *kenosis*, he maintains, allows us to conceive of how this could be the case. Rather than focusing on the generic "divine nature of God" in the theology of the incarnation, von Balthasar thinks it is more theologically fruitful, as well as congruent with the theology of the New Testament in general, and Johannine theology in particular, to use the conception of trinitarian persons who are selfless "pure relations in the love within the Godhead" as a key for seeing how the eternal Word of God can freely become a silent nonword that communicates eternal divine love in creation.[115]

It is von Balthasar's conviction that finite creatures (faithful Jews excepted) have no access to the glory of eternal divine love except through personal participation in the paschal mystery of Christ, which, as a sacramental mystery, carries its own internal logic.[116] Moreover, in the case of the paschal mystery, the internal logic is the revelation of the Trinity freely opening itself to creation and drawing it into the inner divine sphere of self-giving.[117] Von Balthasar explains that the prophets of the old covenant were able to discern that the inner-life of God is love but not that it is trinitarian because the inner-realm had not yet been fully opened to the created order. "The full accomplishment of the covenant . . . becomes possible only when the immanent Trinity becomes the economic Trinity," he writes, "when, therefore, the righteousness (*sedek*) of the Old Testament, as relatedness affecting the whole of man's being, is transcended and deepened to a communication to the creature of the relationality of the triune life which affects the whole being within the Godhead."[118] The mystery of the Trinity becomes fully accessible only through the sacramental event of the incarnation.[119]

Fulfillment, however, does not mean forfeiture. Von Balthasar contends that the old covenant's conceptions of justice and righteousness are not only preserved but intensified in the new covenant's theology of trinitarian revelation. As I will discuss more below, he uses the metaphor of a trinitarian "circuit" to describe the nature of the relationship between the openness and self-giving of divine persons in eternity, and the opening up of this inner-trinitarian communion for creaturely assimilation in the economy of salvation. In opening the eternal trinitarian circuit to human participation, the transcendent God works within the created realm to enable human recipients to incarnate Yahweh's *chesed*, *rachamim, sedaka,* and *mishpat.*

At this point it will be helpful to return to the issue of the "qualitative" difference between the old and new covenants and von Balthasar's belief that when the Word takes on flesh in Christ he fulfills the inner telos of God's covenant with Israel. Von Balthasar considers death as the major boundary in the old covenant preventing its fulfillment because it is closely connected in Hebrew thought with the reality of sin and the loss of divine glory.[120] Asserting that the new covenant is the recapitulation and the fulfillment of the old covenant inherently implies that in the incarnation the Son does not simply take on "creatureliness" in general, but rather he recapitulates humanity's full existential condition as fallen creatures who have turned from the glory of God's love and are hence now subject to death.[121] Entering into solidarity with humanity's existential condition of sin necessarily means that the cross and hell—understood as the absolute separation from God—are the necessary consequences of the incarnation.[122] Christ's absolute self-abandonment in undergoing death in full solidarity with the sinful condition of humans is directly related to his status as the eternal, beloved Son who empties himself out of obedient love for the Father.[123] Therefore, von Balthasar writes, "with the removal of the whole superstructure of the incarnation, the eternal will of the Son within the Trinity to obedience is exposed as the substructure that is the basis of the entire event of the incarnation: and this is set face-to-face with the hidden substructure of sinful existence, exposed in Sheol, as the state of separation from God, the 'loss of his glory.'"[124] Yet, this "face-to-face" of obedience and sin, communion and separation was not willed by the Father as a form of punitive wrath against the world through the Son's suffering, but rather as the means of the world's redemption through the Son's establishment of the sacramental form of perfect, universal righteousness (*sedek*) on earth.[125]

This connection between the work of redemption and the incarnation of righteousness on earth in the opening of the trinitarian circuit is central to von Balthasar's entire conception of the sacramental efficacy of the paschal mystery. Moreover, this connection is also the key to seeing why he identifies salvation with deification. Given the importance of this identification in his theology it is not surprising to find him explicitly identifying Irenaeus as his theological source. Von Balthasar quotes Irenaeus to make the point that in Christ's descent to death and hell he encounters "the 'remainder' that could not be absorbed into the Father's work of creation, because he had left man freedom to decide for or against God—the unfinished part of the creation, that it was left to the incarnate Son to finish; and the Son, obedient to his mission, is led by the Father now into the state of existence of this sin that 'remains.' *Descendit ad inferiora terrae, id quod erat inoperatum conditionis visurus oculis* (Irenaeus)."[126] He explains that in encountering this "unfinished part of the creation," the Son completes it by bringing it into the opened space of his empty self where it can participate in the life-giving power of the trinitarian circuit.[127] This participation and completion of the creation in Christ are possible because, paradoxically, the separation of the Son from the Father in death only intensifies their inner-trinitarian communion. This paradoxical claim for the continuity-in-discontinuity of the Father and the Son is itself rooted in the deeper "logic" of the eternal relationship between the trinitarian persons. Because the Son's separation from the Father is undertaken in free self-abandonment, the Spirit is able to come forth from the Father and enter the Son through the bond of his perfect obedience, thereby reinfusing him with eternal life.[128] Yet the trinitarian event of crucifixion, descent into hell, and resurrection is also an event of creaturely redemption because this reinfusion of eternal life in the Spirit gives Christ the power to send out this same Spirit into those who contemplate the mystery of his death and resurrection, thereby transforming the old covenant's theocentrism into the new covenant's christocentrism.[129] In Christ's death, von Balthasar explains, the triune God is at work "seizing fate and destiny . . . wrenching them out of their axes."[130] Von Balthasar explains the redemptive work of the Trinity in Christ's crucifixion, descent into hell, and resurrection not in terms of an idealist conception of human nature or of creation in general but instead in terms of the historical dynamics of fate and destiny: "It is by this that principalities and powers of fate, which keep man subordinate, are absorbed into the realm of grace and freedom, and 'made ineffective' (1 Cor 2.6; 15.24ff.; Heb 2.14)"[131]

The theology of absolute trinitarian love entering history is the most important element of von Balthasar's *corpus triforme* Christology. With Irenaeus as his primary guide, von Balthasar maintains that the connection between redemption and righteousness lies in the gift of freedom that comes from participation in the paschal mystery.[132] In Christ's kenotic transparence to divine will, he illuminates all dimensions of created finitude from within, but most especially he illuminates the true nature of finite freedom.[133] In light of the paschal mystery, the poverty and self-abandonment taught and lived by Jesus become universally relevant because through him human persons learn that "obedience to God and waiting upon his will belong to the fundamental structure of the creature."[134] In recapitulating human reality, Christ does not redeem externally by forensic justification, but rather he comes to "indwell" the creature, and thereby redeems according to the internal essence of that which he recapitulates.[135] In other words, human nature from the very beginning of time, created in the image of the eternal Son within the immanent Trinity, was constituted according to the inner-trinitarian dynamism of mutual *ekstasis* and self-giving so that, from their side of the ontological creator-creature divide, human persons would be able to transcend themselves toward God's self-expression in the Son.[136] Hence in their encounter with Christ in his *kenosis* into the world, human creatures encounter the divine archetype of their own finite nature as ecstatic beings whose created nature orients them toward the poverty and self-abandonment necessary for incarnating the Word in their lives.[137] There can be nothing destructive to human nature or foreign about the human encounter with the divine Word because, despite its asymmetrical character as ontologically Other, it presents humans with what they can recognize—however obscurely—as congruent with their own nature.[138] Von Balthasar writes,

> This ability to be poor is the human person's deepest wealth: this is revealed by the Christ-event, in which the essence of being became visible for the very first time: as glory. In giving up his Son, God the Father has opened up this possibility for all. But the Spirit of God is sent to change this possibility in us into reality. He shows the world that the poverty of the Son, who sought only the glory of the Father and let himself be robbed of everything in utter obedience, was the most exact expression of the absolute fullness, which does not consist of "having," but of "being=

giving." It is in giving that one is and has. This cannot be explained in words—"I have yet many things to say to you, but you could not bear it now"—it can only be done, and be understood in the course of doing it.[139]

This passage allows me now to give more explanatory content to von Balthasar's claim that Christ's establishment of perfect, universal righteousness (*sedek*) on earth achieves both the fulfillment of the old covenant and the redemption of the created realm.

For von Balthasar, the Gospel of John presents more clearly than the other Gospels the theological case for the claim that Jesus Christ gives the new covenant an educational advantage over the old covenant. He believes John's theology has a deeper understanding of the incarnational curriculum of God's pedagogy; the Johannine teaching that "the Word became flesh" is thus the central interpretive key to the old covenant, as well as to the canon as a whole.[140] This is also because John's theology is more explicitly trinitarian than the synoptic authors.[141] Johannine theology rightly recognizes, von Balthasar argues, that in the old covenant God was gradually educating the Jews away from a pagan religiosity and toward the incarnational religiosity of holiness fully manifested in Jesus.[142] This religiosity reaches its highest expression in Jesus' crucifixion and resurrection. Here God's love for the world and desire to become incarnate in it are most evident. Von Balthasar affirms all these aspects of Johannine theology and interprets them in terms of his theological aesthetics.

Von Balthasar explains that like many of the imperfect forms the Word assumed in the lives of the prophets, its perfect form in Jesus was shattered by murder. Unlike the prophetic forms, however, the "Christ-form" did not permanently dissolve in formlessness, leaving in its wake a paralyzing sense that righteousness is futile and history is chaos. Instead the Christ-form was resurrected "*as form*, as the form which now, in God himself, has definitively become one with the divine Word and Light which God has intended for and bestowed upon the world."[143] In the light of the resurrection, von Balthasar believes, the trinitarian God reveals himself as a mystery of absolute love and fidelity toward the finitude, materiality, and temporality of the created order.[144] For him this means that "Christianity becomes *the* aesthetic religion *par excellence*."[145] When interpreted together, von Balthasar believes, Jesus' crucifixion and resurrection salvage the old covenant's teaching that ethics is the quintessential incarnational activity because they vindicate the God of Moses as ultimately trustworthy and faithful to his creation. Moreover, they vindicate a joyful attitude about life and hope for the ultimate perfection of the world.[146] In Christ, God reveals himself as the perpetual presence of divine love in history, a love that affirms the "light and truth and goodness and beauty" of the finite, sensory world even in tragedy and death.[147] For von Balthasar, the anti-Gnostic message of the risen Christ's "glory" is clear: all future human efforts to incarnate the divine Word on earth are eminently worthwhile because the Father and the Spirit are working to guarantee their ultimate eschatological success. In this sense, and only in this sense, von Balthasar asserts, Christianity is a "utopian" religion.[148]

This message provides the new covenant community with a major advantage over the old covenant community. A utopian view of life on earth was not a real possibility for the Jews.[149] True utopianism requires the perspective on eternity bestowed in the full incarnation of the Word in Jesus. Von Balthasar describes this perspective as seeing "the mystery of the coincidence of genuine time and genuine eternity: the entry of genuine eternity into time (the incarnation of God), the entry of genuine time into eternity (the resurrection of Christ and of the creation in him)."[150] The Jews in the old covenant could not have anticipated God's full-scale intervention into the fallen world to eradicate the power of death and evil.[151] The Jews could have never imagined that God would save his creation by inspiring it with a utopian hope based on the full and permanent union of eternal life and finitude in Christ. In the terminology of his theological aesthetics, von Balthasar explains that the new covenant fulfills the old by assimilating the reality of death into the incarnate form of God's glory. The crucified and risen Christ thus becomes an "imperishable and indivisible form" that transcends all "corruptible and human beauty (Jas 1.10 = 1 Pet 1.24)."[152] Hence in a world currently dominated by wickedness the Christ-form is the most powerful inspiration in history for resolutely preserving Judaism's belief that ethical activity is the quintessentially incarnational activity. By surrendering to death and sin, the Word demonstrated that fate and evil are weaker than divine freedom and love.[153] In the paschal mystery of the incarnate Word, von Balthasar maintains, God revealed the "absolute power" of love to overcome all human tragedy by entering it and triumphing over it from within.[154]

At this point von Balthasar's interpretation of the new covenant becomes innovative. He argues that rather than exempting Christians from the lesson of faithfulness in abandonment, the Christ-form teaches it by a different means. Instead of undergoing a historical exile and abandonment by God, Christians learn it through seeing exile and abandonment demonstrated by the persons of the Trinity. This demonstration occurs in Christ's crucifixion and descent into hell.[155] The cross is a symbolic window on an exile within the Godhead. Von Balthasar contends that the point of the cross's lesson in trinitarian exile is to prepare Christians for participation in this unity-in-difference of the Trinity. The symbolic power of the Son separating himself from the Father through death and hell teaches the paradoxical trinitarian "logic" of communion through separation.[156] It is important to notice that although von Balthasar's trinitarian theology of the cross and descent to hell is novel in some respects, it does have some precedent within patristic theology. For example, Irenaeus taught a doctrine of Christ's descent into hell.[157] Even if von Balthasar does go beyond Irenaeus and the other church fathers in his trinitarian interpretation of Good Friday and Holy Saturday, he nevertheless follows the patristic practice of interpreting the Christian Scriptures in light of the Old Testament. In this case the story of the Babylonian Exile provides him with a major hermeneutic resource.

The primary source of the trinitarian theology in von Balthasar's interpretation of the cross and descent to hell, however, is the Gospel of John. He interprets Johannine theology as teaching that the cross reveals an inner-trinitarian exile. Von Balthasar refers to this teaching in John's Gospel as the doctrine of a trinitarian "circuit." According to this doctrine, the incarnation, death, and resurrection of the Son opens a space between the trinitarian persons that humans can enter and "dwell."[158] This trinitarian circuit becomes open to human participation through a contemplative focus on Christ, particularly his crucifixion and resurrection. The aesthetic power of the sacramental Christ-form draws those who contemplate it into imitation of it, and hence into Christ's love for the Father and Spirit.[159] It also draws believers into the abandonment and exile of the Son. The cross therefore teaches the same paradox God tried to teach the Jews through the exile, but the cross teaches this lesson aesthetically. (Von Balthasar's paradoxical monotheistic-incarnational understanding of aesthetics must, of course, be kept in mind.[160]) The cross teaches aesthetically by the mysterious "attractiveness" of the Son's obedient love. This attractiveness "saves" because it enraptures and compels those who see it to transform their lives according to the pattern of Christ's absolute fidelity to the Father's will. The attractiveness of trinitarian love on the cross invites members of the new covenant to share in Christ's sufferings, thereby drawing them into the process of on-going incarnation.[161] Insofar as they incarnate the Word, the members of the new covenant will be incarnating on earth the trinitarian paradox of communion-in-exile.

For von Balthasar, therefore, the old covenant's theology of Yahweh's glory finds its fulfillment in the new covenant's theology of paschal mystery. By implication, the old covenant's prophetic ethos of obedience to the law finds fulfillment in the new covenant's understanding of faith.

This is clear in von Balthasar's contention that "the Christology of the New Testament as a whole" only makes sense if we understand it in the context of Paul's concern to connect the righteousness of God with human faith in the crucified and risen Christ.[162] On this point, God's promise to Jeremiah to write the law on human hearts is particularly important for von Balthasar. He asserts, "What is new in the New Testament is the fulfillment of God's promise in the Old Testament that he would write his law (of love) on human hearts, so that they would know God from within (Jer 31.33f.; 2 Cor. 3.3). This law of love is the Spirit: he himself."[163] Yet, for von Balthasar, the work of the Spirit can never be separated from Christ, the archetype of created human nature, who reveals the love of the Father in the economy of salvation. Following 1 Cor. 15:45, he asserts that the risen Christ "becomes" a life-giving spirit, and hence the Son is "the Lord of the Spirit," and the Spirit is the "*Pneuma* of the Son."[164] The qualitative difference in the form of revelation from the old to the new covenant—the visible form of the written Law, on one hand, and the invisible presence of the Holy Spirit of the crucified, risen Christ, on the other hand—also implies therefore a radical difference in the degree, locus, and efficacy of divine grace. This difference not only preserves the creation-affirming ethos in the prophetic tradition's conception of *kabod*—including all that this implied with regard to establishing and maintaining structures in society that ensured justice for the poor and marginalized—but also fulfills it by bestowing the freedom from sin necessary for incarnating Yahweh's *chesed*, *rachamim*, *sedek*, and *mishpat*.[165] The Holy Spirit makes this freedom possible by allowing people to be "liberated into [their] own freedom" as finite creatures in the world.[166] But the connection between Spirit and righteousness remains only implicit in von Balthasar, and making it explicit requires examining his connection between grace, faith, and ethics.

This connection is suggested by von Balthasar's use of the terms "expropriation" and "appropriation" to discuss the dynamism of rapture and self-transcendence in the encounter with the Christ-form. He often uses the term "expropriation" to describe the rapture that occurs when grace opens the closed sphere of the self and draws one toward the paschal mystery.[167] Although in ordinary usage the term expropriation connotes confiscation, and hence an act of taking or seizing, in von Balthasar's theological application it means an act of giving and liberating. This application is intentionally ambiguous precisely because von Balthasar is trying to make a point about the paradoxical relationship between grace and faith. He contends that God's expropriation of the self in grace is simultaneous with our free appropriation of this expropriation.[168] In this paradoxical usage, expropriation is in fact God's act of giving God's self in grace, and appropriation is the finite recipient's act of making a responsive gift of self. In other words, God's expropriation of the finite self can be described as a gift of grace that works from within the finite self to create freedom on two levels, each characterized by von Balthasar as a movement of faith: (1) faith as freely enacted receptive openness to the offer of divine love; and (2) faith as freely offered self-giving in a responsive praxis of righteous obedience to the Father's will that seeks to institute the divine *chesed, rachamim, sedek,* and *mishpat* in the created realm.[169] Although von Balthasar does not explicitly thematize this connection between grace, faith, and ethics, if we closely examine the two dominant ways in which he uses the word "faith" throughout *GL7*, it becomes obvious that this is his operative understanding.

First of all, he describes faith as receptivity—receptive faith that accepts the offer of divine love by allowing God to transform one's interior life. This transformation occurs through an act of submission and the handing over of one's self in complete surrender to grace.[170] Second, von Balthasar also describes faith as an ethical response to the grace offered in Christ. Responsive faith obediently endeavors to incarnate God's love through a life of righteousness and active love for others.[171] Moreover—and here is von Balthasar's connecting presupposition— receptive faith is indispensable for ethical faith and vice versa. It is evident that he sees precisely this connection between both senses of faith when his theological analysis of faith becomes explicitly trinitarian.[172] In his trinitarian theology he holds the two senses of faith closely together in a mutually supportive relationship.

At this point we can now conclude that von Balthasar's basic intention in his christological and trinitarian unification of grace, faith, and ethics is to articulate a modified Irenaean understanding of faith as "true gnosis" and salvation history as a *paidagōgos eis Christon*. He interprets the paschal mystery in terms of the progressive unity between created finite freedom and the liberating work of infinite freedom in the order of redemption. In other words, he believes that only through the "supernatural" revelation of trinitarian mystery can the prophetic model of "creaturely" righteousness be fully activated and consistently sustained. This is because the prophetic forms of the Word could not communicate strongly enough God's power over moral decay, tragedy, and death. Hence the incarnation of the Word in the old covenant was impeded because the Israelites lacked sufficient motivation to risk a genuine act of self-transcendence into Yahweh's glory, or to risk this over time despite failures and tragic setbacks. Only the full presence of trinitarian self-giving in Christ makes human self-transcendence possible and sustainable; consequently, only the full presence of trinitarian self-giving in Christ makes possible long-term, irreversible work to establish *chesed*, *rachamim*, *sedek*, and *mishpat* on earth.

Nevertheless, this difference between the covenants presupposes their unity. Von Balthasar believes that the Christian conception of trinitarian glory removes mystery from a purely epistemological frame of reference and places it in a monotheistic grace-freedom frame of reference. Like the prophets' stress on the presence of *kabod* in the form of the covenant, the new covenant stresses free receptivity and practical obedience to the Christ-form as the bridge between the ontologically asymmetrical realms of God and creature.[173] When interpreted christologically, therefore, grace is given a finite sacramental point of origin with a pedagogic orientation. Sacramental grace in the new covenant, von Balthasar contends, refers primarily to the positive gift of infinite love offered in Christ that leads one more deeply into the mystery of God, thus perfecting finite freedom by working with it rather than against it. This perfection does not absorb or negate finite freedom, but rather, as the prophetic tradition illustrates, trains finite freedom to be itself according to God's will in creating it.

For von Balthasar this theology is obviously Irenaean. The meaning of faith in the new covenant is inseparable from a doxological understanding of the creature's free act of glorifying the divine glory that has first glorified it through the free gift of grace. It is important to recall in light of this point that von Balthasar believes that the theme of "'glory' as the mutual glorification of God and man" is the "central concept" of Irenaeus's entire theology.[174] Reading the New Testament with his Irenaean presuppositions, von Balthasar concludes that its theology of faith is dominated by a glory-glorification theme: he reports that the word "glory" is used 116 times and the phrase "to glorify" is used over 60 times.[175] In all cases the direct referent is the glory of God's inexhaustible trinitarian grace which comes from Christ. Glorifying the Father in the Christ means living an active life of ethical righteousness under the guidance of the Spirit.[176] Von Balthasar sums up this doxological conception of grace, faith, and ethics when he explains that in the New Testament,

> δοξάζειν no longer has the δόξα of God as its object, but as its inner principle. Thanks to the glory of God's love, which has become visible in Jesus Christ and in his Cross and resurrection, we are drawn into this love through his grace and are empowered to give it the response that has been planned and attained by God himself. . . . Faith, love and hope are the divine life that is lived in us, a life that comes from divine glory and

enables us to live the Christian life . . . and thereby has as its inmost goal . . . "the praise and glory and honor" of the divine life (1 Pet 1.7), while God's wisdom has always aimed beforehand at *our* own glorification. . . .[177]

In acting upon us in grace, the triune God glorifies humans with the gift of finite freedom which makes it possible for them to glorify God in return by engaging in worldly praxis. Precisely because von Balthasar is trying to be an Irenaean thinker it cannot be said that he sees an either/or, inversely proportional relationship between contemplation and praxis. Moreover, it should also be clear at this point that von Balthasar definitely does not interpret grace as a purely spiritual reality that concerns only the inner, private self, but rather as a reality that has a sacramental origin in Christ and sacramental expression in the church.

### Notes

1. Von Balthasar explicitly invokes Irenaeus on this point in *TD3*, 366–67 n. 10.

2. The following biographical discussion of Marcion is drawn from David Chidester, *Christianity: A Global History* (San Francisco: HarperCollins, 2000), 45–49.

3. For a discussion of Marcion's theological views, see Jaroslav Pelikan, *The Christian Tradition: A History of the Development of Doctrine: The Emergence of the Catholic Tradition (100–600)* (Chicago: University of Chicago Press, 1971), 71–81.

4. Pelikan cites Tertullian arguing that for Marcion "it was the purpose of the coming of Jesus to abolish all the world belong to 'this world' and to its Creator, the 'ruler of the universe'" (ibid., 73).

5. Pelikan cites Irenaeus making this point, and then he cites Tertullian arguing that Marcion considered the creator god "evil" and "equivalent to the devil" (ibid., 74).

6. Following Tertullian's discussion, Pelikan explains that Marcion believed "Christ could not have assumed a material body that participated in the created world, for such a body would have been 'stuffed with excrement.' A material body and a physical birth belonged to the Creator and were unworthy of the true Christ. If he had become a man with a material body, this would have meant the end of divinity" (ibid., 75, 78).

7. Ibid., 76ff.

8. *GL1*, 656; see also *GL1*, 540–41. Cf. *SI*, 3;. *MP*, 62–63; *TD3*, 367.

9. *SI*, 3. This point raises an interesting question about the relevance of Tertullian to von Balthasar's retrieval of Irenaeus, but this issue is too complex to be dealt with here.

10. *TD3*, 367.

11. For a discussion of this patristic hermeneutic model, see de Lubac's *Catholicism*, 165–216.

12. *GL2*, 65, 82. See also *TD2*, 143.

13. See *TD3*, 361–401.

14. It is interesting to note that von Balthasar, like de Lubac, does not think it

necessary for Jews to convert to Christianity. They have their own special role to play in the incarnational process. He writes, "[T]he only relevant question is whether they [the Jews] are prepared to find their salvation in Christ or prefer to wait for another Messiah, who (according to Peter's preaching in Acts 2:38f. and 3:17ff.) will be the same one" (*TD3*, 366). He also argues, for example, that "an inner, pneumatic element" is alive in Israel today (*TD3*, 376).

15. *GL2*, 82; *GL6*, 412.

16. *GL2*, 91–92.

17. *GL2*, 81; cf. *TD2*, 143; *SI*, 9. For Irenaeus, von Balthasar writes, human beings are trained by God to become "accustomed" to obedience and to the Spirit (*GL2*, 79).

18. *GL2*, 82. This Irenaean pedagogical point is clear in von Balthasar's frequent references to Jesus' "hour" of death when he became the crystallizing *kairos*. See *GL6*, 404; *GL7*, 145, 202, 216, 247, 378.

19. *TD3*, 366–67; *GL6*, 384. Cf. *GL7*, 24–25, 90, 105–6.

20. *GL2*, 90–92; see also *GL1*, 624; *GL6*, 402–14; *GL7*, 33–40.

21. *GL6*, 403–9; *GL7*, 203–4.

22. *GL6*, 415. This movement indicated that for von Balthasar there are "many ways in which grace trains the creature to be capable of confronting this glory at all" (ibid., 10).

23. Ibid., 10ff.

24. Ibid., 13.

25. Ibid., 32–33.

26. Ibid., 61–73.

27. Ibid., 162.

28. Ibid., 10ff., 37–41.

29. Ibid., 14.

30. Ibid., 62–73; 149.

31. When there is a question of the primacy of the prophetic "speech event" or the priestly and cultic "blood event" in the Old Testament, von Balthasar consistently and unequivocally decides for the former. See *GL6*, 375–401. The old covenant's prophetic emphasis on the need for a loving response to God's self-gift of love was never fully eclipsed by legalism or ritualism (*GL6*, 375, 379).

32. Ibid., 240–41.

33. Ibid., 245.

34. *GL6*, 185; cf. Deut 7:6–7; 8:17; 7:9; 10:15.

35. Ibid., 156–57; cf. 365–401, where von Balthasar discusses the various ways in which postexilic Judaism lost sight of this Deuteronomic emphasis on love alone.

36. *GL6*, 146–47. Cf. ibid., 205, 207, 209, 211; *GL7*, 90, 391–92, 415ff.

37. In his discussion of Deuteronomy's commandment to return God's love with the whole self, von Balthasar is careful to note that this means putting one's response in the form of practical obedience (ibid., 185–86).

38. See *GL6*, 215–24.

39. Cf. *GL2*, 63–64, 75–76.

40. Cf. *GL6*, 65, 302ff., 365–74.

41. See in its entirety part III of *GL6*, "The Long Twilight," 301–413.

42. Ibid., 9ff., 31–51; *GL7*, 269–71; *SI*, 9.

43. See *GL6*, 14, 10, 154; *SI*, 17–18.

44. *SI*, 8; *GL6*, 87–103.

45. Von Balthasar cites Irenaeus saying "the Word protects the invisibility in such

a way that humans are always given something that draws them towards God; he shows God to humans by dispensing many hints so that they do not lose all sense of God, completely fall away from him, and thus cease to exist" (*TL2*, 63–64). See also *TL1*, 143–44; *GL6*, 104–43.

46. *GL2*, 76. See his reading of Irenaeus on this point in *TD2*, 142–43. For von Balthasar, Irenaeus presents the "basic outline" of the later theological tradition's conception of human nature as an "autonomous finite freedom operating within an encompassing Providence. . . ." Von Balthasar adds, "The emphasis on the *autexousion* in all the early Fathers must be understood as a specifically Christian position (in opposition to the united front of determinism and Gnosticism) . . ." (*TD2*, 217). He argues elsewhere along Irenaean lines that it has been a mistake of traditional Greek and Augustinian patristic theology "to locate man's character as God's image wholly in his aspect as spirit," as it is a mistake of the Reformation tradition to believe man lost his image of God by sinning (*GL6*, 96). It is more accurate, following Sirach, to recognize that the image "includes both the bodily sense and the spiritual faculties of man" joined in the praise of God (*GL6*, 97).

47. *TD2*, 215.

48. *GL1*, 504–5; see also *GL7*, 282.

49. *GL1*, 635, 645, 648.

50. *GL7*, 268–69. "Among the pagans, the god before whose glance one comes and in whose sight one lives is a dispenser of 'gifts': life, health, and so on; but never does he, above all, give himself, as is the case with the God of Israel" (*GL6*, 72).

51. *GL6*, 361–62.

52. *GL7*, 105; see also 497.

53. ". . . the primary meaning of grace must be, not that God bestows on the creature, from the far distance of his heaven, a new 'quality,' but rather that he bends down to the earth and raises man up to himself, making space for him in God's own realm in a manner that goes beyond all his qualities and possibilities, in, that is to say, an act of rapture" (*GL6*, 149). Grace is always, "pure and one-sided grace" (*GL6*, 152).

54. Ibid., 54, 71–72.

55. Ibid., 146–47.

56. Ibid., 294.

57. Ibid., 88.

58. *GL2*, 66, 75. The basis of the covenant from the start, von Balthasar writes, was "obedience, out of reverent and thankful love, to the God of promise and of salvation (Ex 19.5; Deut 7.8f), and it was here that life in accordance with God's directives had its ground and unity" (*GL6*, 169). Cf. also *TD2*, 207–13, 216–17.

59. *GL6*, 59.

60. *GL6*, 185–86. This is precisely the Johannine message von Balthasar detects in the book of Deuteronomy, and it sets the pattern for receptive, obedient prophetic existence as—in an apt physical and spatial metaphor—a "stairway of obedience" upon which God descends into the created realm (223–91, 398).

61. *GL1*, 36.

62. *GL6*, 225; cf. 231–34. For von Balthasar's reading of Irenaeus on this point see *GL2*, 62–64, 75–76.

63. *GL6*, 234.

64. *GL6*, 144; 174–75.

65. Ibid., 175.

66. *GL6*, 162.

67. Ibid., 160–64.

68. God desires a special living relationship with Israel that "is not something that is merely 'interior' and 'ethical' or 'cultic,' but at the same time the whole external, 'legal' and 'political' existence of the group. Precisely this exclusiveness of the relationship between God and the people which is now shaping itself requires, if it is to be incarnated fully, the inclusion of the legal-political sphere" (*GL6*, 152).

69. "The Prophets' word of judgment is predominately a socio-ethical and socio-political word. The manner of man's life is purified and rectified by the fire of God's indwelling Word. We can already begin to see here the basic form of the New Testament: man's right relationship to God has its measure in his right relation to the world, to his neighbor. The doxa of the gracious God who descends on the sanctuary of creation is, in essence, the man who has been conformed to God" (*GL1*, 455).

70. *Chesed* is "a matter of a personal, benevolent, loving attitude that indicates and opens up a sphere of mutual trust." God offers his grace, and man's only possible response is the "free gift of his heart" (*GL6*, 160; cf. 68).

71. For just one of many examples, von Balthasar notes that the prophet Amos typifies this theme of holiness as sharing in God's concern for the poor and needy. For Amos, he contends, "God is in solidarity with the poorest" (*GL6*, 237–38).

72. Ibid., 316.

73. Ibid., 163.

74. Ibid., 165.

75. Ibid., 168.

76. Ibid., 177. This is made clear in Isaiah, he later explains, where all the people are called upon to follow "the ethics of the one who allows himself to be humbled by God and, standing before him in littleness, has the ability to perceive the directives that come from God's sublimity." Ibid., 252.

77. Ibid., 170.

78. Ibid., 170–71.

79. Ibid., 172.

80. Ibid.

81. Ibid., 407. See also *GL7*, 105; *TD2*, 111.

82. With regard to the radical difference between God's incarnation in the two covenants, on one hand, and God's incarnation in Jesus, on the other hand, von Balthasar is careful to make clear that the eternal Word's own *kenosis* in response to the will of the Father is "of qualitatively different kind than the readiness of all free creatures; were there no such difference, then the Cross of Christ would be nothing more than the realization of the purely creaturely attitude to God . . ." *GL7*, 217–18. Compare to his claim about the "indwelling Word" in *GL1*, 455.

83. *TD3*, 367.

84. See, for example, *TD3*, 361–70, 391–401.

85. Ibid., 367–70.

86. Ibid., 366.

87. Ibid., 376–91, especially 384–86.

88. Ibid., 398.

89. Ibid.

90. Interestingly, von Balthasar qualifies this point by noting that "Israel has an advantage in that its religion has neither a Magisterium nor actual dogmas. This gives it an opportunity vis-à-vis mankind that the Church does not have" (*TD3*, 399).

91. Von Balthasar writes, ". . . we must always bear in mind that Christ, as man,

owes a great debt to his own nation's tradition of salvation history—for 'salvation is from the Jews' (Jn 4:22) . . ." (*TD3*, 366).

92. *GL7*, 78–81; see also 55–76, and *GL6*, 192–93. For von Balthasar's reading of Irenaeus on this point, see *GL2*, 51–55, 68–69, and *TD2*, 84, 139–44.

93. *GL7*, 115, 89. In his essay "The Symphonic Unity of His Theology: An Overview," Thomas Norris makes this important connection between Irenaeus and von Balthasar with regard to their understanding of Christ's recapitulation of both the history of Israel and the fullness of human nature. See *The Beauty of Christ*, 236.

94. *GL7*, 39–40.

95. *GL1*, 505.

96. *GL7*, 126.

97. Ibid., 87.

98. Ibid., 132–33, 195.

99. Ibid., 133.

100. *GL7*, 143–45. In the poverty of his obedience, Jesus "lets his entire form-less and therefore wordless existence (as 'flesh') be yielded up in an ultimate gesture, so that it may become something that God's hand can form in its entirety . . ." (47). Von Balthasar goes so far as to use the term "liquefied" to describe Jesus in his self-abandonment to the Father's will (ibid., 151).

101. Ibid., 118.

102. *TD3*, 366.

103. *GL7*, 130.

104. This point indicates why von Balthasar spends so many pages in *GL6* making the case that the prophetic model of obedience ultimately was not efficacious in challenging incipient Gnosticism and tendencies toward an ethos of resignation that haunted much of postexilic Judaism. See *GL6*, 301–413.

105. *GL7*, 144.

106. Ibid., 142. This point explains why for von Balthasar the cross and resurrection always belong together in the New Testament. See *GL7*, 151, 493.

107. Ibid., 14, 125.

108. Ibid., 126.

109. Ibid., 143, 147–48.

110. For a helpful introductory exposition of von Balthasar's trinitarian theology and its relation to his theology of the paschal mystery, see Anne Hunt, *The Trinity and the Paschal Mystery: A Development in Recent Catholic Theology* (Collegeville, Minn.: Liturgical Press, 1997), 57–89.

111. *GL7*, 149–50. Von Balthasar obviously holds that all four evangelists remember and write about the pre-Easter Jesus from the perspective of the resurrection and the sending of the Holy Spirit into the early church (97, 156–57). This is the case because as the Word made flesh, the divine glory of Christ remained essentially hidden during his pre-Easter life (157). Hence von Balthasar describes the incarnation by saying the Word "enters and vanishes in the flesh that is utterly dependent on God" (150). The flesh, he later says, "as such is not Word, but is the form of the Word in emptiness and silence" (161).

112. Cf. ibid., 156, 159–60. As sacramental symbol of self-giving, Jesus' paschal transition from death to life is for the disciples an invitation to take on an "existential participation in [his] self-abandonment" through the grace of the Holy Spirit. See ibid., 151.

113. Ibid., 146–47.

114. Ibid., 269–73.

115. Ibid., 213–14. The Son's kenotic self-emptying in the incarnation "becomes the decisive act of the love of the Son, who translates his being begotten by the Father (and in this, his dependence on him) into the expressive form of creaturely obedience," hence indicating "something of the law of the immanent Trinity" by a bringing "to light of the inner-trinitarian mystery in the dispensation of salvation." Ibid., 214–15.

116. Von Balthasar understands himself to be upholding a shared Johannine and Pauline theological conviction on this point. Following what he takes as the core of their theological projects, von Balthasar frequently contrasts the inner-worldly logic of fallen creatures with the inner-trinitarian logic of divine love. Because the redemption of the created order consists in the participation of the finite in the infinite trinitarian life, a christocentric theology of salvation history has its own internal, self-interpreting trinitarian logic (GL7, 97, 113, 175, 208, 227–28, 248, 316, 360, 365) with its own inner "law" known to us only through Christ (GL7, 249–50, 256, 257, 259, 397, 399–400, 488).

117. Ibid., 377.

118. Ibid., 311; cf. 107.

119. Von Balthasar asserts that the "essential basis" of what is the "decisively Christian element in a theological aesthetics" is the "inner Trinity of God and the coming-forth of this Trinity in the Incarnation" (ibid., 314).

120. GL6, 404–5; GL7, 81–82. "The classic theology of the Old Testament characterizes this death as the loss of the living relationship to God; . . . Paul summarizes this definitive lot of guilty mankind in the statement (which is indebted to Jewish theology), 'All have sinned, and have lost the glory of God' (Rom 3.23)" (GL7, 229).

121. Ibid., 210–12; cf. 143. This is, for von Balthasar, the content of the Pauline claim that God made Christ "to be sin for us" (2 Cor. 5:21) (GL7, 208).

122. GL7, 229–34. This indicates a uniqueness in von Balthasar's understanding of Christ's descent to hell. For him, the descent is not a militant and triumphant descent and conquest of hell but rather a "'sinking down' into the abyss of death, a passive 'being removed.'" Here Jesus participated "in the absolute passivity of being dead" (GL7, 230).

123. Ibid., 225.

124. Ibid., 231.

125. Ibid., 204–6. See also 34, 36–37, 39–40, 93–94, 113, 296–99, 316–17.

126. Translation of Irenaeus quote: "He descended to the lower parts of the earth, to see with his eyes that part of creation which was inactive" (AH 4.22.1; GL7, 233).

127. This participation in the trinitarian circuit is closely connected with the traditional doctrine of sharing in Christ's "sacred heart." Von Balthasar writes, "The place of his heart is open, empty, for all to enter; in this self-emptying, the kenosis has reached its fulfillment" (GL7, 226).

128. GL7, 234, 362–65, 389.

129. Ibid., 311, 363, 389–90.

130. Ibid., 234.

131. Ibid.

132. According to von Balthasar's interpretation of Irenaeus in Against Heresies, redemption means that the human creature receives a gift of finite freedom allowing it to enter into relationship with God's infinite freedom. He maintains that humans can only "attain perfect freedom" through the Son's death because it brings the full-

ness of freedom, a "New Covenant of freedom" (3.12.14; 4.33.14). The newness brought through Christ's death is "the gift of freedom" (4.34.1), "glad tidings of freedom" (4.34.3). The apostles are "apostles of freedom" (3.15.3). *TD2*, 144; cf. 143–45, 215–17. Von Balthasar believes that this Irenaean conception of redemption as the gift of finite freedom sets the basic paradigm followed by other church fathers, such as Clement of Alexandria, Origen, Gregory of Nyssa, Ephrem, Maximus, and Augustine. *TD2*, 215ff.

133. *GL7*, 403. On this theme, see the extremely insightful analysis in Mark McIntosh, *Christology from Within: Spirituality and the Incarnation in Hans Urs von Balthasar* (Notre Dame: University of Notre Dame Press, 1996).

134. Ibid., 217. It must be reiterated that Christ is not for von Balthasar merely one model of human religious potential or an instance of a nonbiblical spiritual law of the cosmos, but rather the fullest incarnation of the second person of the Trinity, who vicariously bears and redeems the collective sin of the world. See *GL7*, 83, 160, 217–18, 214–15.

135. Ibid., 310–11.

136. Ibid., 391, 408–9. For Irenaeus as well, human creatures made in the image and likeness of God have a trinitarian nature; see *GL2*, 66.

137. Ibid., 396–97. See also *TL3*, 169ff. for a discussion of the theme of divinization (*theosis*) in patristic theology.

138. Ibid., 407–9.

139. Ibid., 391; cf. 311.

140. *GL6*, 188–89.

141. *GL7*, 279. Von Balthasar takes as his own starting point the assumption that the central focus of the New Testament is "the absolute trinitarian love of God, which discloses itself and offers itself in Jesus Christ" (*GL7*, 15).

142. "The God of the Bible is neither a *tremendum* nor a *fascinosum*," he asserts, "but first of all an *adorandum*. He is and remains the unutterable first origin from which everything that exists, everything that is good and full of grace, comes forth—he is the Father who gives only good gifts (Lk 11.13)" (ibid., 268).

143. *GL1*, 216.

144. *GL7*, 16–19; *GL1*, 460; *GL4*, 16.

145. *GL1*, 216.

146. *GL7*, 532ff.

147. Ibid., 158; cf. 384.

148. See ibid., 526–29.

149. Ibid., 400; see also 33, 87–89, 91. Cf. *GL2*, 66.

150. *GL6*, 412. Cf. *GL2*, 58, 62.

151. *GL6*, 416, 222, 390–91; *GL7*, 82, 91–92.

152. *GL7*, 14, 19; cf. 81–84, 205–6, 228.

153. Ibid., 213–14.

154. Ibid., 306.

155. Ibid., 202–35.

156. Ibid., 239–55; 389–415.

157. Ibid., 233.

158. Ibid., 525–26.

159. Ibid., 391–99.

160. It must also be noted that seeing aesthetically does not mean for him seeing theoretically. Hence, von Balthasar argues, John did not see in the cross an abstract "juridical or physical law of vicariousness" (ibid., 207–8; see also 151, 232). For

Paul in particular, von Balthasar argues from his reading of 2 Cor. 5:14, the cross has its own internal "logic" of love. In seeing the attractiveness of Christ's love on the cross, we accept Christ's death for us, and "ratify" it by dying to ourselves. In John the "logic" of love revealed in the cross leads us to a readiness to take on Christ's form of love in laying down our lives for others (1 John 3:16). Von Balthasar comments that in each case, this aesthetic theology of the cross dominates and contextualizes all other interpretations (ibid., 208).

161. There is a minor Irenaean influence here on von Balthasar's interpretation of Johannine theology. Von Balthasar writes, "Here truly the axiom that Irenaeus laid down against the Gnostics is valid, that axiom which has it that Christ could not demand of his disciples any suffering that he had not experienced himself as Master" (*MP*, 125).

162. *GL7*, 299ff.; cf. 195–96.

163. Ibid., 399–400. See also 316–17, 363; *GL6*, 275, 262–63.

164. *GL7*, 362–63, 389–90, 405.

165. *GL6*, 171–72.

166. *GL7*, 403–4.

167. Ibid., 399–415, 420. "The power of this act of drawing in is the expropriation of our privacy, i.e., in concrete terms, of our sealed-up egoism, or our addiction to the desires . . . that seek to draw everything to ourselves; it is the liberation that brings us into freedom (Gal 5.1), for 'where the Spirit of the Lord is, there is freedom' (2 Cor. 3.17). This freedom is the opposite of addiction . . . it is essentially service—service first of the self-expropriating love of God, and, coming directly from this, service of all this for whose sake God has expropriated himself" (ibid., 403). See ibid., 115, 287–88, 293, 407, 456–57 for von Balthasar's characterization of faith as rapture.

168. Ibid., 407.

169. For an informative background discussion of von Balthasar's understanding of faith in the context of twentieth-century Catholic theology (particularly French theology), see John Riches, "Balthasar and the Analysis of Faith," in *The Analogy of Beauty*, 35–59. One limitation of Riches's essay is that it overlooks the Old Testament prophetic elements in von Balthasar's understanding of faith that I am emphasizing here.

170. This description of faith is present throughout *GL7*. See 150, 196, 385, 304–7, for faith as receptivity; 385, 404, for faith as acceptance; 160, 293–94, 379–80, 401–2, 407, for faith as allowing grace to transform one's life; and 198, 305–6, 308, 530, for faith as submission, handing over one's self, and surrender.

171. This description of faith is also present throughout *GL7*. See 292, 458, for faith as answering, responsive love; and 299, 418, 445, 453, 456–57, 528, for faith as obedience, righteousness, and practical works of love for others.

172. See ibid., 368, 326, 377–80, 384, 453, 472, and 521.

173. Ibid., 312, 406.

174. *GL2*, 74.

175. *GL7*, 239.

176. Ibid., 397–98, 297; cf. 260–61.

177. Ibid., 398–99.

# Chapter IV

# Christ and Church

The third corollary of *corpus triforme* Christology is the unity-in-difference of Christ and church expressed in the doctrine of a directly
proportional relationship between the institutional church and the Holy
Spirit's work in history. For von Balthasar, the unity of Christ and the
church in *corpus triforme* Christology necessarily implies a conception
of the church as a social and communal body concerned with incarnating God in word and deed. Moreover, he believes this ecclesiology is
Irenaean because it presupposes that the church is a pedagogical institution committed to training its members to incarnate the supernatural.
This training is a type of doxological mystagogy in which the church
trains its members to perfect the created order.

### The Church as the Institutional Form of Christ

Von Balthasar believes he is working from within the presuppositions of
Irenaean theology to articulate an understanding of the church. According to von Balthasar, Irenaeus defines the church as both the "structure"
and "epitome" of the total Body of Christ, and hence is a "living organism" with the risen Christ dwelling in it as its "greater Self."[1] This Irenaean ecclesiological presupposition is extremely important for von
Balthasar. In *GL1* he draws an analogy between Christ's relation to the
church and a soul's relation to its body.[2] He continues this line of thinking in *GL7* when he notes that "the glory of the divine love is experienced in the reciprocity of Christ and the Church" because there is
necessarily an "indissoluble nexus" between the Christ-event and the
church's interpretation of it in faith.[3] Hence he refers to the church as a
"mystery" that shares in the mystery of Christ.[4] In other words, his
ecclesiology brings into systematic coherence the *corpus triforme* corollaries of the unity-in-difference of creation and redemption and the
unity-in-difference of the old and new covenants.

Von Balthasar discusses Irenaeus's doctrine of the *paidagōgos eis
Christon* exclusively in terms of a developmental historical process in

the old covenant that prepared Israel for the coming of Christ. Nevertheless, he indicates in the context of a discussion of Irenaeus's eschatology that he believes Irenaeus also applied the notion of divine pedagogy to the post-Easter church. He refers to the "great Irenaean theme" of an eschatological "last 'training' and 'accustoming' 'for the contemplation of the Father's glory.'"[5] He also contends that it is the "particular insight" of Irenaeus to have seen that even in the post-Easter church human freedom requires education, and hence, he explains, it "must undergo the testing experience (*peira*) of the unnatural 'alienation' from God in order to reach an inner understanding of the Good, that is, of the love of God"; thus, an experience of suffering is necessary "if man's freedom is to attain an inner maturity."[6] Moreover, in *Theologik* he quotes at length a passage from *Against Heresies* suggesting that the human relationship to God is always and necessarily a relationship of teacher and pupil, even in the resurrected life of heaven.[7] The ontological fullness of revelation in Christ, therefore, does not imply that Christians automatically have a full knowledge of God. Baptism does not confer wisdom but rather the conditions for the possibility of wisdom.

In both *GL1* and *GL7* von Balthasar works with this Irenaean understanding of post-Easter pedagogy. This resonance is directly due to the fact that he assimilates the theme of *paidagōgos eis Christon* from Irenaeus's theology and develops it in two closely interrelated ways. First, he explicitly shifts the theological discussion of God's pedagogical activity away from preparation for the future coming of a new covenant to the present ecclesial situation in which the risen Christ and the Holy Spirit are now training Christians in receptivity to grace. Second, in adapting the pedagogy model to new covenant Christology and pneumatology, von Balthasar does not conceive of the human response to the "vertical" gift of grace as a preparation for a future coming messiah, but rather as the horizontal response to an already vertically bestowed grace. This horizontal response takes a dual form: a contemplative movement focused on the full divine presence in the paschal mystery, and an active movement outward into the world. For von Balthasar, therefore, the old covenant's developmental pedagogy becomes a post-Easter ecclesial mystagogy in which the church first contemplates and then lives out the form of the crucified and risen Christ. These two movements allow the church to share in the attractiveness of divine holiness communicated in Christ. This sharing has an internal and an external expression. The church as a community of the baptized provides a sacramental system for believers to gradually become—according to the pace set by their own free consent—more receptive to the participation in the trinitarian circuit and more adept at incarnating the Word. The church as a global community is itself a sacrament of the trinitarian communion drawing members of all nations and races away from paganism and into the incarnational pedagogy of the church's sacramental system.

Obviously, therefore, von Balthasar does not interpret Irenaeus's theology of divine pedagogy as providing anything like a theoretical teleological theodicy. Instead, its primary value for him is that it provides an account of how Christology can be synthesized with ecclesiology. This synthesis is entirely based on von Balthasar's understanding of the incarnation as the doxological unity-in-difference of the divine and human natures in Christ and not on any aspect inherent to the church itself as a human community. This is an important point because, as we will see below, von Balthasar makes some very strong claims about the deifying presence of the divine in the sacramental life of the church, while remaining committed to the ontological difference between the divine and the human. Even when von Balthasar describes the acts of worship that result from contemplative receptivity as a type of creaturely "collaboration" with God, he does not reduce to symmetry the permanently asymmetrical relationship between God and the creature.[8] Doxology is inherently monotheistic for von Balthasar because it is the paradoxical action of God affirming humans in their nature as finite, and the action of humans affirming God in God's nature as divine. Therefore, post-Easter mystagogy is not a developmental or evolutionary linear progress toward deification that could view Christianity or the church in triumphalist terms as the historical pinnacle of absolute religious knowledge.[9] On the contrary, post-Easter mystagogy is essentially characterized by a monotheistic and doxological curriculum that necessarily precludes such ecclesiastical hubris. The content of this curriculum in von Balthasar's ecclesiology is a christocentric process of trinitarian training in which human persons are formed into an ethical community that mirrors God's holiness. For von Balthasar, then, the church exists to sacramentalize Christ in its works of love in the world and in its hope for the redemption of human history, not to teach the world abstract theoretical lessons about God.

The internal logic of von Balthasar's entire theology is committed to the principle that sensory reality, and only sensory reality, communicates grace. Ultimately his analogical use of aesthetic form and his commitment to the institutional nature of religion are grounded in this principle. For him, aesthetic contemplation always requires a particular form that interprets itself for a receptive observer who, given human finitude, can only receive meaning from within a specific historical, cultural, social, and religious context. Thus the criticism that von Balthasar's theology is simultaneously noncontextual and excessively contemplative is not coherent.[10] This criticism is based on a failure to understand that, for von Balthasar, speculation and contemplation are in fact antonyms; his retrieval of classical aesthetics is specifically intended to resist noncontextual speculative theologies that lack epistemic humility. Von Balthasar believes speculative theologies are Gnostic but contemplative ones are doxological. He thinks doxological monotheism is characterized primarily by its belief that the rational intellect cannot operate outside the context of human finitude. One only understands the transcendent God by surrendering to the limitations of finitude and contemplating a particular form from within a pregiven temporal, cultural, and religious environment. Theological aesthetics, therefore, prioritizes a contemplative method in religious discourse precisely because it celebrates these limitations.

Von Balthasar assumes that these limitations are essential for a genuinely sacramental encounter with Christ within the context of the institutional church. Contemplating Christ in his *corpus triforme* totality requires the total context of the church, including the scriptural canon, communal worship, and a sacramental tradition because von Balthasar believes that Christ is first and foremost a sacramental phenomenon. Only secondarily can he be discussed in abstract theological language.[11] Hence, von Balthasar maintains that belief in Christ's real presence in the church's sacramental life is not only legitimate but necessary for knowing the trinitarian reality of God. This means, of course, that one cannot take an external perspective on Christ as if revelation was a past, finished event, or as if commitment to the ecclesial locus of grace and faith was a hindrance to objective understanding.[12] According to von Balthasar, therefore, authentic spiritual understanding requires that one take up a participatory stance of involvement with and commitment to the praxis of the church's sacramental life, with all that this implies about the limitations of the particular institutional religious tradition that provides the interpretive context for this praxis.[13]

Having said this, it is also true that von Balthasar himself occasionally seems to take a negative view of the limitations imposed on Christianity by its "objective" institutional religious tradition. This occurs in his affirmative discussions of Paul's claims about the "utopian" nature of the church as a "wandering people of God" (Hebrews 3-4), and as "the transcending 'remnant' of Israel" (Rom. 9:27, 29; 11:5) that is bound by no rituals or laws other than "the law of divine love and the dying and rising with Christ."[14] Commenting on Paul's ecclesiology from 2 Corinthians, von Balthasar writes of the church:

She may drape herself in ever new garments—those of a static institution with official hierarchies, books of law, regulations for cult and sacraments, theologies closed firmly in on themselves, etc.—but all of these attempts to give herself form cannot do away with this incomprehensible oscillation that belongs to her existence in the world: her glory lies not in her, but in the gospel—she serves [the gospel], and the gospel has glory to the extent that it is the inexplicable "presentation" of the one who (as past and future) is absent; but the presence is the work and the self-attestation of the *Pneuma*.[15]

Von Balthasar does not think this passage should be read as an attack on the principle that religion must be institutional. The issue at stake here is Paul's concern for maintaining the vertical dimension of the church. Von Balthasar thinks Paul never doubted that the church needed to be institutional to carry out its universal mission to the world. He was concerned with making it clear that this universal mission transcends the parochial aspects of Israelite religion (including theocratic politics and laws concerning ritual purity and animal sacrifice). Von Balthasar believes this certainly does not mean that Paul's ecclesiology sees the church as a less, rather than a more, concrete religious community than was biblical Israel. On the contrary, he reads Paul as arguing that law and institution must be relativized so that they do not rigidify and compete with the new incarnational forms being born in the church.[16] Ultimately, this means for von Balthasar that we must admit the fact that the church sins by attempting to embody purely human values; the church's official hierarchy is not immune to this type of sin, and theologians have a duty to challenge the hierarchy when it commits this sin.[17] Nevertheless, despite its sinful nature, genuine faith is always present in the church as the living, on-going reality of the Christ-form in history—the church is permanently accompanied by the Holy Spirit, and hence by grace.[18]

### Public Esotericism and Anti-Gnostic Wisdom

Von Balthasar believes that the institutional form of the church implies that it is public and accessible to all people. His thinking is based on a Johannine christological ontology. For him, a Johannine ontology implies that salvation opens the Trinity to all of humanity. The Word is becoming incarnate so that all humanity can share in the "indwelling" of the Father and the Son in the Spirit, and thereby form a human community united by an analogous trinitarian "indwelling." This is the core theme of his "trinitarian logic." This logic presupposes that in the *kenosis* of the cross, the Son surrenders the "form of God" out of obedient love for the Father, thus glorifying him by this act of self-giving. The Son is in turn glorified by the Father and the Spirit in the resurrection.[19] The risen Christ is then able again to glorify the Father because he extends the inner-trinitarian sphere of the Father's sovereignty out into the world. In a deeply Johannine reflection, von Balthasar explains that this extension of the Father's trinitarian reign of love from within the immanent Trinity into the economy of salvation renders the *kenosis* of the Son "fruitful" in accordance with the inner-trinitarian law of self-giving. The fruitfulness of the *kenosis,* he contends, is not solely the work of the Son or the Father, but it is the work of the Holy Spirit, who is the mutual love between Father and Son in the immanent and economic Trinity. Von Balthasar refers to the Spirit as the "the fruitfulness of the love of Father and Son" who is the source of the Trinity's endless fruitfulness in the world.[20] This fruitfulness of the Trinity in the world is the work of the Spirit glorifying the Father and the Son through the church. Basing his argument on a close exegesis of John's Gospel, von Balthasar notes that Jesus simultaneously links the salvific coming of the Spirit to his own departure in death and promises that he will return to the believers with the Father in the coming of the Spirit. Von Balthasar then turns to the Johannine metaphor of the vine and its fruitful branches to make the connection between the presence of the risen Christ in the church and the Holy Spirit as the fruit of trinitarian love.[21] Jesus returns in the life of the church as both the vine and the fruit it bears. Christ's dual role as both vine and fruit is possible because, as the vine planted in the church by the Father, Christ sends the Spirit, who is the fruit of the love between Father and Son. This is the concrete meaning of the Father and Spirit's glorification of the Son in the resurrection: the Father and the Spirit glorify the Son cooperatively in his disciples. "The Father does this, by accomplishing and revealing the identity of obedience and eternal love, of Cross and Resurrection; the Spirit does this, by instituting in the Church, and so making known before the world, the unity of the love between Father and Son that was lived out in the distance of the Passion for the sake of the world—for he himself *is* this unity of love."[22] The Spirit thus prepares a "dwelling" in the temporal order for the Father and the Son, which ultimately means, he adds, "that a dwelling is prepared for the Church (and thereby for the world) by the Son in the Father." For von Balthasar, then, if the church is to participate in eternal glory, then the "*eternity* of glory" must be instituted in the temporal sphere by the Spirit of the Father and Son.[23]

This last point makes it clear that in von Balthasar's doxological trinitarianism the church integrates the eternal and the temporal, and the infinite and the finite. This trinitarian ecclesiology simultaneously maintains a commitment to the ontological difference between creator and creatures and an insistence that the creator has specifically chosen and designated a particular community of persons as the exclusive site for full divine disclosure in creation. This monotheistic paradox between God as fully Other and fully non-other underlies von Balthasar's willingness to advocate "esotericism" in the church. "Even so truly a 'church of the people' as the Catholic Church does not abolish genuine esotericism. The secret path of the saints is never denied to one who is really willing to follow it."[24] Von Balthasar realizes that this kind of rhetoric brings him into the province of Gnosticism. But he enters as a subversive, not as an ally. In using the terms "esotericism" and "secret" he does not mean to suggest an elitist conception of gnosis, but rather a public conception of gnosis in which there is a directly proportional relationship between the personal and the social.[25] We know this because he interprets the institutional church and its sacramental traditions as the indispensable mystagogic context in which the Christ-form sacramentally imprints and expresses the trinitarian paradox of personal difference in the unity of love.

In holding together the church's public call to follow Christ openly and the intensely personal spirituality this requires, von Balthasar is following an Irenaean precedent. He notes that for Irenaeus the church is an "esoteric mystery" while at the same time it is "the most public and anti-sectarian body known to history."[26] Von Balthasar examines this paradox in his discussion of the "hiddenness" of the risen Christ.[27] In the Son's public overcoming of death, the glory of God is made fully manifest, but this manifestation is also "hidden" and not available to the eye of the neutral observer.[28] This "hidden" glory of the risen Christ both originates and is permanently renewed only in the context of the public community of faith. Both origination and renewal are the work of the free trinitarian God who is the divine pedagogue patiently dispensing "hints" to attentive pupils.[29] In the new covenant, dispensing hints is the task of the Spirit, or, as von Balthasar puts it, the Spirit's task is to interpret the risen Christ in the lives of the baptized.[30]

Von Balthasar sometimes argues that the Spirit trains Christians in wisdom. Like "esotericism," however, the term "wisdom" has a Gnostic connotation that von Balthasar is careful to avoid. As a *corpus triforme* theologian it is inescapable for him to affirm some type of notion of a progressive growth of religious wisdom in history. Yet as an anti-Gnostic thinker he is at pains to qualify his understanding of progressive wisdom. For example, he holds a negative view of the idea of a progressive education of the human race in general (which he equates with Hegelianism, evolutionary philosophy, and theological supersessionism[31]), as well as a highly critical interpretation of theologies of "wisdom" that are speculative and nonchristocentric.[32] In both cases, however, he is working with the Irenaean distinction between true and false gnosis, in which the former is based on a cross-centered and ecclesially contextualized spirituality, while the latter is based on noncontextual, detached, and abstract philosophical reflection.[33] Thus, in the pedagogy of true gnosis the "wisdom" imparted by the Spirit is always christocentric in three important senses. First, it involves personally sharing in Christ's suffering. Second, it implies a paradoxical movement toward creaturely autonomy through dependence on grace. Third, the pedagogy always takes a public, ecclesial form.

### Sacramental Imprinting in Baptism and Eucharist

For von Balthasar, baptism and the eucharist are the two most important forms of God's sacramental pedagogy in the church. He interprets baptism as a mystagogic initiation into the form of the crucified Christ because by being initiated into the church in baptism one enters into the sphere of the Spirit, who trains believers in receptivity to Christ.[34] By adding a strong pneumatological dimension to the theology of baptism he makes explicit the connection between sacramental and trinitarian theology.[35] Baptism is clearly, for von Balthasar, not simply the initiation into a human community but also an "esoteric" initiation into the inner-life of the Trinity. In a particularly strong assertion, he maintains that in baptism the human spirit is "drawn into the event of the eternal generation of the Son."[36] It is important to keep in mind, however, his commitment to a monotheistic discourse of doxological asymmetry: he is not blurring the ontological difference between creator and creature, nor is he confusing a doctrine of human sanctification by grace with a doctrine of the immanent Trinity.[37] Even if he is less than careful in his rhetoric, he is more than clear elsewhere that the sacramental imprinting of baptism does not involve—as some Gnostic philosophies assumed—the recovery of one's own divine form which has been lost. Instead, in baptism one attains a wholly new form in which one becomes a new creation in Christ.[38] This wholly new form is inseparable from the overall form of the church in salvation history; becoming a new creation in Christ means for von Balthasar that one takes on a fully ecclesial existence.

This point brings out the significance of von Balthasar's Irenaean claim that the sacrament of the eucharist is the epitome of the church.[39] The eucharist is the symbol of inner-trinitarian glory. Moreover, it is the form of the world's redemption in that it is the visible expression of the encounter between infinite and finite freedom. Recall that the pedagogic model assumes the importance of patience and the right timing of lessons. Von Balthasar believes that the timing of Jesus' death in the overall pattern of God's pedagogy was perfectly chosen for maximal educational effect. He explains that Jesus' "hour" of death became the *kairos* crystallizing all God's previous lessons in incarnational religiosity.[40] Hence, it is highly significant that von Balthasar closely links the Last Supper and the cross as together constituting the "hour" of Christ's *kairos*.[41] Both in the crucifixion and in sharing a meal with his disciples Jesus taught the "compelling and transparent logic" of his incarnation, namely, the power the Father has given Jesus to share his life with others so that, through this sharing, the Father's love may come into the world. There is a mutual glorification of the trinitarian persons here in which the Son glorifies the Father by allowing himself to be the one through whom the Father's love comes, and the Father and Spirit glorify the Son by raising him from the dead. The resurrection renders the church's eucharistic celebration a doxological event between the Father and the Son because it is here that, out of obedience, the Son is "liquefied" and poured into human hearts.[42] Von Balthasar is quite clear that the "eucharistic liquefying" of Christ is a communal reality with communal effects. Thus, he argues that the Last Supper is a "form for the Church, since the form—the meal—is a social act intended to constitute the interior form itself of the Church."[43] Here in the Last Supper Jesus gestures toward the eucharistic surrender of his humanity on the cross, a gesture that indicates that God will be incorporated in the human community through his flesh. As a *"memoriale passionis Domini"* the eucharist constitutes the church as social body arising out of the risen Christ's glorified body.[44]

Von Balthasar both clarifies and amplifies the social dimension of the eucharist by connecting it with trinitarian theology. "The Church," he explains, "with all that goes to make up its social context, is the disclosure and the exposition of Christ, and thereby of the social life within the Godhead. And since Jesus prays to the Father to permit those who belong to him to dwell where he is and to see his glory (Jn 17:24), and the Church is already the place where he is, the personal and social life of the Church permits one to see into the glory of Christ and of the triune love."[45] The eucharist is thus simultaneously the sacramental imprinting of the inner-trinitarian life on believers and the formation of the ecclesial community as the incarnation of the Trinity on earth. Therefore eucharistic faith cannot be simply an "I-Thou" piety, but rather an "I-Thou-We" activity of community formation.[46] Hence von Balthasar maintains that the ecclesial "I-Thou-We" of the church is not a human construct but rather is "bestowed vertically by God on sinful men" to form them "horizontally" into a human community of love.[47]

The eucharistic community of the church gives visible, bodily form to the Trinity, and points eschatologically to the complete integration of all persons into the absolute love of the trinitarian circuit.

### Sacramental Imprinting in the Scriptural Word

In *Theo-Drama* von Balthasar discusses the basic characteristics of the patristic biblical hermeneutic. This hermeneutic interests him because, unlike modern biblical criticism, it unites Christology and ecclesiology. Von Balthasar believes that the church fathers read the Bible as a sacrament testifying to the Word's real presence in the lives of its authors. The authors encounter the Word and incarnate it in their literary creativity, but the encounters with the Word always occur within the context of a specific covenant community. Moreover, the embodying of the Word in literary form functions like a sacrament for the members of the community, drawing them into the incarnational process.

Regarding the Word's literary form, von Balthasar explains that patristic Christology operates with "an elliptical structure."[48] He means that patristic theology assumes that a genuine understanding of Christ is possible only if there was direct correlation between the revealed content or object of faith and the form given to this content in apostolic preaching. Premodern Christology takes as a given that there is a "complete reciprocity" between the form of Christ presented by the church and the believer's personal encounter with the content of this form. The self-revealing content is the "absolutely radiant and self-evident" divine Word who interprets himself to those who enter the "circle" of an ecclesially formed faith.[49] In other words, the patristic and generally premodern christological ellipse presuppose that in order to encounter genuinely the objective reality of the self-revealing Word of God, one must enter the highly biased, completely nonneutral world of apostolic and ecclesial faith. Because the apostles and evangelists were formed by their personal encounters with the reality of Christ, their very human and faith-based literary interpretations of these encounters are in fact accurate expressions of Christ's true nature and identity.

Von Balthasar retains all these elements of the patristic hermeneutic in his advocacy of a "theodramatic hermeneutics" in *TD2*. He insists that the biblical canon cannot be read outside of its historical context but rather must be interpreted as a multidimensional literary testimony to the divine Word that is continually spoken in new ways by God the Father in the church.[50] Hence as testimonies to God's on-going incarnational process, the canonical Scriptures are not simply a written record of past historical events but are instead pointers to the living divine

Word who is "continually moving" and witnessing to himself in history. Factual historical accuracy is important to the biblical writers only insofar as it illuminates the deeper spiritual understanding of the Word's self-interpretation in and through historical persons and events. The written texts of the canon are themselves an expression of the Word's on-going real presence as a self-interpreting reality. Von Balthasar remarks that for this reason the closing of the canon "is in truth not a 'closing' at all but the widest imaginable 'opening'" because the Word continues to be present in world history as a living reality "capable of infinite assimilation and interpretation."[51] The Scriptural canon leaves many questions unanswered and events unexplained so that the living Word can interpret them himself in the lives of receptive believers. For von Balthasar, therefore, the Word speaking in the canon does not present believers with "dispassionate knowledge" or "some lofty vantage point."[52] Rather, the Word continues to form believers into vessels capable of receiving and enfleshing him in ever-new human forms. In this way the Word continues to speak in and through contemporary believers just as he spoke in the lives and writings of the scriptural witnesses.[53] Von Balthasar, therefore, sees no theologically relevant distinction between the Jesus of history and the Christ of faith.

In a surprising and unconventional argument, von Balthasar goes on to suggest that modern historical-critical scholars provide an important reason for retrieving the patristic hermeneutic. For example, historical-critical method has rightly shown that the early church's objective truth claims about Christ and its biased subjective faith were closely interwoven. Modern critical scholars, however, have not always recognized the theological value of this insight. They fail to grasp what was an axiom for premodern Christology: it is the nature of the risen Christ to create an ecclesial tradition of faith to present his objective reality in sacramental forms. Von Balthasar believes that the books in the canon have such sacramental status because they are the products of an incarnational process. Modern critical scholarship, however, tends to harbor a Gnostic disdain for the very notion of sacramental incarnations of the supernatural and hence casts a suspicious eye on the church's christological tradition. From out of these suspicions, the historical-critical scholars of the eighteenth and nineteenth centuries developed and fostered two new christological assumptions: (a) neither the church's canonical Scriptures nor its doctrinal tradition express the true reality of Christ, but instead they cover it over with distorting biases; and (b) the only way to know the "real" Christ is through a completely neutral historical scholarship that gets at the true facts about Jesus.

As flawed as von Balthasar believes these two christological assumptions are, he has greater concerns about the Gnostic assumptions guiding many of the hostile reactions to the historical-critical method. He thinks that Friedrich Schleiermacher began a tradition of resistance to the historical-critical method that completely ignores *corpus triforme* Christology. This approach, von Balthasar contends, raises more christological difficulties than it resolves.[54] According to him, Schleiermacher rightly attempts to refute the historical-critical method's disconnection of objective revelation and personal faith, but he also erroneously leaves unchallenged its attempt to disconnect the form of Christ presented by the ecclesial tradition and the content of christological reality. This means that in reasserting the ellipse of revelation and faith, Schleiermacher, as well as the many nineteenth-century Protestant scholars who shared his agenda, in effect misidentified the revelation pole of the ellipse by focusing on the personal charisma of the pre-Easter Jesus rather than on the unity of the pre- and post-Easter Jesus Christ mediated by the canon and the church. Rather than seeing Jesus Christ as a necessarily and intrinsically ecclesial form that only interprets itself in the context of the church's Scriptures and sacramental life, Schleiermacher put the emphasis on the believer's experience of the pre-Easter Jesus in the depths of the self. This experience of Jesus' personal charisma exists *in* the church but is not necessarily mediated by it.[55]

Von Balthasar maintains that the dominant figures of nineteenth-century Protestant Christology all work from "within the fundamental perspective created by Schleiermacher, that is, within the ellipse formed by the unique personality of Jesus, living in history, the prototype of a man totally inhabited by God, and the pious consciousness of the believer within the Church."[56] This position seems to be congruent with Scripture and the patristic tradition of hermeneutics because Schleiermacher is obviously presupposing the on-going historical reality of the person of Jesus. Von Balthasar, however, does not think that Schleiermacher's position is congruent because for him the risen Christ is in fact not a person in the sense that he exists objectively in history with the same personal identity as the man who lived, died, and was raised from the dead. Rather, for Schleiermacher Christ is a static icon from the past who lives on in the history of religious consciousness as a memory to which we devote ourselves in mind and heart. In other words, Schleiermacher assumes a gap between *Historie* (the collection of facts about the past attained through neutral study) and *Geschichte* (the living reality of the past as it continuously shapes and informs the present). He opts to interpret the on-going historical reality of Christ primarily in terms of *Geschichte* and treats *Historie* as if it were not really relevant to modern faith.[57] Moreover, for Schleiermacher, the historical person of Jesus includes only his ministry up to and including the passion—the resurrection and ascension, he insists, "cannot be laid down as properly constituent parts of the doctrine of his person, and thus are eclipsed in soteriology by the "personality" of the pre-Easter Jesus.[58] This "personality" is relevant in salvation history interpreted as *Geschichte* only insofar as it enlivens the divine core in humanity, causing it to awaken from its dormant state.[59]

Von Balthasar considers Schleiermacher's philosophical Christology the source of Rudolf Bultmann's Gnostic distinction between the "Jesus of history" and the "Christ of faith." Like Schleiermacher, Bultmann rejects only one of the two basic assumptions of the historical-critical method: he opposes historical-critical neutrality but not the separation of the church's Christ and the "real" Christ. Hence, Bultmann correlates the ecclesial kerygma with personal faith but leaves this separation unchallenged. Von Balthasar therefore does not believe that Bultmann's understanding of "kerygma," despite his claims to the contrary, actually involves an ecclesial mediation of the reality of Christ. This is why Bultmann views the ecclesial form of Christ presented in the canonical Scriptures as the product of a "mythological" way of thinking that is no longer relevant today, and which hence must be "demythologized."[60] Von Balthasar thinks this language is highly misleading. Despite his rhetoric against mythology, Bultmann is in fact offering a Gnostic reinterpretation of Christ. For him, von Balthasar argues, Christ is not the original historical Jesus (in the sense of *Historie*), but rather he is a "formless" spiritual "idea of humanity" brought to human consciousness by remembering the figure of Jesus of Nazareth. According to von Balthasar, Bultmann believes that the canonical and dogmatic "mythology" of Jesus created by the early church was the result of a process of apotheosis through the unconscious projection of humanity's essentially divine human nature onto him.[61] Hence although the formless "Christ of faith" did take on form in a particular ecclesial kerygma about Jesus, its universal relevance can be regained by reversing the projection through a process of demythologization, which will then make the "Christ of faith" for us today what it really was in the first century, namely, a formless divine reality latent in the human soul. In Bultmann's rigorously antisacramental and anti-incarnational Christology, therefore, the "historical Jesus" must be kept "pale and 'formless.'"[62] Von Balthasar interprets Bultmann's idea that the "facts" about the historical Jesus are ultimately irrelevant to faith as Gnostic hostility toward the fact of God's incarnation.[63] Indeed, he explicitly identifies Bultmann with second-century docetism.[64] Moreover, von Balthasar thinks Bultmann's scriptural hermeneutic is typically Gnostic because it fails to understand that the true reality of Christ is only accessible insofar as the church mediates it.

His critique of Bultmann reveals von Balthasar's theological agenda. Above all he wants to establish the sacramental traditions of the church as historically permanent and essential dimensions of the total Christ-form. Von Balthasar's claim that the Word interprets itself means that no neutral interpretation of the church (and the canonical Scriptures are for him part of the church) will be adequate. To see the real Christ is to see Christ in all phases of his incarnational process, including the church. Thus, membership in the church means participating in God's on-going incarnation. Framing the issue in this way allows von Balthasar to maintain that the doctrine of Scripture's divine inspiration and the Chalcedonian doctrine that Christ was fully human and fully divine are both testifying to the sacramental embodying of the divine Word in receptive human beings. Only baptized participants in the incarnational process can understand it and truthfully comment on it. As von Balthasar might put it, without the eyes of ecclesial faith Christ is incomprehensible.[65]

This returns us to von Balthasar's odd and curious claim that historical-critical scholarship enriches Irenaeus's patristic theology by confirming its best intentions. In direct contrast to his generally negative reading of Bultmann, von Balthasar highlights the positive contributions of modern historical-critical scholarship in order to forge an alliance between it and Irenaeus's battle against Bultmann's abstract Gnostic Christology. For example, he argues that historical-critical method is certainly right to assume that theology must avoid ahistorical, noncontextual, culturally and sociologically naïve readings of the biblical texts. In this sense, historical-critical scholarship is anti-Gnostic. However, once this point is made against Bultmann, von Balthasar turns against his historical-critical allies. He believes that a historical-critical interpretation of Scripture outside its ecclesial context does not in the end foster the genuinely historical, contextual reading the historical critics themselves advocate. This is because, von Balthasar believes, historical-critical scholars themselves almost always have a Gnostic disdain for monotheism and/or the doctrine of the incarnation. Hence they attempt to go behind the monotheistic and christological meaning of the text to find some other meaning (sociological, psychological, pantheistic, deistic, and so on). In the case of the New Testament, historical-critical method usually immediately rules out the possibility that the text could be testifying to real, historical human encounters with the Jewish God incarnated in the life, death, and resurrection of a Jewish rabbi. Instead, von Balthasar charges, historical-critical method sets out to strip the Bible of its supposed kerygmatic overlay in order to uncover the real historical Jesus buried beneath what it takes to be layers of ecclesial distortion and superstition.[66] The "real" Jesus turns out to be just an extraordinary human being who has no claim to absolute religious status. Recall here von Balthasar's theological commitment to de Lubac's doctrine of grace: the supernatural has in fact entered history and therefore it is impossible to bracket out for analysis a "pure nature." De Lubac always defines the supernatural in terms of Jewish monotheism and not pantheism or deism. Following this line of thought, von Balthasar is compelled to argue that historical-critical scholars are historically naïve when they bracket out the presence of the supernatural in the lives of the authors who produced the canonical Scriptures. The historical critics betray their own ideals with their a priori bias that the supernatural was not a real historical presence for the authors of the canonical texts. Claiming to be a historical scholar while ignoring the real historical presence of the supernatural in a particular place, person, and time, von Balthasar would argue, is a contradiction. Rather than facing this contradiction, historical-critical scholars often try to salvage the religious (but not supernatural) meaning of the biblical texts. They argue that there must be some other nonsupernatural source for the events and teachings presented in the text, a source which is different from the text's own claim that the Jewish God is their source. The exact type of alternative, nonsupernatural source they assert exposes the types of metaphysical bias guiding their supposedly neutral analyses. For von Balthasar, then, insofar as historical critics fail to read the biblical texts as testimonies to historical encounters with the paradoxical mystery of the supernatural, they, like Bultmann, operate within the parameters of false gnosis.

### The Doxological Curriculum of the Church's Mystagogy

The sacramental imprinting of the Word in the church's sacraments and Scriptures is both the product of and the impetus for the church's mystagogy. For von Balthasar, of course, the mystery of Jesus Christ is the primary object of the church's mystagogy. He believes, however, that the theological virtues of faith, love, and hope constitute the concrete curriculum of the church's mystagogy into Christ. Following Irenaeus's principle that "the glory of God is a living man, and the life of man is the vision of God,"[67] von Balthasar argues that these virtues are, like the Son in his trinitarian relations, inherently doxological. Therefore the curriculum of ecclesial mystagogy involves being trained in a doxological praxis of receptive learning in which one is guided by Christ and the

Spirit in the inner-law of trinitarian self-communication.[68] The institutional church teaches spiritual openness so that God can write the inner-law of the trinitarian circuit on one's heart, and it teaches spiritual literacy so that one can read and follow this law. The church, therefore, enables its members to glorify God freely and creatively by making it possible for them to be imprinted by divine love and to embody it in the world. For von Balthasar, this praxis of receptive learning and free expression is the concrete meaning of the virtue of faith as it exists in an inherently symbiotic relationship with love and hope.

Von Balthasar understands the connection between grace and faith as contemplative receptivity and active response. For him, therefore, faith is an inherently ecclesial virtue with its own particular context and sacramental object of contemplative focus. The church is both the arena where the Christ-form in all its complex multidimensionality is presented to believers for faithful contemplation and where their faithful response to it originates. This understanding of faith is directly connected with a prophetic ethos of incarnating Yahweh's *chesed, rachamim, sedek,* and *mishpat* in the social realm. This connection between ecclesial faith and the old covenant's prophetic ethos explains why von Balthasar insists that the church must be not only an essentially social and communal body but also one that is necessarily concerned with justice in the world. In a remarkably synthetic passage von Balthasar brings together the core themes of his theology of the paschal mystery:

> Interior self-renunciation (*Entselbstung,* literally, "unselving") has not only its effect, but its basis and constant verification in self-renunciation for the purpose of serving of the world—serving the historical Christ, whom I encounter through the Church and in her, and, if I have understood the Gospel, also in every neighbor and in every situation in the world. This objectivism, which is proper to the Catholic principle . . . is the result of taking seriously the *ekstasis* of love, its going out of itself: only in this way can man achieve an act of serious love which corresponds to God's own act of taking love seriously—the act of the divine Eros which goes out of itself in order to become man and dies on the Cross for the world. . . . To do this the Christian need not wait until his physical death, but must begin his work at once; already in baptism he has died radically and had risen unto God, and he then spends the rest of his life training himself in this reality and living it out.[69]

The "Catholic principle" means in this context an ecclesiological understanding of spiritual life that integrates trinitarian monotheism with interpersonal and institutional praxis. Although von Balthasar uses the phrase "training himself," he certainly does not understand mystagogical initiation into the paschal mystery as an activity carried out by indi-

viduals acting alone. Rather, Christians can only be said to train themselves in the sense that they freely submit to formation by the sacramental community of the church. The internal logic of this belief leads
von Balthasar to make the striking claim quoted earlier in chapter 2:
human fulfillment takes place "not in the glory of paradise, but in the
crucifying encounter of the crucified Lord in the sin-distorted face of
one's fellow-man."[70] This assertion is extremely important and requires
further explication.

First, the use of the term "sin-distorted" must not be taken as a reference to the sinfulness of the other, but a reference to the sins of injustice
perpetrated against the other that are expressed in his or her suffering
face. This is why von Balthasar describes it as an encounter with the crucified face of Christ. Second, von Balthasar believes this understanding of
the other's "sin-distorted face" is the key to understanding the New Testament's theology of the paschal mystery. The "face" of Christ in the sin-
distorted face of the other becomes the locus of the Spirit's call for us to
ratify the paschal Christ-form. Moreover, this implies that participation
in the Trinity's mystagogic work of redemption does not mean a purely
individual, interior piety, but rather a faith that seeks to foster justice on
earth through cooperation and dialogue with others. Moreover, because
the church participates in the unity-in-difference of the trinitarian persons, it seeks to affirm and love "the other precisely as *other*."[71] Hence,
the church is the mystagogic context where the doxological training in
affirming the other as other occurs. This training centrally involves contemplative "study" of the paschal mystery, which expresses the trinitarian receptivity and self-giving that is the doxological archetype of all
respect for the otherness of the other. This explains why von Balthasar is
highly critical of any Christian metaphysical attempt to express the glory
of God that does not take seriously enough the personal Otherness of
God or the personal otherness of our fellow human creatures.[72] Further,
it illuminates in a deeper way the social—and even political—implications of von Balthasar's ecclesiology. As the incarnation of trinitarian
love, the church necessarily has an impetus toward justice and righteousness on behalf of the other. Moreover, for von Balthasar, this impetus is
the root meaning of Jesus' "message" for the church:

> Jesus' message has . . . authority over all commissions given to men in rela-
> tion to the Creation too—the establishment of a just order upon earth that
> is worthy of man, the struggle against injustice and inhumanity—and it is
> he who will utter the definitive word to bring in the harvest of the endeav-
> ors of the world, which will be laid at his feet. Jesus' authority does not
> relieve mankind of the exertion to assume full concreteness: now that his
> word and example have been among us, active human love—individual

and social, personal and acting through structures—cannot be post-poned.[73]

Von Balthasar thinks this "active human love" on the individual and social, personal and structural level is itself the direct result of the incarnational dynamic of the economy Trinity working in finite human persons to perfect their creaturely freedom from within.[74]

According to von Balthasar, the pneumatological aspect of the incarnational process consists in fostering the virtue of love as the inner telos of faith. The Johannine theology of the fruitful vine and branches serves as von Balthasar's vehicle for articulating this pneumatological symbiosis between faith and love.[75] The Spirit's activity in the church is to form believers into the form of the crucified Christ so that they will be willing to lay down their own lives for each other as Christ laid his down for them. The essence of the church is imitating the cruciform self-giving of Christ on the cross. In von Balthasar's mystagogic conception of the church, believers are prepared by the Spirit to make an "attempt at total self-renunciation, at dying to all self-will" so that they will be able to bear divine fruit in love for one another through concrete deeds.[76] All roads in von Balthasar's theology lead back to the monotheistic axiom that ethical activity is the quintessential incarnational activity.

Von Balthasar's rigorous and repeated distinction between speculative, abstract spiritual understanding and a practical, christocentric ethos of love clearly indicates his reliance on Irenaeus's distinction between true and false gnosis. A paradigmatic instance of his application of this distinction comes in his exegesis of 2 Corinthians 8, where Paul discusses his collection from the churches of Macedonia for famine relief in the Jerusalem church. Von Balthasar's interpretation of this chapter is extremely revealing of his own understanding of the church as the context where the infinite freedom of trinitarian self-giving takes on a concrete form that makes no distinction between body and soul, matter and spirit. He believes that in this passage the New Testament's theology of divine "overflow" reaches its full christological and trinitarian dimensions.[77] He argues that the alms given by the Macedonian churches are the fruit of the grace they have received from Christ, a grace that is directly connected to their sacramental formation according to the pattern of Christ's *kenosis*. In his commentary on Paul's text von Balthasar explains that in his *kenosis* Christ's riches and his act of self-giving are identical. Therefore in the poverty of self-abandonment Christians give themselves away and become rich, just as Christ emptied himself of his riches to give himself to the world. Paul's encouragement of the Corinthians to give to Jerusalem as generously as the Macedonians illustrates something essential about the Christian understanding of poverty and riches, namely, the "lack of distinction between what is spiritual and what is material as regards the fruitfulness and the establishment of 'equality,' . . . especially when this is considered against the background of the Trinity and the Incarnation."[78]

If, for von Balthasar, ethical activity is the quintessential incarnational activity, then hope is its precondition. For him Christian hope always exists in a symbiosis with faith and love. This is the case because the ecclesial initiation into the trinitarian dynamism of receptivity and active responsive love originates in hope, while hope requires faith and love. Hence he assumes all three theological virtues work together in a circular dynamism of mutual support that educates believers into an ever-deeper participation in the paschal mystery. Indeed, believers incarnate the Word to the extent that they integrate these three virtues. Hence, von Balthasar believes that the church is mystagogical both for its members and for the world because it is the concrete embodiment of the unity of faith, love, and hope in human existence.[79] As witnesses to the Father's love for his Son in their own hearts, in the church community, and in the world, Christians know that the glory of God is glorious not only because of its immediate power but also because of its eschatological trajectory. This knowledge gives Christians "the certainty that their Christian 'patience' is no mere waiting until the process of time matures by itself and reaches its end."[80] Contrary then to teleological theories of history, Christian hope does not understand the Spirit as a timeless void that will eventually absorb all the chaos of history, nor does it understand the Spirit as a blind, impersonal evolutionary process leading creation to some "perfect" end that has nothing to do with those who have died along the way. Rather, hope allows Christians to live in the Spirit in a truly eschatological sense, willing to risk everything in faith and love as if God's will reigned fully now on earth, but also knowing that the dead have not yet been raised, and that all tears have not yet been wiped away.[81] Hope gives Christianity its nonworldly perspective without allowing it to degenerate into an other-worldly contempt for finite, bodily, and historical existence.[82] Through the self-interpreting reality of the *corpus triforme*, Christians are able to resist all forms of historical determinism that see temporal life as nothing but a relentless march toward death and oblivion. In von Balthasar's view, therefore, the goal of all ecclesial mystagogy is to train people in this resistance.

## Notes

1. *TD2*, 145-46; see also *TL3*, 268-81.

2. *GL1*, 559. It is important to notice that this analogy preserves the difference between Christ and the church. "Nothing in the Church—not even the Church her-

self—can lay claim to an autonomous form that would compete with the Christ-form or even replace it" (GL1, 576).

3. GL7, 113-15. See also TL3, 224-33, 268-78.

4. GL1, 571.

5. GL2, 93.

6. TD2, 143.

7. "God must be greater than everything outside of himself, . . . and not only in this world, but also in that which is to come, so that he always remains the teacher, and man always remains God's pupil. As the apostle says, when everything else has passed away, these three alone will remain: faith, hope, love. So our unshakable faith remains in our teacher who gives us certainty that He alone is the one true God, and that we should always love Him because he alone is our Father; while we hope ever to be receiving more and more from God, and to learn from Him, because He is good, and possesses boundless riches, a kingdom without end, and teachings that can never be exhausted" (cf. AH 2.28.3). TL2, 254-55.

8. See GL1, 563.

9. His disdainful, highly negative comments about Hegel and Hegelian Idealism throughout GL7 give a good indication that something very different is going on in von Balthasar's theology. Von Balthasar associates Hegelianism with Gnosticism (86, 178) in its search for a "purely philosophical" knowledge of God (315), an "absolute knowledge" of the divine (524). For this reason, von Balthasar charges Hegel with being anti-Semitic (440-41) and asserts that Hegel's philosophy is the exact contrary of a truly Christian understanding of redemption in Christ (13-14). I will return to this critique in the next chapter.

10. Craig Arnold Phillips contends that von Balthasar's theology is ahistorical and noncontextual because it is contemplative. See "From Aesthetics to Redemptive Politics: A Political Reading of the Theological Aesthetics of Hans Urs Von Balthasar and the Materialist Aesthetics of Walter Benjamin" (Ann Arbor, Mich.: UMI Dissertation Services, 1993), 118-19, 166-81.

11. For a discussion of this point, see von Balthasar's OPSC, 131-45.

12. For von Balthasar it is a mistake to "look on historical revelation as a past event, as presupposed, and not as something always happening, to be listened to and obeyed." See "Theology and Sanctity," in Explorations in Theology 1: The Word Made Flesh, trans. A. V. Littledale (San Francisco: Ignatius Press, 1989), 205.

13. See, for example, TL3, 294-330.

14. GL7, 488-90, 526-28.

15. Ibid., 490-91.

16. GL1, 559, 561-70, 576. Von Balthasar makes a very similar point when he contends that for Irenaeus the totality of the Christ-form cannot be exhaustively captured in creedal formulas or dogmas, even if they do "sum up and 'epitomize' revealed truth." For Irenaeus, the church rightly organizes the truths of the faith, but this is only in service of the revealed truth that is "so living and transcendent—since God's ever-greater love is its core—that words and formulas can never master it" (TD2, 146).

17. Von Balthasar makes this point with force in his essay "Sponsa Verbi," in Skizzen zur Theologie II, Eng. trans., Church and World, trans. A. V. Littledale with Alexander Dru (New York: Herder and Herder, 1967). See also GL1, 570, and OPSC, 145-57. Nevertheless, he maintains that although empirically the church can be disfigured and distorted beyond recognition, in its depths it is immaculate and infallible (GL7, 102).

18. *GL1*, 567, 569. Von Balthasar quotes Irenaeus (*AH* 3.24.1) to make this point in *Theologik*: "Wo die Kirche ist, da ist auch der Geist Gottes, und wo der Geist Gottes ist, da ist auch die Kirche und alle Gnade; und der Geist ist Wahrheit" (*TL3*, 15).

19. *GL7*, 239ff.

20. Ibid., 252.

21. Ibid., 253ff.

22. Ibid., 255-56.

23. Ibid., 256. "The trinitarian love is the only ultimate form of all love—both the love between God and men, and that between human persons" (ibid., 484).

24. *GL1*, 33-34.

25. See *GL7*, 432-84. Von Balthasar's position in these pages is nearly identical to de Lubac's arguments for the unity of person and society in the church. See *Catholicism*, 326-66.

26. *GL2*, 87.

27. *GL7*, 318-85.

28. Ibid., 493.

29. See ibid., 95, 136. See also *GL2*, 75, 77.

30. *TL3*, 268ff. It is therefore not surprising that Irenaean pneumatology receives affirmation in this text. See also *TL3*, 153-56.

31. *GL6*, 412; *GL7*, 13-14, 111, 508-11.

32. *GL7*, 222, 362-63, 400. See also *MP*, 55, 66; *TL2*, 147.

33. Ibid., 525-26; *GL6*, 357; *MP*, 38-41.

34. Ibid., 308, 405.

35. Ibid., 405.

36. Ibid.

37. See Cyril O'Regan's carefully argued essay on von Balthasar's reading of Meister Eckhart, "Balthasar and Eckhart: Theological Principles and Catholicity," *The Thomist* 60, 2 (April, 1996): 203-39; see esp. 210-13.

38. *GL7*, 293-94.

39. *TD2*, 145-46; *SI*, 92.

40. *GL6*, 404; *GL7*, 145, 202, 216, 247, 378.

41. "The supper and the Cross together constitute the 'hour' for which he had come (Jn 12.27)" (*GL1*, 571).

42. *GL7*, 152, 226.

43. *GL1*, 571.

44. Ibid., 573-74. Hence he asserts that "the fellowship of followers which is called together by Jesus has an internal structure that is designed to go out beyond itself to mankind as a whole" (*GL7*, 96).

45. Ibid., 467.

46. Ibid., 432. Von Balthasar argues that an ecclesial life cannot be a "private 'spirituality'" for individuals because "[i]n the *mysterium* of the Church no individual member can be successfully isolated from the whole living organism." This is so because believers are imprinted with Christ's form; because Christ "cannot be detached either from his trinitarian or from his salvation-historical ecclesial context," neither can believers who share his form be separated from this context (*OPSC*, 132). Moreover, because Christ now "stands in an indivisible whole within a constellation of his fellow men" all those who share in his form share in this constellation (136ff.)

47. *GL7*, 433.

48. *TD3*, 59ff.
49. Ibid., 59-60.
50. See *TD2*, 102-15.
51. *TD3*, 105.
52. Ibid., 114.
53. Ibid., 109-15.
54. Ibid., 60-68, 71-73. Scholars could reasonably question von Balthasar's reading of Schleiermacher. My point, however, is not that he is accurate in what he claims about Schleiermacher. My point is that his claims indicate how he thinks about scriptural hermeneutics.
55. Ibid., 60-61.
56. Ibid., 71.
57. Ibid., 68ff.
58. Ibid., 72-73.
59. Ibid., 65.
60. Ibid., 64-68.
61. Ibid., 64.
62. Ibid., 67-68
63. Ibid., 69; cf. 76. Von Balthasar notes that Bultmann believed that "'the life of Jesus was unmessianic'" (ibid., 67).
64. *GL1*, 52, 314.
65. "The first prerequisite for understanding is to accept what is given just as it offers itself. If certain excisions are practised on the Gospel from the outset, the integrity of the phenomenon is lost and it has already become incomprehensible" (ibid., 467).
66. Ibid., 466ff.
67. *GL2*, 74-75; *TD2*, 149; *TL2*, 207.
68. "In the Gospels . . . 'christology' occurs only in the framework of 'ecclesiology' [because] this variegated 'Church' of men around Jesus is gathered, held together, and determined in its behavior *only* through his person and presence" (*GL7*, 100). As we will see in later chapters, this is a crucially important point for understanding von Balthasar's extreme resistance to the idea that the church can or should align itself with any particular partisan political agenda.
69. *GL1*, 216-17.
70. *GL7*, 470.
71. Ibid., 447.
72. Ibid., 440-41.
73. Ibid., 129.
74. Ibid., 457.
75. Ibid., 419-20.
76. Ibid., 257.
77. Ibid., 424, 427ff.
78. Ibid., 430.
79. Ibid., 521.
80. Ibid., 511.
81. Ibid., 178-80, 508ff.
82. Von Balthasar argues that this is why in Christianity the redemption of the body matters, "for it is only together with the body that we are saved" (ibid., 513).

# PART THREE

# THEOLOGY IN AN AGONISTIC CONTEXT

# Chapter V

# The Making of Modern Gnosticism

In chapter 1 I asserted that von Balthasar sees many modern theological trends as variations of second-century Gnostic doctrines, and he intends his entire theological project as a contemporary reprise of Irenaeus's project in *Against Heresies*. In this chapter I will defend this assertion. Von Balthasar believes that salvation history is rife with dramatic tension resulting from a competition between the church and its "post-Christian" Gnostic enemies over conflicting symbolic systems, contradictory claims of absolute truth, and rival conceptions of the good. He identifies one of Gnosticism's primary characteristics as its practice of presenting abstract theory as if it were Judeo-Christian theology. It borrows heavily from both the Bible and the Christian doctrinal tradition, thereby concealing its antimonotheistic and anti-incarnational agenda. Second-century Gnosticism retained some external elements of the *corpus triforme* while rejecting its core beliefs in monotheism and the real incarnation of eternity in time. It produced Christologies that resembled metaphysical philosophy more than doxological sacramentality. In the second century, Gnosticism's deceptive practices were extremely successful, and it infiltrated and contaminated the early church.[1] Von Balthasar sees this same Gnostic practice at work in Christianity today.[2] He is generally uninterested in the question of whether Gnosticism is consciously carrying out a demonic plot to sabotage God's plan for creation or whether its speculative reinterpretations of Christianity are simply naïve and inadvertently heterodox. His rhetoric seems to suggest that he favors the former, more paranoid option.[3] In any case, he sets himself the tasks of retrieving Irenaeus's critique of second-century Gnosticism and applying it as a diagnostic tool in the contemporary context to explain the practice (conscious or not) many modern theologians use in their hostile reinterpretations of *corpus triforme* Christology.

## Epic Theology Then and Now

Von Balthasar uses the term "epic" theology to refer to the speculative "false gnosis" opposed by Irenaeus in the second century. He describes epic theology as having two poles:

> At one extreme, there is the mythological view in which God (or the gods) is embroiled in the world drama, which, with its own laws of operation, thus constitutes a third level of reality above God and man; at the other extreme, God is seen as dwelling in philosophical sublimity above the vicissitudes of the world, which prevent him from entering the dramatic action.[4]

Von Balthasar believes that there is a clear connection between second-century epic theology and modern theologies that have been influenced by Georg Wilhelm Friedrich Hegel (1770-1831):

> Where is the path that leads between the twin abysses of a systematics in which God, absolute Being, is only the Unmoved before whom the moving world plays out its drama, and a mythology which absorbs God into the world and makes him to be one of the warring parties of world process? The two extremes meet: they are both incorporated into the gnosticism of the second century and once more in that of Hegel.[5]

The "second-century Gnosticism" in question here is certainly Irenaeus's nemesis, Valentinianism,[6] but the connection between second-century Valentinianism and modern Hegelianism that von Balthasar asserts here requires more explanation than he supplies. Assertions about the connections between Hegel and Gnosticism in general are not rare in von Balthasar's writings,[7] yet explicit explanations of the connections between Hegel and Valentinianism are absent. In his theological aesthetics von Balthasar did draw a direct parallel between Hegel and Valentinianism, observing that Valentinus's system "is often very reminiscent of Hegel."[8] But here too the connections are left only implicit.[9] Yet, the lack of explicit comparisons between Hegel and Valentinianism does not cast doubt on my thesis that von Balthasar identifies many contemporary theological trends as being variations on the Irenaean theme of "false gnosis." It is obvious, however, that this thesis requires several preliminary qualifications. First, von Balthasar has so internalized the positive norm of the *corpus triforme* that he uses it to critique speculative theological systems, whether or not they are continuous with second-century Valentinianism. This means that some of the links in the conceptual chain from Valentinianism to Hegelianism are not always as strong as he presumes. Second, because von Balthasar is far more interested in identifying willed deviance from the *corpus triforme* standard, he often overlooks both the details of the deviance and the specific distinctions between various types of deviance. The connection between Valentinianism per se and Hegelianism per se is less important to him than the general connection between ancient types of speculative theological discourse and modern types. In both cases he sees a fundamental hostility to *corpus triforme* Christology. Third, although in the passage quoted above von Balthasar seems to suggest a perfect analogy between second-century Valentinianism and Hegelianism, it is clear elsewhere in *Theo-Drama* that he recognizes that the modern situation is much more complex. Although he sees himself as being in an agonistic situation with many similarities to Irenaeus's second-century context, he does not necessarily assume that all the modern types of Gnosticism can be reduced to Valentinianism. Nor does he think it necessary to make this reduction to draw relevant parallels between ancient and modern types of speculative false gnosis. Fourth, it is reasonable to believe that the lack of a perfect analogy between second-century Valentinianism and modern Gnosticism is itself a condition for von Balthasar's repetition of an essentially Irenaean critique of false gnosis. If the analogy between the second century and modernity were perfect, this would be a denial of the historical uniqueness both von Balthasar and Irenaeus wished to defend from erasure by ahistorical epic theology.

Therefore, the best place to begin tracing the connections in von Balthasar's thought between second-century false gnosis and modern post-Christian epic discourse is not in his interpretation of Valentinianism but in his interpretation of Marcionism.[10] In what appears to be a reference to Valentinianism, he explains, on the one hand, that ancient Gnosticism in general was "too fantastic" in its grandiose speculations to be a credible rival to the biblically grounded, historically oriented Christianity advocated by Irenaeus.[11] Marcionism, on the other hand, was a populist, intellectually unsophisticated variant on Valentinianism.[12] Marcionism proved to be a unique case because its seemingly down-to-earth, apparently common-sense approach to theology earned for it a special kind of permanent status in Western Christianity. Nevertheless, as I noted in chapter 5, von Balthasar considers Marcion an arch-Gnostic whose ideas are anything but commonsensical. He argues that Marcion taught the "most dangerous form" of Gnosticism because its abstract speculative assumptions were cloaked in a "mythical" discourse resembling the biblical narrative, and hence it seemed "closest to Christianity and the least burdened by fantasy."[13] For example, Marcion describes the struggle between the tyranny of Yahweh and the freedom of Jesus Christ in dramatic terms. Von Balthasar, therefore, considers Marcion an epic thinker who denies the first and second corollaries of *corpus triforme* Christology. Once he disconnected the old and new covenants it made perfect sense for him to also disconnect creation and redemption. This second disconnection necessarily follows from his dichotomy between the old covenant's exterior religion of works and earthly justice and the new covenant's religion of spiritual interiority. Thus Marcionism set an important example that later Gnostic movements followed: the veiling of an essentially speculative Gnostic discourse behind nonspeculative theological gestures.

Von Balthasar clearly believes that all types of Gnosticism have continued to exercise influence over non-Christian religious thought since the first century.[14] However, the conviction that the mythic, Marcionist type of Gnosticism reemerges in the Christian Middle Ages with Joachim of Fiore's doctrine of the "three phases" of history is at the center of his agonistic interpretation of salvation history.[15] Just as with Marcion's ancient mythic system, Joachim's type of Gnosticism credibly masqueraded as a biblically grounded Christian theology while simultaneously dismantling the *corpus triforme* system of meaning. Joachim's Gnosticism, however, becomes a more serious and profoundly influential player on the world stage than either Marcionism or any of the purely speculative forms of ancient Gnosticism had been.[16]

Joachim, abbot of a Franciscan monastery in Calabria, taught that the history of the world can be divided into three sequential periods: the age of the Father, the age of the Son, and the age of the Spirit.[17] Von Balthasar insists that this division of history into discrete trinitarian epochs poses a direct challenge to the Christian system of meaning. For example, although Joachim appears to maintain the unity of the old and new covenants by putting the age of the Father and the age of the Son in a sequential relation, he in fact speculatively reinterprets the unity of the old and new covenants to erase the unity of trinitarianism and monotheism intrinsic to the *corpus triforme*. Joachim's doctrine of history, unlike some types of ancient Gnosticism that undervalued history, attempts to take seriously the linear historical orientation of the old covenant prophets' expectation of a coming messiah. Von Balthasar does not think Joachim really succeeds. Taking seriously the prophet's expectation of a coming messiah would mean recognizing the historical *kairos* of the incarnation as the fulfillment of the old covenant's promise of a coming messiah. Joachim, instead, offers a theory of historical stages that presupposes there is no redemptive axis of history where vertical and horizontal intersect, but only a forward-flowing movement beyond the historical epoch of the Son toward an ever-deeper interiorizing of the Spirit. This way of thinking undoes the new covenant's soteriological integration of eternal and temporal reality and replaces it with a conception of Christian faith based only on the latter. For Joachim, the created order has not yet been redeemed but must instead progressively move forward into a future historical age when redemption will be realized.

In addition to Joachim's disconnection of the unity between the old and new covenants and the unity of creation and redemption, von Balthasar sees him making a similarly hostile move against the third corollary of *corpus triforme* Christology, the unity of Christ and the church.[18] Joachim's purely horizontal conception of the Trinity assigns the reality of the church only to the "era of Christ." This intellectual maneuver renders the institutional church, with its dogmas, sacraments, liturgies, and clerical hierarchy, "a mere episode, to be followed and transcended by an era of the Spirit" when there will be a total interiorization of religion. In this new age of the Spirit the truly spiritual adepts will have a direct and pure knowledge of God without the mediation of law, faith, ritual, institution, or any other determinate religious phenomena associated with positive religion in the ages of the Father and the Son.

Again, von Balthasar's main concern is that Joachim's doctrine, although appearing to take history seriously as a source of religious understanding, in fact undermines the full historical determinacy of faith in favor of an a priori theory of history. More precisely, Joachim replaces the divinely revealed a posteriori reality offered in the concrete historical event of Christ with a speculative human construct. In this sense, Joachim's doctrine is really only a variant of the general Gnostic practice of posturing as Christianity on the world stage while at the same time rejecting the contemplative aesthetic ethos intrinsic to the Christian system of meaning. This rejection of the contemplative ethos led both Joachim and the ancient Gnosticism to dismantle the unity of the *corpus triforme* and replace it with a purely internalized interpretation of Christian faith based on a subjective and human speculative construct. These explanatory reinterpretations of the *corpus triforme* belong in the category of what von Balthasar terms "theological rationalism," which he defines as a mode of theological reflection that "treats God and his grace like some component that can be manipulated by human thought."[19] As noted above, however, he thinks that this type of rationalism is more serious and has more lasting effects in its modern, Joachimite form, because this form is able to veil its ahistorical, speculative, and indeterminate conception of faith behind a specious commitment to a historical perspective. On this point, he contends that "Joachim's successors in this field are as innumerable as the sand of the sea."[20]

Von Balthasar believes, for example, that it is the direct result of Joachim's influence that modern Gnosticism develops the "ideology" that human redemption can be attained at some point in the future through a progressive, inner-worldly historical praxis.[21] Recall that he considers the desire to attain total control and mastery over reality through a priori metaphysical theories to be a core feature of Gnostic discourse. Under the sway of Joachim's disconnection of Jewish messianic hope and the new covenant's theology of redemption, the Gnostic explanatory ethos shifts the focus away from a static metaphysics of pantheistic monism and toward a dynamic metaphysics of historical progress. This shift results in an increasing intensity in the Gnostic desire for power over reality. It is as if Gnosticism, after centuries of repression by the Constantinian church, came to realize that it could win its war against Christianity by advocating humanity's progressive self-redemption through its self-liberation from nature, altar, and throne.[22]

In von Balthasar's capacious interpretation of modern Gnosticism, therefore, an ethos of stoic resignation gives way to an ethos of Promethean power and control. Gnosticism becomes synonymous with the claim that the eventual full rational discernment of all the laws of nature and history will allow the human race finally to take away the sins of the world and establish a universal reign of peace, justice, and happiness on earth. In this sunny humanism we see a clear instance of the Gnostic reinterpretation of the *corpus triforme* theology of the incarnation: human nature itself—and not the human nature of the person of Jesus Christ—becomes the agent of the world's redemption. It carries out this reinterpretation by borrowing heavily from Christianity's belief that, in secularizing the cosmos, Christ liberates human freedom from servitude to pagan deities and the cosmic law of death. Gnostic forms of humanism are "post-Christian" because their anthropology is culturally credible only after the redeeming work of Christ, who fully liberates humanity into its creaturely autonomy and freedom from cosmic determinism.[23] Because modern Gnosticism interprets the creaturely freedom made possible by Christ outside the context of the *corpus triforme* system of meaning, von Balthasar charges it with being radically anthropocentric and with being driven by a "Titanic" or "Promethean" principle of power.[24] Modern Gnosticism, however, is ultimately internally conflicted and unstable because of the evolutionary presuppositions in Joachimite progressivism. The question of whether progress is entirely dependent on human effort or if it is an inevitable evolutionary process beyond human control is never resolved in modern Gnosticism. As a result, despite its often strident optimism about humanity's ability to control its destiny, a strong undertow of evolutionary determinism haunts modern Gnosticism, constantly threatening to transform its celebration of human freedom into an ethos of resignation. Yet in modern

Gnosticism's epic narration of humanity's self-emancipation from tragedy and suffering, the ethos of resignation does not originate from the cyclical cosmic process of particular beings arising from and merging back into a sea of nothingness, as was the case in ancient Gnosticism. Rather, its ethos of resignation arises from the inevitable march of the mechanistic and technological ordering of social and political life that sacrifices the freedom—and perhaps even the lives—of individual persons to the rationally discerned, anonymous laws of history.[25]

## Hegel and Modern Gnosticism

As this point suggests, and as I will discuss below, von Balthasar's intention in his analysis of post-Christian Gnosticism is to offer theological resistance to political forms of Gnostic discourse. It is important to keep in mind that this resistance originates from his more primary resistance to Joachimite and Hegelian theology. But of all the modern Gnostic advocates of the "myth" of human progress, Hegel is the one who most interests von Balthasar. He considers Hegel's grand system to be the most representative, influential, and theologically dangerous development of Joachimism.[26] This is not to say that he thinks Hegel's thought can be exhaustively reduced to the influence of Joachim; as I mentioned earlier, he believes that Valentinianism is also a very strong presence in Hegel. Unfortunately, he does not supply much explanation for his view that there is a complex symbiosis of Marcionism, Valentinianism, and Joachimism in Hegel.[27] Mapping out the details of this symbiosis is less important to him than generally sketching the big picture that he believes many contemporary theologians have failed to see. In this big picture, von Balthasar wants to show that Hegel's insistence that it is possible for humans to attain an "absolute knowledge" of the totality of reality best exemplifies the modern form of the "false gnosis" Irenaeus opposed in the second century.[28] Therefore, when he contends that Hegel's understanding of Christianity "jettisons the very aspects which are of theological significance to us," this must be read as an Irenaean indictment of Hegel as a Gnostic thinker who rejects *corpus triforme* Christology and all its corollaries.[29] But because he does not discuss Hegel's philosophical theology explicitly in terms of the *corpus triforme*, my hermeneutic edict requires some further justification.

Von Balthasar begins his indictment of Hegel by first critically examining his thesis that Christianity has abolished art.[30] While this may seem an oddly nontheological issue, he thinks that it clearly illustrates Hegel's hostile, epic reinterpretation of Christianity. For example, he believes that Hegel's claim that speculative philosophy sublates art is made possible by Christianity's prior claim that God's incarnation in history sublates art. In Hegel's view, he argues, "Christianity is not only coextensive but identical with the human (which in turn is the manifestation of the divine). . . . [T]he identity of God and man is the point of absoluteness which interprets the whole process of Spirit."[31] This monistic equation of the divine and human is at the basis of Hegel's opinion that "Christianity replaces art," an opinion which von Balthasar suspects is a veiled way to claim that Christianity abolishes the dramatic meaning of history as an interaction between God and humanity. Although Hegel intends to challenge Enlightenment rationalism, he consistently affirms its core assumption that the contingent events of history are ultimately irrelevant for theology's universal truth claims.[32] Von Balthasar makes the same charge again later when he criticizes Hegel for attempting to fit Christianity "into an all-inclusive history of the human spirit," which makes it inevitable that Christ's life and death on earth are reduced to merely an "imaging" of a wider historical process of the human spirit in such a way that "the recalling of this special event is in fact only 'devotion' on the part of the 'mind and heart'" to what is essentially a past event.[33] The implications of this reading of Hegel are clear: Hegel has abandoned a *corpus triforme* understanding of the unity of old covenant promise and new covenant fulfillment because he has forfeited biblical monotheism's belief in a transcendent, personal God whose pedagogical providence guides history. In other words, von Balthasar is convinced that Hegel's idealistic reinterpretation of salvation history reduces the God-world relation to a mythological type of pantheism.[34] In the Hegelian system, God is an immature deity whose developmental process corresponds exactly to the tragedies that unfold in human history. It is precisely here that von Balthasar thinks the epic presuppositions of Hegel's thinking become clearest: for Hegel the ultimate meaning of created temporality is not a dramatic interaction between God and humanity (or between the church and its enemies) but rather an epic interaction between God and God. In this epic theological system, the created order is ultimately the projection of God's self-alienation and need for self-expression in an other.[35] Hegel is found guilty here of a brazenly hostile reinterpretation of the incarnation: he wrongly conflates the eternal procession of the Son from the Father with the doctrine of creation out of nothing, with the result that the temporal finite creation is the "incarnation" of God's alienated Other. Thus history is for Hegel a three-part process of divine self-development: God's descent into pathology and alienation, God's moment of turning away from alienation and toward psychic wholeness, and God's journey back toward psychic wholeness through the overcoming of God's alienated self. In this epic system, the cross merely symbolizes the midpoint of this process, and thus is no more than simply "the highest 'representation' of the most general law of being." This general law of being, however, is ultimately for Hegel a law of nonbeing: the cross symbolizes the turning point from God's divine alienation to divine wholeness, a turning point in which God's alienated self begins to be reabsorbed into God. Thus the "law" represented by the cross is that, as God overcomes the self-alienation of finitude, creation is inexorably moving toward its annihilation in the infinity of divine nothingness.[36]

Von Balthasar's critical reading of Hegel's philosophy as a speculative reduction of God and creation to the mythology of a dynamic developmental pantheism also indicates that he believes it is guilty of subverting the *corpus triforme* unity of creation and redemption. For Hegel, there can only be an inversely proportional relationship between God's inner psychic healing and the independent autonomy of the created order. For Hegel, then, God must be both the subject and the object of theological discourse; there can ultimately be no analogy between infinite and finite when they are reduced to identity in a monistic system. Von Balthasar makes this point by explaining that Hegel held the a priori assumption that bodily resurrection and the redemption of individual persons are impossible, and to believe otherwise is simply a form of human "egoism."[37] He believes that the basis of Hegel's opinion here is directly rooted in his speculative theory of history as inner-divine process. This theory reduces history to merely God's act of contemplating God's own alienated self as it journeys back into the monistic "identity" of the World Spirit, a process in which the World Spirit must completely subsume all individuals who contribute to it along the way. Therefore, in Hegel's epic theology of history all finite reality is ultimately "absorbed in identity," and all personal reality is in the end overcome by "the impersonality of destiny."[38] As a consequence of this view, in Hegel's system "there is no role for the individual in his distinctness"—the redemption of the "individual" does not mean resurrection and personal communion with God, but rather "a perfect integration . . . of the particular individual into the totality of the spirit . . . ; for Hegel, the step-by-step journey toward this is a ruthless process whereby all that is particular is stripped of its illusion of being able to reach truth in and for itself."[39] Von Balthasar is aware that Hegel uses personal language for God, such as the language of selfhood and love, but he advocates suspicion here. He notes that Hegel defines God's "infinite love" as follows: "Infinite love is seen in that God has identified himself with what is alien to him in order to kill it."[40] Moreover, von Balthasar argues that Hegel's claim that Christianity abolishes drama reveals his true Gnostic agenda:

there is really no point to make dramatic art about action on the world stage because Christians know that, in the face of the impersonal destiny of the Spirit, humanity can do nothing but cultivate "devotion in mind and heart" to the past event of Christ's death and must do so in complete resignation to their coming eschatological oblivion. Since the cross shows that negation and death are intrinsic to God, internal devotion to Christ as the image of God's death means that Christians must cultivate a spirituality of self-annihilation because this is the most apt existential posture in the face of the impersonal destiny of "infinite love." Hegel's understanding of Christianity, however, fosters not only an ethos of resignation to destiny but also a Promethean ethos of explanatory power that can dictate the necessity of submission to the whole process of history. In other words, it is possible for Hegel to interpret contemplation of the crucified Christ in terms of a spirituality that has nothing to do with action in the world because his philosophy takes a God's-eye, absolute perspective on the totality of world history and sees that it will all be absorbed into the Spirit's self-understanding. For von Balthasar, it is difficult to imagine a more effective way to drain away the theological relevance of finite, particular acts of personal engagement in history's struggles.

Moreover, it also indicates the anti–*corpus triforme* presuppositions of Hegel's ecclesiology. Von Balthasar contends that Hegel does not take seriously the idea of the church as the "body" of Christ where the Spirit works to harmonize personal uniqueness and universal mission. On the contrary, he sees a definite Gnostic political agenda at work here. Hegel disconnects Christology from Christianity's pneumatic ecclesiology and attempts to spiritualize the political community, in effect making it the incarnation of the Spirit in history. In this transformation of the church into the state, Hegel forfeits the christocentric-ecclesial balance of personal individuality and communal universality.[41] As a result, von Balthasar explains, "Hegel puts the nation, 'the generalized individual,' at the center of his thought, to which anything 'particular' is a contrasting element."[42] He observes that, for Hegel, "the individual can look forward to no other immortality than that of service to the nation or the state" because (in Hegel's own words), "The individual as such is nothing."[43] In complete contradiction of Irenaeus's conception of the ecclesial *communio*, Hegel insists that the individual knows him or herself only in sacrificing all individuality to the totality of the Spirit as it takes form in the nation, and without this total sacrificial act the self can only know alienation. Thus, on von Balthasar's reading, the center of Hegel's entire argument in the *Phenomenology of Spirit* is that the fulfillment of the self lies in its negation and absorption by the state, which is the historical bearer of the World Spirit. Therefore on religious principle, Hegel will allow neither individual rights nor dissent based on individual conscience from the will of the state. Quoting the words of Hegel's text, von Balthasar demonstrates that Hegel believes that the particular individual must make an act of absolute surrender to the "generalized individual" of the nation or the state. This act of surrender requires the "the overcoming of the point of view of one's immediate happiness . . . ; the overcoming of the point of view of insane self-conceit, which undertakes to improve the world according to the 'law of one's own undisciplined heart' . . . ; the overcoming of the point of view of private virtue, which is 'conquered by the world's onward course.'"[44] Von Balthasar goes on to explain—directly quoting Hegel's highly pejorative terminology—that this overcoming of self in surrender to the state requires also that one surrender all personal care for anything that one could call one's own, the desire to be recognized by others, and the "hypocrisy" that one's "conscience" is absolute.[45] Thus for Hegel, on von Balthasar's interpretation, reconciling the finite particular and the infinite universal requires the complete relinquishing of personal existence in a total surrender to assimilation by the "absolute spirit" as it is expressed in the "community of the nation" in its political organization by the state; this total surrender finds its highest expression in the individual's willingness to undergo death as a sign of solidarity with the nation.[46] We see here the merger of ancient Stoicism's conception of personal freedom as surrender to the necessity of destiny and modern totalitarianism's conception of personal freedom as surrender to the will of the state.[47]

Clearly, then, von Balthasar contests Hegel's thesis of the death of art not out of an aesthete's interest in preserving the arts or the theater. Rather, von Balthasar's concern is, as he puts it, to allow for the "continuance of the dramatic dimension beyond the 'end' allotted to it by Hegel."[48] This concern is strictly theological because it is about preserving the meaning of faith as a Christian individual's personal involvement in the church's dramatic action on the world stage, an action that cooperates through the Holy Spirit with the universal and on-going redemptive work of the crucified and risen Christ. If there is truth in Hegel's claim that drama is dead, von Balthasar remarks, this is only because Christianity has wrongly forfeited its universal mission in the world and has instead allowed itself to make peace with secularism, which he describes as "the leveling-down of everything, Christian or non-Christian, under the universal, impersonal, dialectical law of 'die and become.'"[49] It is precisely this secular "leveling down" of all personal reality in the face of impersonal destiny that von Balthasar identifies as the most important element unifying both second-century Gnosticism and Hegelianism. For von Balthasar, the real issue at stake is whether a monistic or a monotheistic interpretation of existence ultimately will have regulative control over the church's understanding of its relationship to world history. This leads us finally to perhaps one of the most interesting aspects of his argument for an agonistic theology of history—his attempt to interpret the rivalry between the Christian and the Gnostic players in political terms. He does this by generally asserting that Hegel's epic theology has an "inner logic" that "leads directly to Marxism."[50]

## Marxism: A Quasi-Gnostic Religion

Von Balthasar is entirely aware that both right-wing Hegelians and orthodox Marxists have always bristled at the assertion of an "inner logic" connecting the avowedly Lutheran and politically conservative Hegel with the atheistic and revolutionary Marx. After all, Marx's entire intellectual agenda was to turn Hegelian idealism "on its head" by replacing its abstract speculative explanations of the world with a concrete project for changing the world. Granting this point, von Balthasar remains nonetheless convinced that, on the most fundamental questions, Marx's supposed disagreements with Hegel are mere distinctions without a real difference: Hegel is Marx's intellectual father in the line of Joachimite Gnostic thought, and if Marx intended an Oedipal rebellion, his success is more rumor than reality.[51] Certainly Marx distinguished his historical "materialism" from Hegel's abstract idealism, but this only signifies that the former was more thorough and direct in his hostile reinterpretation of Christianity than the latter. The gist of von Balthasar's reading of Marx is that, despite his polemical insistence on practical economic and political activity in the material world, Marx's atheism is not reducible to a simplistic positivist materialism. On the contrary, Marx always pays as much attention to humanity's spiritual life as to its material existence, and Marx is just as interested in metaphysical theories of history as he is in empirical analyses of economic practices. Therefore Marx's theories function as an alternative religion insofar as they offer themselves as a humanist catechism that claims to be a holistic solution to the problem of human suffering. Before beginning this discussion, however, I will note that it is unfortunate that von Balthasar does not do more to elucidate his provocative theological reading of Marxism. He suggests and insinuates more than he troubles himself to fully explain. Nevertheless, it is possible to bring together the various pieces of his critique into a coherent indictment of Marxism as a case of Gnostic plagiarism from the *corpus triforme* system of meaning.

Von Balthasar believes that Marx follows Hegel in jettisoning the *corpus triforme*'s theology of vertical redemption while presupposing its horizontal understanding of history, as well as its secularized conception of human freedom as liberation from the magic and superstition of pagan cosmology. But Marx's "materialist" philosophy also retrieves two central elements of old covenant religion that Hegel had generally ignored, thereby giving it a more biblical flavor and a more deceptive resemblance to the *corpus triforme* than Hegelianism. The first element is the old covenant theme of justice for the poor. In putting the intellectual spotlight on the needy and destitute victims of economic exploitation, Marx "rediscovers" a fundamental concern in both Christianity and the Old Testament's prophetic tradition.[52] But, in a typically Gnostic procedure, Marx takes this fundamental concern out of its overall biblical context and places it in the framework of a purely horizontal theory of history. There is something unique here, however, that is directly related to old covenant religion: contrary to Joachim and Hegel's emphasis on realized eschatology, Marxism retrieves and secularizes the old covenant's future-oriented messianism. This retrieval allows Marxism to preserve more successfully the worldly orientation of the old covenant's eschatology—that is, Judaism's messianic hope for an earthly kingdom of political and economic justice—which Hegel and Joachim abandon in their Marcionist eschatology of pure Spirit.[53]

> The effective challenge [to Christianity] comes from a secularized Israel that, frustrated in its Messianic hope, tries to promote salvation in and through the technological age. It is explicitly atheistic and anti-theistic vis-à-vis the ancient God, Yahweh, who has failed; and it is explicitly anti-Christian, insofar as Jesus' claim to fulfill this salvation in himself is proved to be a pitiful failure, doomed in its very concept. Marxist anti-theism organizes and channels all the pagan, diffuse, anti-Christian atheism and gives it a shape, a plan, a striking force. It may do this by interpreting the Messianic expectation as a dialectic that presses forward with iron necessity; or it may take the "watching and waiting" that is built on a concrete faith in Yahweh's promise, substituting for it an abstract "principle of hope" that is empty, cheerless and grounded on nothing but itself.[54]

In other words, Marxism follows the standard Gnostic practice of disconnecting the old and the new covenants. But Marxism is atypical in that it reverses Joachim and Hegel's Marcionist order of priorities and favors the concrete prophetic discourse of justice in the old covenant (albeit in secularized form) over the supposedly other-worldliness of the new covenant.

This interpretation of Marxism helps explain a claim von Balthasar makes in *TD4*. He observes that Marxism's reading of Christianity overlooks the reality that Christianity in fact always argued on behalf of justice and human rights, but it did so based on a notion of human dignity, not on a theory of historical "progress." "Now, however, out from under the Christian message came the Old Testament hope of an earthly future, in the form of the Messianic expectation; it was this that imparted a final religious tincture to the technological notion of progress."[55] He adds a little later that, "The entire modern ideology of progress, even where it wears a religious mask, represents a history of the relationship between earth and heaven that has been tipped up so that heaven is 'in the future.'"[56] There is a great deal implied by this reading of Marxism as secularized Jewish messianism that von Balthasar leaves unexplained.[57] However, if we look at it in the context of his understanding of modern Gnosticism as an attack on the second corollary of the *corpus triforme* (the unity of creation and redemption), the overall indictment of Marxism becomes more focused. According to von Balthasar, Marxism remains within a Gnostic framework on the issue of the unity of creation and redemption because it assumes a nondoxological, either/or relationship between divine transcendence and human redemption. As in Joachim and Hegel, Marx reinterprets the *corpus triforme* unity of creation and redemption in purely inner-worldly terms. But Joachim and Hegel's implicit atheism becomes explicit in Marx: it is necessary to break "the alienating spell cast by a tyrant in heaven" in order to affirm "the absolute freedom of man."[58] Once belief in a transcendent redeemer God has been overcome, a Promethean humanism will then be free to carry out the redemption of the earth through the construction of a secular utopia.[59] Von Balthasar insists that this atheistic theory of redemption is doomed to failure because it cannot preserve the integrity of created human freedom. Von Balthasar explains that, for Marx, human alienation is only overcome when the "abstract" distinction between individual and society is dropped and the personal identity of individuals becomes merged into the "ideal totality" of the collective.[60] This point exposes the abstract and ahistorical nature of Marx's supposedly concrete and historical philosophy. Rather than empirically interpreting the world, as he claimed to be doing, Marx was simply applying his a priori anthropological and political theories to history. When the contingencies of reality do not conform to Marx's neat theories, he solves the problem by erasing the contingencies.[61] For example,

Marx makes historical "progress" into an a priori law of nature, and then identifies this progress with the revolutionary socialist state. In this system it is inevitable that an individual person or group of persons who refuse to conform to the law of historical progress will be interpreted as unnatural. Thus in Marxism, "personal freedom is so absorbed into the over-riding interest in mankind's total development that anyone who refuses to surrender his personal drama to the latter is regarded as immoral and ripe for liquidation."[62] This willingness to eliminate persons who do not fit into the system indicates that, contrary to its humanistic rhetoric, Marxism is a form of epic theology that privileges abstract and general metaphysical laws over the concrete particulars.

Hence von Balthasar interprets Marx (along with Hegel) as belonging to the category of epic thinkers who believe all human action in history is merely a "puppet play" conducted by blind, transhuman forces.[63] At times von Balthasar argues that in Marxism the role of the puppeteer is played by blind economic forces, and at other times he argues that the puppeteer is the totalitarian socialist state.[64] Because Marx reduces politics to economics, the two puppeteers are really the same. In any case, for Marx all the human conflicts in history are ultimately revealed to be irrelevant illusions in the face of the wider, universal laws of absolute necessity. Given this epic perspective, it was inevitable that the Promethean humanism of Marx's early writings would give way in Marx's later writings (particularly in *Das Kapital*) to a darker deterministic vision in which human beings are inextricably caught up in economic dynamics beyond their control. Von Balthasar has no doubt that this was a predictable outcome because any philosophical system that denies human beings access to a transworldly freedom has only two options: posit a Prometheanism in which humanity is free from nature and God and in total control of its own destiny or posit an ethos of resignation that honestly accepts the power of transhuman forces over human self-assertion and admits the closed, tragic nature of finite existence without God. It is an open question whether Marx ultimately chose the latter option, but it is clear that the majority of his later disciples chose the former.

This leads us finally to von Balthasar's greatest area of concern regarding Marxism's Gnostic agenda. Of the three corollaries of the *corpus triforme* von Balthasar perceives as being under attack by Marxism, he worries most about the unity of Christ and the church. Without naming Marxism directly, he refers obliquely to it at one point in *TD2* in a discussion of political movements that are "post-Christian parodies of the 'Body of Christ,' the Christian Church." The passage continues,

> in the post-Christian age, political edifices arise in competition with her; they claim the right, theoretically and practically, to administer the total-

ity of salvation and truth, and they do so explicitly as one sociological part or "party" (*pars*). They also use force to implement their program (methods to which the Church herself, contrary to her true mission, once resorted), and, from their secularized standpoint, such use of force acquires an appearance of legitimacy. For, in the plan of "positive humanism," the common good is the freedom of mankind, which is to be pursued in all circumstances and hence with all available means.[65]

The "political edifices" mentioned here certainly include both Marxist regimes and anti-Marxist fascist regimes; von Balthasar believes that what is merely theoretical in Hegel's political philosophy becomes a concrete plan of action in Nazi and Soviet totalitarianism.[66] It is also clear in *Theo-Drama* that von Balthasar considers Marxism a better rival to the Christian church than racist and nationalist fascist regimes. This is the case because Marxism offers a messianic theory of transhuman historical forces of progress incarnated in enlightened proletarian revolutionaries. This quasi deification of historical law, and exaltation of those who discern and enforce it, has enough traces of Joachimism in it to qualify organized Marxist political parties as Gnostic "churches" of pure "spirit." Recall that Joachim negates the value of the institutional church by identifying it exclusively with the epoch of the Son, which is surpassed by the epoch of the Spirit. In Hegel's theology (arising out of a Reformation context) this disconnection of the institutional Christian church from the Holy Spirit allows the Spirit to migrate into purely secular affairs, where it now primarily operates in (German) political institutions. It is a short step from here for Marxists to interpret their revolutionary political parties as charismatic movements in competition for moral authority in world history with a defunct and reactionary Christian church. Marxist political parties, however, do not celebrate the death of the Christian church as a victory for intellectual nihilism, cultural relativism, and moral anarchy, but instead they move to fill the vacuum with their own doctrinal catechesis, proletarian internationalism, and moral universalism. For von Balthasar, therefore, there are two main characteristics that distinguish the crypto-church formed by Marxist political parties from the Christian church. First, it disdains the power of sacramental grace in human affairs precisely because it is based on the rejection of the Christ-form as an efficacious power in history. Instead, revolutionary violence led by the chosen few, coupled with scathing moralistic rhetoric about economic injustice, will be the engine driving history to the eschatological kingdom of a classless society. Second and consequently, the crypto-church of Marxism easily degenerates into a puritanical regulatory system of external controls based on violence and/or the threat of violence to maintain moral order and compel submission to its sectarian agenda of class warfare. In contrast, for von Balthasar, the Christian church believes that grace is both efficacious and universal, and consequently it relies on public contemplative worship of the beauty of the Christ-form to foster moral goodness and universal solidarity.

## Notes

1. Von Balthasar writes, "'So-called gnosis' was an enormous temptation in the early Christian Church. By contrast, persecution, even the bloodiest posed far less of a threat to the Church's continuing purity and further development. Gnosticism had its roots in late antiquity, drew on oriental and Jewish sources, and multiplied into innumerable esoteric doctrines and sects. Then, like a vampire, the parasite took hold of the youthful bloom and vigour of Christianity. What made it so insidious was the fact that the Gnostics very often did not want to leave the Church. Instead, they claimed to be offering a superior and more authentic exposition of Holy Scripture . . ." (*SI*, 1).

2. As one piece of evidence to prove this claim von Balthasar asserts "the clearest proof of the continuing relevance of the second-century struggle against Gnosticism is the fashionable interest, within the Christian Churches, in Zen meditation. This is essentially anti-Incarnational" (*SI*, 5). See also his claim in *OPSC* that "the spectre of Plotinus" is haunting the church today. He asserts, Plotinism "is more alive today than ever before, because it is, in effect, that religiosity which holds the essentially real and ultimate to be ineffable and beyond concepts. Hence, it negates the Word of God who became flesh. One meets this Plotinism everywhere in Catholic thought today . . ." (121).

3. For example, von Balthasar considers Marcionism as epitomizing Gnosticism, and he labels it a "demonic contrivance" (*GL1*, 656). Moreover, as I will argue later in this chapter, he views Marxism as a type of Gnosticism. He charges that its "satanic falsehoods" fascinate many Christians, and "this fascination so weakens the Christian organism that the alien wasp [of Marxism] is able to inject its anaesthetizing sting and lay its eggs right inside it, with the result that the body, hollowed out from inside, serves as welcome food for the enemy" (*TD4*, 441).

4. *TD2*, 9.

5. *TD1*, 131.

6. See *GL2*, 33–44.

7. Von Balthasar explicitly asserts in *GL7* that Hegel's thought is a form of Gnosticism (86, 178). He also makes this connection in *TD1*, 131; *TD2*, 34–35, 40, 89, 256, 423; *TD3*, 136–37. In *The Scandal of the Incarnation* he is quite explicit. In the context of a brief and general discussion of the history of Gnosticism from the second century to today, he argues that there is "a fundamental tendency in Hegel's philosophy which can be called Gnostic. For Hegel, everything material remains phenomenal and only finds its truth in the spiritual. The religious 'dualism' which distinguishes between pious consciousness and the Absolute is a mere 'image' (Vorstellung), which, even in the case of the so-called 'absolute religion' of Christianity, has to be rejected in favor of all-encompassing absolute 'knowledge.' Ultimately, for man, there can be no more mystery about divine Spirit" (5).

8. *GL2*, 39.

9. The passage in question runs as follows: "The logical and metaphysical dialectic of being and becoming [in Valentinianism], which if often very reminiscent of Hegel, is turned into a personal drama. Every concept becomes an aeon, every conceptual tension becomes a male-female relationship, every example of intellectual 'alienation' becomes an episode of tragedy. However the personalisation cannot be maintained; the personalised principle must instead be constantly reabsorbed, and constantly are, into the progressive unity of becoming. This is shown very clearly by the christology, which deliberately talks not about four Christs, but about one under four aspects. Nor is there an adequate distinction between the physical and the moral, the substantial and the accidental, as states solidify into substances, but are not really substance and may either evaporate into nothing or be expelled as waste. So in all this it is the final category which leaves no choice and is interesting for having been bought at this price. The divine becomes interesting because it so much resembles the human, because in God too there is an abyss, a suffering, a darkness and a drama, infinitely deeper than in man and yet (as Schelling will say later) always already overtaken and past and conquered by the light. And the human is interesting because of the extent to which the divine displays itself and its life in man, because man himself is a part of the eternal drama and his small passing passions here receive an absolute character. This means that nothing is finally fixed; before it is fixed seriously or irrevocably it is already canceled, withdrawn, eclipsed by the arrival of the next vision. But what a sense of intoxication to look into the inner mechanism of being itself! This aesthetic spiritual frenzy is the constant element that holds the rest of the system together and, as Irenaeus will show, leaves its mark on people even in their general disposition; it is this that marks them out as sectaries. Irenaeus judges them as Kierkegaard judged the Hegelians and Nietzsche the Wagnerians" (*GL2*, 39).

10. In *Mysterium Paschale*, he explicitly identifies Hegel with Marcionism, particularly with Marcion's anti-Semitism (*MP*, 62–63). This matches his claim in *GL7* that Hegel is an anti-Semitic thinker (440–41).

11. Cf. *TD4*, 457.

12. In his discussion of Irenaeus in *GL2* von Balthasar explains that "Valentinian Gnosis" was the religious system "with which Irenaeus wrestled first and in most detail, treating the others as no more than variants or illustrative sources" (33). He then quotes Irenaeus saying, "Once the Valentinians are bested, the whole crowd of heretics will be refuted" (*AH* 2.48.1).

13. *SI*, 3. This point raises an interesting question about the relevance of Tertullian to von Balthasar's retrieval of Irenaeus. This issue, however, is too complex to be dealt with here.

14. "Gnosticism was rampant in Irenaeus' day, and is constantly reviving in all the non-Christian religions and philosophies" (*SI*, 8).

15. Von Balthasar mentions "the Jewish Kabbala and Gematria of the Middle Ages and the Renaissance" and as being rooted in Gnostic thought, but he is far more interested in Joachim of Fiore as a conduit of Gnosticism into modernity. He credits Henri de Lubac with demonstrating the extensive influence of Joachim of Fiore on modern Western religious thought. See his *The Theology of Henri de Lubac: An Overview* (San Francisco: Ignatius Press, 1991), 123–24. In both this text and in *TD4* von Balthasar praises de Lubac's two-volume work *La Postérité spirituelle de Joachim de Flore* (Lethielleux, 1979) for tracing the origins of the Enlightenment, German Idealism, and Marxism in Joachim's theology (*TD4*, 458). See also *SI*, 4–5. See also *OPSC*, 99ff.

16. *TD4*, 457.

17. Ibid., 428, 446; *TD3*, 400, 512.

18. *TD3*, 400; cf. *TD4*, 458. On this point von Balthasar seems to be closely following de Lubac's analysis of Joachim's attempt to disconnect the incarnate Christ and the institutional church. Indeed, he is so persuaded by de Lubac's analysis of the pervasive intellectual influence of Joachim's purely pneumatic ecclesiology that he is moved to remark that "there is no other subject that is theologically more exciting or decisive than this" (*The Theology of Henri de Lubac*, 125).

19. *TD2*, 53; see also *TD3*, 26.

20. *TD4*, 446.

21. "The entire modern ideology of progress, even where it wears a religious mask, represents a history of the relationship between earth and heaven that has been tipped up so that heaven is 'in the future'" (ibid., 92).

22. Ibid., 87; cf. 446–47.

23. Cf. *TD2*, 243ff.

24. *TD2*, 420ff.

25. See *TD2*, 39–40, 47–48; *TD4*, 87–92, 444.

26. Von Balthasar both directly (*TD3*, 45, 400; *SI*, 5) and indirectly (*TD4*, 446, 458–59; *OPSC*, 101) equates Hegel's philosophical theology with Joachim's theology.

27. Although von Balthasar does not himself explain how the disparate thinkers Valentinius and Joachim both could have a high degree of influence on Hegel's thought, such explanations are possible. For example, see Cyril O'Regan's *The Heterodox Hegel* (Albany: State University of New York Press, 1994) and *Gnostic Return in Modernity* (Albany: State University of New York Press, 2001). O'Regan's interpretation of Hegel confirms many of von Balthasar's assumptions and assertions about the Gnostic influences that inform Hegel's philosophy.

28. He makes this point indirectly in the following passage: "The totality [of revelation] . . . rooted in and resting on the Father's eternal decision, is expressly called 'mystery' (Eph 1:9; 3:9; and so forth); and this mystery, even when it has been revealed (*apocalypsis*), is not some configuration that can be grasped in its totality by earthly understanding. It remains a mystery of faith. The deeper our knowledge of it, the more unfathomable (Eph 3:8) the divine love becomes. . . . And for this knowledge . . . we need the 'eyes of faith.' Lest the object of our beholding should turn into an 'absolute knowledge,' however, it was necessary to distinguish our endeavor from that of Hegel in particular. . . . 'Absolute knowledge' is the death of all theo-drama, but God's 'love which surpasses all gnosis' is the death of 'absolute knowledge'" (*TD2*, 89). See also *TD1*, 66–70; *TD2*, 42, 119–20, 126, 423; *TD3*, 64; *TD4*, 446; *TD5*, 225–26; *GL7*, 524, 525.

29. See *TD1*, 55 and 131.

30. See ibid., 59–62.

31. Ibid., 61–62.

32. Ibid., 62; cf. 322

33. Ibid., 65; cf. 457.

34. For a more detailed discussion of this point, as well as the discussion in the remainder of this paragraph, see *GL5*, 572–90. See also *TD5*, 223–29.

35. It is also interesting to note that von Balthasar believes that the argument for a "cosmogenesis and anthropogenesis" out of God completely contradicts the monotheistic doctrine of the *analogia entis*. He also associates it with Gnosticism, the Kabbalah, and Spinozaism (cf. *TD2*, 420). Here we also see the root of his rejec-

tion of any type of Neoplatonic speculative metaphysics that puts God and creation on the same ontological plane through an *exitus-reditus* schema.

36. This interpretation explains why von Balthasar believes Hegel's philosophy of history lacks all appreciation for divine mystery, and hence is ultimately a form of atheism (cf. *TD4*, 11, 459; *TD2*, 423).

37. *TD1*, 65.

38. Ibid., 67. Von Balthasar argues later that Hegel's idealist philosophy must "dissolve the empirical, personal 'I' in the 'essential,'" the 'ideal'" (*TD1*, 558). For von Balthasar, this is the link between both the Enlightenment and Marxism's rejection of the historical individual as having absolute value (611). On this point he praises Franz Rosenzweig for his anti-Hegelian defense of the "individual human being" against "all system-building" that replaces the personal I-Thou of humanity's relationship to God with an impersonal third-person epic narrative (637–39). This affirmative discussion of Rosenzweig suggests interesting connections between von Balthasar and Emmanuel Levinas.

39. Ibid., 578–79; cf. *TD2*, 375.

40. *TD1*, 60. The Hegel quote comes from *Philosophy of Religion* 12:246–51.

41. Ibid., 588.

42. Ibid., 579.

43. Ibid., 584.

44. Ibid., 586.

45. Ibid., 587.

46. Ibid., 587–88.

47. Ibid., 502–3.

48. Ibid., 121.

49. Ibid., 68; cf. *TD4*, 128.

50. Ibid., 589.

51. Although Marx may have intended to negate Hegelian philosophy, von Balthasar explains, "as is always the case with violent negations, the 'No' remained closely bound to that which was rejected, a fact that decisively influenced the worldwide movement which he began and essentially formed" (*GL5*, 590). He later adds that even when focusing on the biblical theme of economic justice, Marx "borrows all his conceptual material . . . from the Hegelian Philosophy of Spirit" (*GL5*, 591).

52. Ibid.

53. See *GL5*, 591, 596; *TD4*, 91–92.

54. *TD4*, 440.

55. Ibid., 91.

56. Ibid., 92.

57. For example, von Balthasar does not bring out the interesting fact that Marx's understanding of human progress toward communism is quite similar to the general form of Christianity's narrative of salvation history. For example, in texts such as *The Communist Manifesto* it is relatively easy to notice the following parallel themes: (1) the primal sin of egoistic greed causes man's fall from the paradise of primitive communism; (2) the fall's consequences: man's alienation from himself, others, and society; (3) history progresses in an ordered, quasi-providential pattern; (4) the proletariat class function as the agents of epochal, messianic redemption; (5) the suffering of the proletariat in Late Capitalism functions in Marx's narrative of redemption as a socio-economic Good Friday; (6) the proletariat revolution functions in the narrative as the resurrection of the crucified class and its ascent to redemptive political control over society, becoming history's right hand; (7) the

dictatorship of the proletariat as a Last Judgment of the wicked; (8) the period of Socialism as a millenarian period of goodness on earth before (9) the arrival of the final future classless communist society as the eschatological New Jerusalem. In addition to these formal similarities we can also point to another even more basic parallel: for both Marx and Christianity there are universal moral values that will ultimately triumph at the end of history, e.g., the priority of the human race as one family over racial, national, or cultural differences, the priority of community over individualism, the centrality of practical ethics, and the imperative for material, social justice for the poor.

58. *TD4*, 441.

59. Ibid., 444.

60. *GL5*, 593. Cf. *TD4*, 128; cf. 91, 144–45, 299, 444.

61. Von Balthasar is basic agreement here with Karl Popper's interpretation of Marx. See *The Open Society and Its Enemies* (Princeton, New Jersey: Princeton University Press, 1950), 274–397.

62. *TD2*, 40.

63. *TD4*, 74.

64. In *GL5* von Balthasar describes Marx's view of history as a "drama" in which capitalists and proletarians "play the utterly passive role of persons who are driven, in their relationship to the sole active power, which is capital" (*GL5*, 596). In *TD4* he asserts (unfortunately with little supporting explanation or textual documentation) that Marx's evolutionary theory of historical progress gives rise to a totalitarian society in which everything is reduced to technological control, including ethics and politics (91ff.).

65. *TD2*, 425.

66. *TD4*, 145, 439. Von Balthasar writes, "If one considers that Hegel's earliest concern was the concrete (i.e. national) Spirit of the People (*Volksgeist*) which mediates between total Spirit and the monad, and that this indeterminate Spirit of the People appeared to him later as the formed Spirit of the State, then it is clear that Hegel had to become the intellectual point of departure for the later socialism of the Left and of the Right, both of which in their own way have gathered the glory of absolute Being into the absolutist claims of their own 'party'" (*GL5*, 590). This point from the theological aesthetics goes a long way toward making sense of von Balthasar's attempt in *Theo-Drama* to put Hegel and Marx in the same intellectual category as Lenin, Hitler, and Stalin. See *TD4*, 145.

# Chapter VI

# Refuting Ahistorical Theologies of Salvation History

Throughout *Theo-Drama*, von Balthasar critically analyzes various modern theologians and theological movements for failing to articulate adequately the depth and breadth of the Christian system of meaning in response to the challenge posed by its Gnostic rivals. Given his conviction that modern Gnosticism is a parasitic discourse that gains cultural credibility through its hostile reinterpretation of Christianity, one might be tempted to conclude that von Balthasar sees himself as a prosecutor indicting betrayers of the true Christian faith when carrying out his critical analyses of various modern theological inadequacies. This is not the case, however. Although he follows Irenaeus in drawing clear lines between Gnostic discourse and Christian doxological discourse, he does acknowledge the complexity of borderline cases where categories seem to blur. Moreover, he sees the necessity of making relevant distinctions within the Christian category between strong and weak resistance, and between differing types of strong and weak resistance. With regard to the latter, he allows for a great deal of theological latitude in *Theo-Drama*, and even when he decides that a particular theologian or theological system has forfeited certain aspects of the *corpus triforme*, he can be remarkably exculpatory if he believes the transgression does not involve a total repudiation of the entire Christian system of meaning. In these cases, he treats the theology in question as redeemable, and his criticisms are meant to be constructive. Hence, rather than reading all of von Balthasar's critical forays as exposés of theological treason, it is more accurate to interpret them as inquiries into the reasons why a particular theologian or theological movement failed to offer sufficient resistance to the modern Gnostic attack on the *corpus triforme*. Moreover, he does not think all those who offer insufficient resistance deserve the same level of criticism: he realizes that there are various degrees of inadequacy that may mitigate culpability.

It is possible, therefore, to see in von Balthasar's critical discussions of weak resistance to Gnostic reinterpretation something like a ranking process in which theologies are graded according to their level of insufficiency. This ranking process is not announced, and its clarity is obscured by the ambivalence that often characterizes his critical analyses of particular cases. Nevertheless, it is possible to identify the presence of such a process, as well as to discern some of the criteria he uses to evaluate and distinguish levels and types of insufficient resistance. These criteria are implicit in the questions at work in all his critical analyses of modern theologies: To what extent does a particular theological system recognize the agonistic context in which Christianity must defend its system of meaning from hostile reinterpretation? To what degree does it accurately discern the nature and strategies of the Gnostic antagonist? What internal resources does the theology in question have for giving a strong articulation of each element of the *corpus triforme* system of meaning? To what extent does the ignorance and/or naïveté of a theological system leave itself vulnerable to Gnostic reinterpretation? Reading von Balthasar's critical discussions with these questions in mind allows us to see how he ranks theologies according to their degree of insufficient resistance.

I will focus attention in this chapter on the four most important theologies he counts as weak attempts to resist Gnosticism's ahistorical epic theology. These are Karl Rahner's theology, Karl Barth's theology, liberation theology, and Jürgen Moltmann's theology. These four examples cover a wide range of theological options, and therefore discussing them will illustrate the complexity and sophistication of his critical-analytical approach. I will discuss these four models as borderline cases that occupy a gray area between resistance to Gnostic reinterpretation and capitulation to it. In the case of Rahner, von Balthasar sees an internally conflicted project that cannot come to terms with the deep historical impact of the Word's incarnation in Jesus. In Barth's case, von Balthasar sees an admirable project of theological reform in danger of subverting itself because of its failure to understand doxology in a sufficiently Irenaean sense. In the case of liberation theology, he sees a dangerously weak level of resistance to the Marxist variety of Gnostic discourse, and in the case of Moltmann he sees a dangerously weak level of resistance to the Hegelian variety. Rahner and Barth score high in von Balthasar's ranking, but not high enough to count as offering sufficient resistance to Gnosticism. Both liberation theology and Moltmann score poorly, but von Balthasar does not think they are guilty of the same degree of insufficiency. As I will argue, von Balthasar ranks Moltmann below liberation theology in ability to adequately defend Christian theology from hostile Gnostic reinterpretation.

### Karl Rahner: The Insufficient Resistance of Anachronism

There are numerous points of agreement between Karl Rahner's transcendental theology and von Balthasar's theological aesthetics. These agreements are more theologically relevant than their disagreements. In reading what follows, it is important to keep in mind that von Balthasar shares with Rahner a christocentric conception of supernatural mystery, a critical rejection of neoscholastic rationalism, and a theological anthropology that accents the receptivity of the human creature to supernatural grace.[1] It is also important to be aware of von Balthasar's strong respect for Rahner as a Catholic theologian.[2] This basic respect remained intact despite his reservations about some aspects of Rahner's theology.[3] Finally, we cannot overlook the fact that Rahner and von Balthasar were both deeply committed to a neopatristic theological perspective. All of these factors significantly ameliorate von Balthasar's criticisms of Rahner. Moreover, it is also important to note that von Balthasar had the capacity to be a remarkably tendentious and polemical thinker, and nowhere do these intellectual vices manifest themselves more clearly than in his attacks on Rahner's theology. The lack of hermeneutic generosity is a factor to keep in mind when reading von Balthasar criticisms of Rahner; one wonders if all aspects of von Balthasar's own theology could withstand a similarly unyielding and hostile critique.

Von Balthasar believes Rahner's theology might be christologically inadequate due to its excessive reliance on inherently abstract philosophical methods. In the context of *Theo-Drama's* agonistic interpretation of salvation history, charging any thinker with being "abstract" is tantamount to accusing them of Gnosticism. Von Balthasar, however, presents a highly ambivalent reading of Rahner in *Theo-Drama*. This renders it a particularly pertinent example of the complexity in von Balthasar's distinction between a fully post-Christian discourse and a Christian discourse that fails to immunize itself adequately against hostile reinterpretation. Like many of the other trends in modern theology, von Balthasar believes Rahner's theology is partially infected with ahistorical epic presuppositions. But it is not fatally infected, nor is its remedy drastic. Rahner's failed resistance has a unique status for von Balthasar because it has immense internal resources for healing itself, if only it can adequately come to terms with the precise nature of its disease.

In his critical analyses of the trends in modern theology, von Balthasar discusses Rahner's theology under the title of the "theology of history."[4] This is something of a surprise because von Balthasar often criticizes Rahner's transcendental method for being irredeemably ahistorical. Yet here he praises Rahner's theology of history for opposing "a rationalist-idealist ethics of timelessly valid laws," for recognizing the distinctively christological importance of "the stream of horizontal history," and for emphasizing "the church's particular situation, with its . . . historically distinct viewpoint."[5] After these affirmations, however, von Balthasar effectively qualifies them. Observing that the theology of history assumes that "all historical situations, whether of individuals or of groups, . . . contain a christological a priori, an *existentiale* or transcendent dimension," he expresses the worry that, were this belief in a christological a priori true, it "would mark the most diverse, and externally perhaps contradictory, situations as 'salvific' for 'open' or 'anonymous' Christians."[6] Although only obliquely expressed, the concern here is that Rahner's theology of history shares the same basic deficiency as Bultmann's theology of "event": it too does not adequately understand the relationship of the Old and the New Covenants in salvation history, and hence it also fails to come to terms with the historical reality and theological implications of the incarnation. But, unlike Bultmann's tendency to erase horizontal history in the vertical grace of the new covenant, Rahner's transcendental theology of history comes dangerously close to the other extreme: horizontal history absorbs vertical grace.[7] In other words, von Balthasar charges Rahner's theology of history with operating as if the incarnation and the founding of the new covenant had either not occurred or were fundamentally irrelevant. Rahner's transcendental theology of history, he believes, wrongly assumes that revelation is always and everywhere available in generally accessible categorical phenomena of history, irrespective of the life, death, and resurrection of Jesus. He explains that because the transcendental theology of history does not seem to grasp the "dramatic" change in humanity's existential and religious situation that occurs after the incarnation, it has an "insufficient" grasp of what is unique in biblical revelation, as well as an inadequate conception of the dramatic tension inherent to the vertically transfigured time of the church in history.[8] Clearly von Balthasar is worried that transcendental theology is complicit in the post-Christian attempt to subvert the *corpus triforme* unity of the old and new covenant with an a priori theory of history.

The implications of this critique for the second element of the *corpus triforme* become evident in von Balthasar's discussion of Rahner's understanding of Christ's mediating role between God and humanity.[9] Von Balthasar believes that Rahner allows a deterministic mode of reflection to infiltrate his theology of the relationship between Christ's redeeming grace and creation. For example, after acknowledging Rahner's claim that all people have a "transcendent openness to the absolute," von Balthasar goes on to question whether Rahner is right to equate this openness with "an experience of grace."[10] Contradicting Rahner, he argues that grace can be "withdrawn from the sinner" even if transcendental openness cannot. He then quotes Rahner saying that "supernaturally elevated transcendence . . . [is an] abiding *existentiale:* through the gift of grace, it is always and everywhere operative; it is always present, even under the forms of denial."[11] And later in *TD4,* von Balthasar quotes Rahner's contention that pre- and post-Christian religions are "Christologies searching for a subject," and are undertaking this search "in the Holy Spirit."[12] With regard to these Rahnerian claims (as well as the ones he quotes in the following passage) von Balthasar has several reservations:

> . . . it is questionable whether this (supernatural) transcendence, even if it is a real experience of grace, can be termed an experience of being addressed by the personal God. And . . . even if it can, it is by no means certain that, on the basis of this word, which is addressed "to all times" and which communicates a "formal, nonobjective knowledge of revelation," and given the theological principle that God wills to manifest and give himself to the world solely and definitively in Jesus Christ, we can conclude that this non-objective knowledge must also contain "something specifically Christian," namely "an implicit knowledge of the Trinity." . . . Now it is clear, in a train of thought such as this, that the *conversio ad phantasma* necessary for objective religious knowing can only provide inadequate objects for the nonobjective inner "word."[13]

Although von Balthasar grants validity to Rahner's desire to interpret extrabiblical religions as being in some way oriented toward Christ, he sees potentially serious christological problems in his transcendental explanatory approach to this question, an approach whose dominant tendency is to relativize "objective religious knowing" in relation to a more fundamental "nonobjective inner 'word.'"[14] He believes these potential problems become actual in Rahner's theory of anonymous Christians, which he believes contains "an irreconcilable contradiction" because of its inevitable privileging of the "a priori, transcendental word" over the "a posteriori, categorical revelation" in Christ.[15] Von Balthasar thinks that even though Rahner intends to teach a doctrine of God's absolute, vertical revelation in the incarnation, the transcendental method he uses necessarily supplants "the extraordinary and unique event" of the incarnation in history with a highly abstract theory of the formless religious openness of the transcendental subject.

Von Balthasar brings the same basic set of concerns about Rahner's tendency to prioritize anthropological theory over historical fact to his analysis of Rahner's soteriology in *TD4*. This analysis is a critical exposé of the ways in which Rahner's speculative proclivities render his theology dangerously vulnerable to post-Christian reinterpretation. Von Balthasar begins with the portentous observation that Rahner's heavy reliance on philosophy leads to a "tightly ordered system" of fundamental theology.[16] He then expresses alarm that in Rahner's primarily theoretical system, "many elements of the organism of Christian faith that have been handed down to us must either drop out or be entirely reinterpreted."[17] Then, in a passage that reveals the root of his anxiety about Rahner's soteriology, von Balthasar argues that Rahner shares Hegel's disdain for the traditional interpretations of the cross as a "representative expiation"; like Hegel, Rahner undertakes a massive reinterpretation of Scripture, the church fathers, and Anselm in order to reinterpret the creed's claim that Christ died *pro nobis* in a way that more neatly fits his own a priori anthropological theories. This is certainly not a trivial charge, and so to demonstrate it von Balthasar begins by quoting Rahner's own words: Rahner writes that to interpret the cross as a representative expiation "contradicts a proper understanding of man's self-redemption."[18] After quoting what he thinks is a clearly audacious assertion, von Balthasar then goes on to challenge what he takes to be the faulty arguments Rahner relies on to justify it. He explains that Rahner considers the doctrine of representative expiation to be a distortion of the early disciples' "original" experience of the risen Christ, an experience which Rahner asserts occurred prior to the later belief that Christ's death had "redemptive significance." For Rahner this original experience of the risen Christ is more basic and hence more relevant than the "late" New Testament theological reflections about the preexistent Logos, "explicit soteriologies," and other secondary interpretive schemas. Von Balthasar has no patience for what he sees as Rahner's effort to fabricate a dichotomy between early faith in Jesus and later soteriological reflection on Christ, bluntly accusing it of "downgrading . . . practically the entire high theology of the New Testament—a theology from which members of the church down through the centuries have drawn their spirituality, whether they were ordinary folk or the great saints."[19] Moreover, after making the exculpatory suggestion that perhaps Rahner is guilty only of flawed exegesis, von Balthasar reconsiders and asserts instead that this dichotomy results more from

Rahner's "speculative" approach, which he insists is more "crucial" for Rahner than exegesis.

Von Balthasar believes that Rahner's predilection for making speculative anthropocentric assertions about what is and is not soteriologically possible is responsible for the vaguely post-Christian timbre of his theology. But what troubles him most about this predilection is that it causes Rahner's theology of history to veer dangerously close to an epic mode of reflection. Recall that there are two poles of speculative epic theology: the first pole is mythological and posits a pathetic God helplessly entangled in the tragedies of history; the second pole is philosophical and posits an aloof spectator God sublimely detached from the vicissitudes of history. Von Balthasar thinks Rahner's theology strongly gravitates toward the philosophical pole. For example, he charges Rahner's theology with granting axiomatic status to an a priori speculative principle. This principle is that "God, who is unchangeable, cannot be caused to 'change his mind' by an event in the world like the cross of Christ; he cannot be changed from an insulted, wrathful God to a reconciled God."[20] He cites numerous passages in which Rahner argues that any suggestion that God's mind can change is necessarily a type of "mythology." He remarks that he could affirm Rahner's point that God is "unchangeable" if it meant only that the "whole work of salvation proceeds from the loving Father, a Father who does not need to reconcile himself with the world but undertakes to reconcile the world to himself." But he does not think that this is the dominant animating assumption in Rahner's theology of divine immutability. Instead, von Balthasar strongly suspects that what Rahner intends as a repudiation of speculative theology is in fact a case of one pole of epic theology demonizing the other. In other words, he believes that the assumption at work in Rahner's rejection of divine mutability is derived not from biblical revelation, but instead from an Enlightenment version of epic philosophy: the contingent events of history are in the end irrelevant for theology's universal truth claims.[21] Because Rahner polices biblical revelation according to this epic axiom, he is compelled to insist that no event on the stage of history can ultimately change the inner life of God. The qualifier "ultimately" is extremely important here—the issue for von Balthasar is not that Rahner simply denies altogether the theological relevance of history and refuses to correlate it with eternity (if this were the case, Rahner would not be an advocate of a Christology "from below"), but rather that he denies that the historical event of the life and death of Jesus actually alters in any way the predetermined eternal will of God. This denial is epitomized in Rahner's insistence that "God is he-who-is-always-reconciled" with humanity, irrespective of what happens on the stage of history.[22] Von Balthasar thinks this denial relativizes the salvific value of Jesus' life and death. Moreover, he finds it disturbing that Rahner does not hold that the obedience of the man Jesus to the will of God "is the condition without which neither world nor salvation would be possible," but maintains instead that God's a priori desire to "'be there' for everyone" is the condition for the possibility of salvation, and Jesus' death on the cross is simply an "exemplary" sign of this universal saving will.

Despite its self-promotion as a historical approach, therefore, von Balthasar thinks Rahner's entire method closes its eyes to the real historical interactions between humanity and God and instead constructs an explanatory grid over history and speculatively correlates the human spirit with a general theory of universally accessible divine presence. Von Balthasar thinks Rahner's efforts to contextualize Jesus Christ within the parameters of his anthropological religious theories raise a crucial issue: is the primary locus of grace the historical event of the incarnation in the human form of Jesus Christ or is it something else more general— a supernatural existential—that is only triggered by the historical Christ-form? And if the latter, this implies that Christ does not mediate grace to human persons in the sense that he brings them a grace they lacked, but, instead, when believers recall Christ in their minds and hearts he becomes the occasion for the activation of the implicit grace they already had prior to and independent of the incarnation.[23] Of course the implicit question driving von Balthasar's concerns here is what resources does Rahner's theology possess for resisting the post-Christian effort to disconnect horizontal creation and vertical redemption? Does Rahner's theology stress enough the absolute uniqueness and indispensability of vertical revelation for it to avoid the post-Christian attempt to reinterpret the Christian meaning of redemption as being simply the dissolving of all the "illusions" of categorical phenomena— including personal identity—in the flowing stream of time? Von Balthasar is raising the question of whether Rahner's theology is consistently monotheistic and doxological. But the issue is not whether the *kairos* of Christ totally nullifies history, but whether history totally nullifies the *kairos*.

Given this critique, why is Rahner counted as only a model of insufficient resistance to Gnosticism and not as a patron of post-Christian discourse? Rahner's swerves away from the *corpus triforme* perspective are not consistent or extreme enough to put him in the same category as radical transgressors like Joachim and Hegel. Moreover, Rahner's good pastoral intentions, willingness to listen to alternative points of view, and general (albeit qualified) respect for the Catholic theological tradition mitigate the severity of von Balthasar's evaluation. Nevertheless, as we have seen, his evaluation is quite severe. Rahner does not seem to recognize the agonistic context in which Christianity must defend its system of meaning from hostile reinterpretation. As a consequence, Rahner is unable to discern accurately the nature and strategies of the post-Christian antagonist.[24] Von Balthasar, however, does think that Rahner has immense internal resources for giving a strong articulation of the *corpus triforme* system of meaning were he to overcome his naïveté about Christianity's historical context. Yet Rahner's theology nonetheless leaves Christian theology vulnerable to post-Christian reinterpretation because it lacks a vitally necessary ingredient: a strong biblical emphasis on vertical revelation. But even this lack does not imply for von Balthasar that Rahner's horizontal theology is continuous with the purely horizontal perspective of philosophical epic theology. The key to understanding why not is offered in von Balthasar's remark that "today's transcendental theologians would like to interpret Christ as the 'highest, unsurpassable instance' of a self-disclosure to man on God's part that is coterminous with creation as such. However, this attempt comes too late: the stage's background has already been cleared."[25] The truly surprising implication of this passage is that von Balthasar thinks the real problem with Rahner's theology is not that it is a patron of post-Christian discourse but that it is a patron of pre-Christian religion. In other words, the root of Rahner's insufficient resistance to post-Christian discourse lies in his fundamentally anachronistic mode of theological reflection. What seem to be Rahner's gestures of allegiance to a post-Christian worldview are in fact gestures of allegiance to a pre-Christian worldview—von Balthasar believes the core assumptions of Rahner's theology would not be fundamentally altered if the incarnation had never happened. In von Balthasar's evaluation, therefore, Rahner is not guilty of rejecting Christ but rather of failing to recognize that history has been irreversibly punctuated by the Christ-event. As a result of this failure, Rahner does not see that the ancient pre-Christian world is now defunct because it has been permanently secularized by Christ. The only options now are the post-Christian negation of the pre-Christian aesthetic ethos—with all that this implies for the technological control of nature and technocratic management of society—or the transfiguration of the pre-Christian ethos in the aesthetic holism of the *corpus triforme*.[26] Von Balthasar does not fault Rahner for choosing the wrong option; he faults him for not realizing that a choice must be made.

## Karl Barth and the Siren Song of Gnosticism

In von Balthasar's formative engagement with Karl's Barth's theological system, the analogy of being and Christology are the two issues that dominated and shaped the entire discussion.[27] Von Balthasar was both fascinated and provoked by Barth's forceful arguments on these issues. There can be no doubt on this point: von Balthasar theology's has massive debts to Barth's theology. This point is well documented and incontrovertible. His massive borrowings from Barth's theology, however, must be understood in the wider context of his allegiance to de Lubac's neopatristic project. Von Balthasar borrows heavily from Barth because he sees him as a friendly rival to de Lubac's program of theological reform.[28] For example, he considers Barth *the* spokesman in modern Protestant theology for a strongly patristic theology of God's simultaneous vertical transcendence above creation and sacramental presence within it. In *The Glory of the Lord* von Balthasar unequivocally praises Barth for being an advocate of a genuinely theological aesthetics, as opposed to the aesthetic theology prevalent among some modern Protestant thinkers.[29] This is why, as I noted in chapter 2, he asserts that Barth's understanding of "beauty of God" in the crucified Christ "agrees with [my] own overall plan" in formulating a theological aesthetics.[30] This helps explain his reason for commending Barth for teaching a thoroughly biblical and "radically anti-Platonic" anthropology.[31] As we will see, however, von Balthasar is somewhat undecided in *Theo-Drama* about just how consistent Barth is in maintaining his theological commitment to a biblical notion of vertical transcendence. In his examination of Barth's theology of "event," von Balthasar lauds it for delivering biblical revelation from rationalism's attempt to abstract the meaning of Christianity out of its historical context.[32] Nevertheless, he faults Barth's weak understanding of the relevance of the old covenant's "horizontal time" for the new covenant's theology of redemption.[33] This leads Barth to have an underdeveloped understanding of what it means to believe that the new covenant fulfills the old. Von Balthasar recognizes that Barth asserts a closer unity between the two covenants in his later writings than in his early work,[34] but he still suspects that Barth never fully grasped the implications of this unity. This suspicion is at work when he expresses a doubt as to whether Barth's theology of "event" adequately understands God's vertical descent into history as a *kairos* or a unique "hour" when time is "refashioned" into the uniquely eschatological and nonneutral time of the church. There is a dangerous tendency in the theology of "event" toward interpreting the incarnation as the total erasure of old covenant "law" and replacing it by new covenant "grace."[35] This tendency is so strong that Barth's theology often seems to be interpreting time and eternity as mutually exclusive realities; in other words, the emphasis on realized eschatology is so pronounced in the theology of event that the "already" of the kingdom completely eclipses the "not yet" of horizontal history in both the old and the new Israel. This imbalance leads von Balthasar to suggest that Barth's theology might belong in the same category as "Gnosticism," which also—in contrast to Scripture and the early church—"devalued the Old Testament" and "obscured" its "horizontal relationship" to the New Testament.

The worry driving von Balthasar's claim about the erasure of time in Barth comes into view when he discusses the apparent presence of a doctrine of universal salvation (*apokatastasis*) in his theology. He grants that Barth always denied teaching this doctrine, but von Balthasar finds these denials unconvincing.[36] This is why he often expresses serious concerns about what he sees as Barth's practice of interpreting faith in a way that causes it to resemble Stoicism's love of fate. For example, von Balthasar asserts that "there is something timeless and context-less" in Barth's theology "which does not do justice to the genuinely historical nature of biblical revelation."[37] Von Balthasar then contends that the emphasis in Barth's doctrine of election falls so heavily on the overpowering nature of the redemptive divine love offered in Christ that this doctrine tends at times toward "constraint and systematization," and hence is occasionally inclined "to overstep the legitimate limits and competence of theology, to give in to over-systematization."[38] In other words, Barth conceives of the power of divine love in such strong explanatory terms that it is difficult to see how created human freedom's ability to accept or resist this love can be preserved without violating the logic of his theological system.[39] Von Balthasar thinks it is dangerous to undervalue the human response in this way; he observes that Barth does not think the *Mysterium iniquitatis* has any ultimate theological relevance because God's freedom will simply overpower any sinful resistance to grace.[40] Barth's doctrine of election thus comes perilously close to an epic theological perspective which interprets all finitude, including especially the realities of tragedy and evil, as a web of illusions. Given this predilection for an epic mode of reflection, how can Barth then do justice to historical revelation in general and to the doctrine of the incarnation in particular? Indeed, von Balthasar raises precisely this question. In his book on Barth's theology, von Balthasar finds it difficult to see how Barth can truly be counted as a theologian of the incarnation since in his system he "has not left enough breathing room between creation and Covenant."[41] Barth fails to grasp the doxological unity-without-identity of the entire created order with the divine that is brought into being through the incarnation.[42]

Von Balthasar also sees ecclesiological implications following from Barth's weak understanding of the unity of the old and new covenants and the unity of creation and redemption. These implications first become visible in Barth's failure to take seriously the importance of exegesis for understanding the full meaning of God's incarnation in human form. "With Barth, the neutral 'historico-critical method' . . . is simply regarded as obsolete and put out of action: in sovereign power, the word of God interprets itself directly to faith, scorning all critical exegesis."[43] The point here is subtle, and it must be read in light of the following question von Balthasar raises regarding Barth's assertion of an identity between the self-interpreting Word and personal faith: "In Barth's case . . . we can still ask whether the identity he so strongly asserts is tenable without the mediation of exegesis."[44] It is clear that he does not think Barth fully understands what it means to say God's word interprets itself; ultimately he believes Barth refuses exegesis because he fails to understand that the Word interprets itself through Scripture within the context of the faithful church and not simply within the heart of private individuals. More specifically, Barth fails to come to terms with the full reality of incarnation because he does not fully grasp what it means to say that the incarnate Word necessarily interprets himself in and through the communal reality of the institutional church.[45]

None of the criticisms discussed thus far lead von Balthasar to conclude that Barth is a post-Christian thinker. On the contrary, he believes that the genuinely Christian intentions of Barth's theology cannot be fully developed because of his excessively uncritical reliance on idealist categories. This reliance contaminates Barth's theology with a speculative orientation that weakens his ability to defend adequately the theological relevance of horizontal history, the theological ultimacy of creaturely freedom, and the unity-in-distinction of infinite and finite in the mystical body of Christ. Von Balthasar partially makes this case in *The Glory of the Lord,* where he explicitly charges Barth with holding a doctrine of "theological theopanism" that has a close conceptual proximity with Spinoza's "philosophical pantheism."[46] Once he has asserted this association with philosophical monism, von Balthasar then focuses particularly on Barth's doctrine of election, which he insists is an example of "philosophical apriorism" and a "philosophical-theological concept of God."[47] He resumes this line of criticism in *Theo-Drama* when he argues that Barth's theology is "speculative."[48] The gist of von Balthasar's argument is that Barth interprets the demonic as "nothingness" (following Hegel's thesis that the demonic is "negativity") because

he does not take seriously a theology of the created order in which genuinely free creatures (angels, demons, or humans) can exist as ontologically other than God.[49] In other words, von Balthasar contends that
there are no real demons in Barth's theology because he reduces all reality to a christological monism. Von Balthasar curtly refers to this as
Barth's "re-Christianizing of German Idealism."[50] Moreover, in a particularly damning passage, von Balthasar traces the line influence for
Barth's monistic doctrine of the demonic as "nothingness" back
through Schelling and Jakob Böehme to the Gnosticism of the Kabbalah.[51] In *TD4*, however, von Balthasar retreats somewhat from these
negative associations by noting that Barth's essay "Mysticism and
Atheism" provides a resource for resisting the anthropocentric focus of
idealism.[52] Moreover, in *TD5* he makes a positive reference to "the
transcendent God of Karl Barth."[53] And in a point that could be read
as a reversal of his earlier criticisms, he goes on to assert that Barth's
Christology "is essentially narrative and not a matter of systematic
deduction."[54] All these conflicting claims suggest that von Balthasar
thinks Barth's theology is drawn off course by the conceptual allure of
theological monism, but he does not think it ultimately yields to this
Gnostic siren song.

### Liberation Theology's Insufficient Resistance to Marxism

Contrary to the restrained tone in his criticisms of the Protestant Barth,
von Balthasar's criticisms of Catholic liberation theology are often
remarkably shrill. But focusing exclusively on this tone outside the context of his overall evaluation of liberation theology leads to a skewed
understanding of his real complaint. For example, noting the severity of
his attacks against liberation theology, some commentators have
jumped to the conclusion that he totally opposes anything and everything all liberation theologians have ever written.[55] The thinking of
these commentators tends to run as follows: since liberation theologians
generally advocate the theological importance of themes such as history,
praxis, community, social justice, and Christian political involvement,
von Balthasar's opposition to them must be evidence of an ahistorical,
passive, individualistic, and politically indifferent theological agenda.[56]
A careful reading of *Theo-Drama*, as well as of the essay on liberation
theology that von Balthasar composed while writing *Theo-Drama*, will
show that the matter is not that simple.[57] Such a reading will show that
he identifies two basic deficiencies in liberation theology that are quite
different from what commentators tend to assume: the first deficiency is
the lack of an authentically theological aesthetic perspective; the second

deficiency is liberation theology's chronic naïveté about Christianity's agonistic historical context and about the exact nature and strategies of the Gnostic antagonist.

Von Balthasar's evaluation of liberation theology is fundamentally ambivalent. It is possible to isolate two different types of critique at work in his analysis of liberation theology, a hard and a soft critique. These two critiques are intertwined, but it is possible to disentangle them and gauge the level of importance each has in his overall evaluation. The hard critique, on the one hand, tends to be polemical, caricaturing liberation theology as an intentional collaborator with modern Gnosticism's war against the *corpus triforme*. The soft critique, on the other hand, finds liberation theology guilty of only naïveté about its historical context, a misidentification of Christianity's true enemies, and, consequently, a theologically imprudent and uncritical appropriation of Gnostic modes of reflection. After briefly sketching the substance of the hard critique, I will argue that the soft critique more accurately expresses the conciliatory character of von Balthasar's evaluation of liberation theology. This argument will show that von Balthasar affirms the basic goals and intentions of liberation theology and that he believes —contrary to a purely Gnostic discourse, which is based on a sinful rejection of Christ—that it is truly a Christian discourse, and is, in principle, capable of being reconfigured according to *corpus triforme* categories.

The main substance of the hard critique of liberation theology in *Theo-Drama* is that it is the direct outgrowth of the Joachim-Hegel-Marx line of modern Gnosticism, and as such, it cooperates fully and intentionally in the dismantling of the *corpus triforme* system of meaning. This cooperation is made possible because liberation theology "disregards" traditional theology, and instead it "strives for a radical simplification of theology and has developed its own standpoint by bypassing most of what has become traditional and by reading Scripture in a way that amounts to a wholly new start."[58] This desire to simplify theology makes liberation theology inherently reductive and biased against the complexity of the *corpus triforme*. Along these lines, von Balthasar charges that liberation theology "succumbs in a new way to theological rationalism" because it attempts to interpret all the interactions between God and humanity "within a single system or overview."[59] This type of systematic thought only underwrites a Gnostic speculative dismissal of vertical transcendence, which is the conceptual prerequisite for the disconnection of the *corpus triforme* unity of the old and new covenants. Hence, he explicitly identifies liberation theology with the major perpetrators of this disconnection: Joachimism,

Enlightenment progressivism, German Idealism, and Marxist material-ism.[60] In his essay "Liberation Theology in the Light of Salvation His-tory," he implicitly identifies liberation theology with the Gnostic attack on the unity of the old and new covenants. In a scolding admonition, he suggests that liberation theology disconnects the old covenant's hori-zontal hope from the new covenant's theology of the vertical fulfillment of this hope:

> Whenever a form of Christianity which considers itself enlightened forgets that Christ's Cross and Resurrection wholly fulfilled the Old Testament's "utopian" promise ("God with us"), the result is not a lapsing back into paganism . . . , but a drifting into a Judaizing mentality that now reads the New Testament through the filter of a master-slave ideology and which, consequently, takes into its own control the business of mankind's total politico-religious liberation, entirely contrary to the Old Testament's orig-inal understanding of Israel.[61]

Both the tenor and the context of this passage suggest that, with regard to the first element of the *corpus triforme*, he thinks liberation theology is Joachimite, Hegelian, and Marxist.[62]

Von Balthasar also believes that liberation theology is guilty of col-laborating with the Gnostic agenda to disconnect creation and redemp-tion. We see this clearly in his charge that liberation theology is a type of "monism."[63] Of course, his point is not that liberation theology is monistic in the same way as speculative metaphysical philosophies are. Rather, he argues, liberation theology is monistic because it denies the role of vertical divine transcendence in human redemption.[64] This explains why he often warns liberation theologians against thinking that human beings can free themselves from the evils of unjust social, politi-cal, and economic structures without relying on grace.[65] It also explains why he reminds liberation theology that genuine redemption must be a liberation into one's own freedom, and thus it cannot by definition involve any type of coercion.[66] This point echoes his criticism of Marx-ism's effort to secularize human redemption by merging humanistic theories of progressive liberation in history with cosmological theories of natural law. He believes that because liberation theologians con-sciously assimilate Marxist philosophy, it is necessary to remind them that whenever Marx's abstract theories are put into practice, they inevitably result in the coercion and "liquidation" by an authoritarian state of "immoral" and "unnatural" dissenters who did not fit the rul-ing party's a priori vision of freedom.[67] He worries in particular about what he sees as liberation theology's excessive willingness to justify the use of violence for a partisan agenda.[68]

Von Balthasar's hard critique of liberation theology with regard to its

cooperation in the dismantling of the *corpus triforme* reaches its highest
point of intensity on the issue of its complicity in the Gnostic rejection
of the unity of Christ and the church.[69] Specifically, he is deeply troubled
by what he perceives as liberation theology's polarizing and sectarian
proclivities.[70] Animating these worries is the suspicion that it has opted
for a puritanical ecclesiology in which moralism and violence are the
forces driving history toward the kingdom of God. As in Marxism, liberation theology nurtures a strong distrust of the aesthetic power of the
Christ-form as an efficacious motivator of human ethical action. Von
Balthasar expresses grave concerns that many contemporary Christians
are held "spellbound" by the world Marxist movement, and hence they
import its partisan agenda into the church to reorient its mission in history toward accomplishing a purely human redemption.[71] He explicitly
names liberation theologians as primary examples of such "spellbound"
Christians, and he accuses them of fostering a dangerous fascination
with Marxism that paralyzes the church and renders it unable to resist
the "satanic falsehoods" of communism's hostile reinterpretation of
Christianity. He writes,

> this fascination so weakens the Christian organism that the alien wasp [of
> Marxism] is able to inject its anaesthetizing sting and lay its eggs right
> inside it, with the result that the body, hollowed out from inside, serves as
> welcome food for the enemy. Christians are confronted with a thousand
> pretexts for interpreting their own eschatological hope in purely mundane
> terms; they are urged to put Third World development and liberation the-
> ology before missionary activity, instead of performing "corporeal works
> of mercy" in the all-embracing spirit of the Beatitudes. Why, if we are seri-
> ous about God's Incarnation in Jesus, should we not find "atheism in
> Christianity"? For the latter's norm now resides in this divine impulse in
> man, not in the alienating spell cast by a tyrant in heaven.[72]

By operating under the seemingly neutral banners of "progress" and
"development," he continues, Christian movements like liberation
theology have entered into the service of a "demonic" Gnostic agenda.[73]
Here we see the hard critique at its most acerbic.

The bitter rhetoric of von Balthasar's hard critique is excessive and
misleading because it contradicts his overall interpretation of liberation
theology. If we examine this rhetoric in the context of other claims he
makes elsewhere in *Theo-Drama* and "Liberation Theology in Light of
Salvation History," we see that the overall critique is soft and not hard:
liberation theology is not itself Gnostic but is merely an extreme example of insufficient Christian resistance to modern Gnosticism's hostile
reinterpretation of Christianity. The most helpful passages for gauging
the true proportions of von Balthasar's critique are found in a section in

*TD4* entitled "The Theodramatic Dimensions of Liberation." Here he explains that we must read liberation theology from the "vantage point" of its charter document, the Second Vatican Council's "Pastoral Constitution on the Church in the Modern World," *Gaudium et spes*.[74] When read from this vantage point, he explains, we will be able to "appreciate [liberation theology's] urgency and its complex nature."[75] His interpretation of *Gaudium et spes*, therefore, provides the hermeneutic key for accurately understanding his interpretation of liberation theology. On the central issues he thinks that liberation theology repeats both the strengths and the weaknesses of *Gaudium et spes*. This is hermeneutically important because, although he is not uncritical of *Gaudium et spes*, he definitely does not consider it an example of Gnosticism.

Von Balthasar's worries about the anthropocentric tendencies of liberation theology take on new meaning when we read them in the context of the praise he offers *Gaudium et spes* for its attempt to articulate a christocentric humanism that takes the incarnation as the ultimate source of meaning and truth in human existence.[76] It is also significant that he affirms *Gaudium et spes* for describing human existence as a "battlefield" and notes that "the whole life of men, both individual and social, shows itself to be a struggle, and a *dramatic one*, between good and evil, between light and darkness."[77] *Gaudium et spes* rightly recognizes that each individual person will have to maintain the "dour combat with the powers of evil, stretching . . . until the last day."[78] But in a critical move that signals the content of his later critique of liberation theology, he chides *Gaudium et spes* for not being social and political enough in its teaching about this "dour combat." In assuming a "convergence between the world culture and the Church's catholic ideal," it fails to make any mention of "a corresponding combat at the *social* level, at the level of culture and politics, where the battle is bound to be even more severe. . . ."[79] This failure gives rise to suspicions in von Balthasar's mind about a latent naïveté in the pastoral constitution about who are in fact the church's real enemies. For example, he questions the assumption of *Gaudium et spes* that Christians can make easy alliances with secular psychology and sociology. It is interesting that he expresses exactly the same concern about liberation theology's tendency to naïvely enter intellectual alliances with secular ideologies without first critically examining their underlying axioms about Christianity.[80] Even when rightly recognizing that Christianity exists in an agonistic context, it is still necessary to identify accurately the enemy so that the church's mission will not be subverted by supposed allies who, in reality, harbor deep hostility to the core elements of the faith.

Von Balthasar suspects that the failure to accurately identify the church's real enemy is the root cause of some theological mischief in *Gaudium et spes*. The best example is the document's practice of optimistically correlating efforts to build a humanistic world culture with the church's proclamation of the kingdom of God.[81] He worries that "there is too little appreciation of the problems encountered by Christians in cooperating with such 'Titanist' projects." In particular, he suggests that *Gaudium et spes* has irresponsibly ignored all the problems that the "eschatological passages of Scripture" raise for theories of human religious progress. The direct root of this theological omission lies in the pastoral constitution's working assumption that it could formulate its doctrine of Christian humanism and ecclesial involvement in the world "by setting to one side the apocalyptic law of the ever-growing No that opposes the ever-growing Yes."[82] But since this law is, according to von Balthasar, the fundamental law of world history, by ignoring it *Gaudium et spes* locked itself into an inherently ahistorical mode of reflection that prevented it from understanding the meaning of the theodrama playing itself out on the world stage.

Like *Gaudium et spes*, von Balthasar finds liberation theology too simplistic in its analysis of socio-economic issues and too ready to make alliances with those who advocate seemingly neutral notions of progress. But this does not mean, as the rhetoric of the hard critique suggests, that liberation theology knowingly and sinfully joins in the modern Gnostic attack on the *corpus triforme*. Indeed, in some respects, liberation theology gets a better score than *Gaudium et spes* for more clearly understanding that the church's overall system of meaning implies that the battleground of history must include the terrain of politics and culture. On this point, however, liberation theology needs to be saved from itself. This salvation will be carried out by identifying and highlighting its most redeemable traits. For example, in spite of its self-negating alliance with a priori philosophies, von Balthasar thinks liberation theology's appeal to praxis is inherently Christian, and hence it requires special emphasis. Thus he lauds liberation theology for calling Christians to engage in a "world-transforming cooperation" with Christ's mission, explaining that this call expresses "the heart of Christianity, [and] it reveals the dramatic situation of the Christian in this world as perhaps nothing else does."[83] But because liberation theologians themselves do not give enough attention to real theological, a posteriori reasons for their insistence on praxis, von Balthasar feels compelled to remind them that Christians must insist on praxis not because they believe our only hope lies in human self-redemption but because they believe it is possible for the grace of God to break into the "self-enclosed world" of sin and transform the entire creation with the gift of "God-given freedom." Without this belief, appeals to praxis would be nothing more than a call to waste one's life in an ultimately Sisyphean struggle against evil and injustice. Would Christ have sent his disciples out "like sheep among wolves," he asks, if it were not possible for grace to transform all of creation, including "the public realm that is ruled by the laws of society, of economics and of politics"?[84] In an attempt to turn the tables, he wryly observes that grace cannot be "restricted to the private realm of example and interpersonal influence."[85]

Von Balthasar then goes on to make it very clear that he thinks liberation theology is being fully Christian in rejecting other-worldly interpretations of life, and in directly confronting political and economic injustice. For example, in *TD5* von Balthasar joins liberation theology in insisting that the church must work in the world for the transformation of the world.[86] Moreover, with the liberation theologians, he maintains that the church must understand its mission in terms of praxis in the service of the poor and marginalized; this means for him "the establishment of a just order upon earth that is worthy of man, the struggle against injustice and inhumanity."[87] But contrary to what he sees as liberation theology's underemphasis on the theological virtue of hope, von Balthasar calls for a renewed emphasis on the worldly, liberating dimension of theological hope.[88] He writes,

> Christian hope, theological hope, goes beyond this world, but it does not pass it by: rather, it takes the world with it on its way to God, who has graciously prepared a dwelling in himself for us and for the world. This implies that the Christian in the world is meant to awaken hope, particularly among the most hopeless; and this in turn means that he must create such humane conditions as will actually allow the poor and oppressed to have hope. Hope must never be individualistic: it must always be social. It cannot simply hope that others will attain eternal salvation; it must enable them to cherish this hope by creating conditions apt to promote it.[89]

He clearly intends the phrases "create humane . . . conditions" and "creating conditions apt to promote [hope]" to include conditions of physical well-being in the political and economic realms. This is clear from his insistence in *TD2* that Christianity necessarily must have a "public and political relevance."[90] Von Balthasar goes on to add that simply because Christianity "puts the accent on the individual's call to follow Christ [this] does not mean that Christ's work is always a private matter, concerned only with saving the individual's 'soul.'" Despite the "initial" emphasis on the individual's call, therefore, the church's mission to combat injustice and its "causes" indicates that "the realm of the political fits into the total context" of Christian faith.[91] This total context of faith includes the full range of the church's dramatic struggle with its Gnostic antagonist. Von Balthasar thus argues that the Christian believer must get actively involved in the dramatic process of the church's political struggles in salvation history, which means "exposing oneself to the enemy . . . ; it is not done by immunizing oneself, through meditative, philosophical or mystical techniques, against the world."[92] In *TD4* von Balthasar expands this call to action by including specifically economic issues within the range of church's political struggles. He explains that being a Christian means using human labor to shape earth in the "likeness" of humanity, which is itself the "likeness of God."[93] This work of humanizing the earth necessarily implies resisting the dehumanizing "exploitation of workers, who are regarded and treated as mere means to power."[94] The threat of failure or personal danger cannot dissuade Christians from this struggle, he insists, because it is a "strict Christian duty to fight for social justice on behalf of the poor and oppressed. It is a spiritual and corporal 'work of mercy', a work according to which the Christian, and indeed everyone, will be judged."[95]

All of von Balthasar's assertions about the political and economic imperatives of Christian faith certainly beg important questions about the details of methods and strategy. I will deal with many of these questions in the next chapter when I raise the issue of whether von Balthasar's theology can be interpreted as a political theology. The nature of his critique of liberation theology, however, is the issue at the moment. Given the wide scope of von Balthasar's agreement with liberation theology on the political and economic nature of the church's mission in history, it is obvious that, occasional rhetoric aside, the hard critique does not express his overall opinion: liberation theology is not Gnostic, and it is definitely redeemable.[96] It is true that he thinks that insofar as liberation theology operates in ignorance of the agonistic situation in post-Easter history, it will constantly lapse into an ahistorical perspective that blinds it to the existence and hostile nature of the church's Gnostic rival. This explains its insufficiently critical assimilation of Marxism's abstract theories of history. But liberation theology is not Gnostic in the sense that it completely disdains the power of grace in human affairs. Nor is liberation theology guilty of intentionally and sinfully rejecting Christ and his redemption of the created order.

Nevertheless, the soft critique obviously does not mean that liberation theology's deviation from the *corpus triforme* standard is not serious. Even if liberation theology qualifies as a type of Christian discourse, it remains a borderline case. In particular, von Balthasar remains concerned with three issues: (1) to what degree does liberation theology grant that grace has efficacious power in transforming human affairs; (2) to what extent is liberation theology's understanding of grace christocentric and sacramental (and hence ecclesial); and (3) is liberation theology capable of assimilating a theological aesthetic perspective that reorders the transcendentals so that the (christologically transfigured) beautiful has governing priority over the good and the true? The third issue is perhaps the most important because it will determine the content of the first two. In other words, is liberation theology capable of prioritizing a christocentric contemplative realism as the origin and permanent regulator of its theology of praxis and freedom? We can ascertain from von Balthasar's criticisms of liberation theology that he thinks it assumes an inversely proportional relationship between contemplation and praxis. Insofar as this is the case, he believes, liberation theology's advocacy of praxis will remain in danger of drifting toward rationalism because it is not grounded in contemplative receptivity to the self-interpreting incarnate Word. Moreover, without a grounding in contemplative receptivity, it will be impossible for liberation theology, despite its rhetoric of praxis, to ultimately avoid yielding to an ethos of existential resignation in the face of the overwhelmingly tragic nature of the human condition. In this sense, von Balthasar's criticism of liberation theology is analogous to his criticism of those modern poets and philosophers who sought to retrieve the classical aesthetic ethos. In both cases, there is a strong emphasis on casting a realistic eye on tragedy and human suffering but without a corresponding realistic focus on the Christ-form. So although the aesthetic poets and philosophers advocated contemplation, and the liberation theologians advocate praxis, their common failure to seriously contemplate the praxis of God in the total Christ-form destabilizes their intended resistance to rationalism and abstraction. This is why von Balthasar finds something remarkably ahistorical about liberation theology in its optimistic emphasis on the ability of human praxis to succeed in Christianizing the world. Liberation theology's optimism fails to come to terms with the basic law of post-Easter history, namely, the increasing prevalence on the world stage of players who act out a militant and sinful rejection of the Christ-form and the system of meaning it expresses. Nevertheless, as Catholic thinkers committed to conciliar teaching, liberation theologians, in principle at least, have at their disposal theological resources for overcoming their ahistorical naïveté.

### Jürgen Moltmann: Collaboration or Resistance?

Von Balthasar's reading of Moltmann shows the same willingness to mix affirmation and criticism as in his reading of liberation theology. The accent, however, falls more strongly on critique. Whereas his critique of liberation theology had the tenor of reprimand, the critique of Moltmann is extraordinarily strident and condemnatory. Moreover, contrary to his criticisms of liberation theology, his reading of Moltmann allows for almost no ameliorating factors such as an adherence to official Catholic conciliar teachings. Von Balthasar's commentaries on Moltmann's theology often give the impression that he sees it as being adrift in a sea of modern Gnosticism without compass or map. Von Balthasar formally shares much of Moltmann's theological agenda (such as his trinitarian interpretation of the cross), but he is dismayed by what he sees as Moltmann's irresponsible, naïve, and counter-productive dependence on Gnostic modes of reflection. This is why, in examining Moltmann's theology, he is less ambivalent than he had been with liberation theology: he strongly shifts the balance of his remarks toward criticism because he thinks it has so few internal resources for resisting the hostile Gnostic reinterpretation of Christianity. As in my reading of his critique of liberation theology, I will argue here that it is possible to isolate in von Balthasar's critique of Moltmann a hard and a soft critique. The hard critique is that Moltmann's theology belongs squarely in the category of Gnostic discourse. It is self-consciously Hegelian; it is primarily and intentionally—and not secondarily and accidentally—monistic; and it makes no effort to resist the influence of either Marcionist or Valentinian Gnostic thinkers. Instead, Moltmann brazenly affirms them as resources for reconstructing Christian theology. The soft critique is that many of Moltmann's theological conclusions are more biblical than Gnostic. Hence there are elements in his project that could count as gestures of resistance to Gnosticism. These elements in Moltmann's theology would qualify it as guilty of only grossly insufficient resistance to, and not deliberate collaboration with, Hegelian Gnosticism. Unlike the case with liberation theology, however, von Balthasar does not ultimately make a clear decision between the soft and the hard critique in his evaluation. Indeed, the line between soft and hard critique in his reading of Moltmann is very thin. I will now discuss in more detail both critiques and explain why this is so.

One of the primary characteristics of von Balthasar's hard critique is its consistent and explicit identification of Moltmann's theology with Hegelianism. He also identifies many other modern theologians with Hegelianism.[97] Nonetheless, it is clear in *Theo-Drama* that he reads Moltmann's work as a particularly egregious of example of rampant Hegelianism in modern theology.[98] Indeed, von Balthasar tells us that Moltmann's theology wants to "salvage Hegel" and implant his views "into Christian theology"; Moltmann's project seeks to rehabilitate

Hegel as a Christian thinker "by tracing his thought back to its origins in the *Lutheran* Reformation. . . ."[99] From von Balthasar's perspective, however, it is not always clear that Moltmann has the necessary critical distance to prevent his rehabilitation from becoming simply an expository repetition of Hegel's theology. In purveying Hegelianism as *bona fide* Reformation theology, von Balthasar believes Moltmann allows the parasite of Gnosticism to flourish by feeding off the body of Protestant orthodoxy. For example, Moltmann purveys Hegelianism by interpreting the Trinity "in the Hegelian manner," thereby giving a Lutheran stamp of approval to Hegel's mythological view of God as tragically "entangled" in the process of cosmic evolution.[100] To understand more fully von Balthasar's thinking on this point, we need to look more specifically at how he reads Moltmann's trinitarian theology of the cross as being rife with the Hegel's speculative presuppositions.

Von Balthasar produces an abundance of evidence demonstrating Moltmann's commitment to Hegel's philosophical theology of the cross. The unifying theme of all this evidence is the strong parallel between Moltmann's theology of the cross and Hegel's epic interpretation of history as a three-part process of divine self-development: God's descent into pathos and alienation, God's moment of turning away from alienation, and God's journey back toward psychic wholeness through the overcoming of God's alienated self. As I explained earlier, in this epic system, the cross symbolizes the midpoint of this process. The cross symbolizes the turning point in which God's alienated self—that is, the otherness of the finite created order—begins to be absorbed back into God. It is not necessary here to reproduce all the evidence von Balthasar gathers to demonstrate that Moltmann shares this Hegelian version of epic theology. A few pertinent examples will suffice to make the point.

Arguing from his reading of Moltmann's *The Crucified God*, von Balthasar determines that Moltmann believes that the cross is not primarily about humanity's alienation from God but is instead about the inner life of God. Von Balthasar does not find it problematic that the cross symbolizes inner-trinitarian relationships (he holds a similar view himself), but he does find Moltmann's articulation of it problematic. Moltmann holds that the cross symbolizes that the Son is alienated from the Father to the "utmost degree of enmity and distinction."[101] This means that the entire Godhead is affected by the painful alienation between the Father and Son that occurs on the cross.[102] Von Balthasar suspects that this position makes it difficult for Moltmann's theology to resist falling into an epic, mythological reinterpretation of God as helplessly entangled in the suffering of the world. If he were to resist such a reinterpretation, Moltmann would seriously have to qualify his rhetoric about the suffering and alienation of the entire Godhead. Von Balthasar also worries that Moltmann's rhetoric runs the risk of ontologically identifying the inner-trinitarian suffering and alienation of God with the suffering and tragedies within the temporal order of creation. His worries are not assuaged by Moltmann's assertion that the "bifurcation" of Father and Son contains the "whole turmoil of history."[103] Nor does it help Moltmann's case when he declares that "the Trinity is not a closed circle in heaven but an open eschatological process for men on earth, with the Cross as its origin."[104] This process renders the cross the site of the Trinity's actualization. All this makes it clear to von Balthasar that Hegel's trinitarian theology is at the root of Moltmann's thinking here. Rather than correcting Hegel, Moltmann has assimilated his conflation of the internal trinitarian processions with the process of history, thereby indirectly affirming Hegel's mythological doctrine that history is the linear unfolding of the Trinity. Von Balthasar remarks in *TD5* that, for Moltmann, "The 'immanent' *processio* of the Son (within the Trinity) is identified with his 'economic' *missio*." He immediately adds, "Thus we have arrived at Hegel's view in his *Phenomenology*."[105]

Von Balthasar also sees in Moltmann a disturbing restatement of Hegel's reinterpretation of Luther's *sub contrario* doctrine: we only know God in God's opposites, that is, death, tragedy, godlessness, and evil. Thus in Moltmann's theology, the cross remains the sole locus of our knowledge of God because it is here that we learn about God's true identity as one who undergoes suffering and about the pain of overcoming self-alienation.[106] This is why, von Balthasar notes, Moltmann argues for an understanding of God in terms of a "universal theology of pain": since, as Moltmann asserts, "God and the world are . . . involved in a common redemptive process," it is also true that human history is "at the same time the history of God's passion."[107] As God endures the pain of journeying back to psychic wholeness, the creation too experiences God's pain. Hence, we must interpret all the suffering of history as fully identical with God's suffering and vice versa. Von Balthasar observes that Moltmann attempts to assert the orthodox nature of his trinitarian theology of the cross by calling it "Christian panentheism." But von Balthasar finds it difficult to see how this trendy label significantly distinguishes Moltmann's theology from Hegel's heterodox philosophical monism.[108] Von Balthasar acknowledges that Moltmann does not intend to echo an unreconstructed Hegelianism.[109] Moltmann tries to distance himself from Hegel's ideas by asserting that the Son is not the Father's creation, that there is a distinction between the world process and the inner-trinitarian process, and that the created order has its own space, time, and freedom.[110] Assertions aside, however, von Balthasar does not believe Moltmann succeeds in making a plausible case that his theology is genuinely free of Hegel's influence on these central issues.[111] But if Moltmann's intention was to resist the non-Christian aspects of Hegelianism, why does he seem to fail so utterly? The answer is that Moltmann's own understanding of Christianity was incomplete, and hence he was not able to recognize fully and resist the dangers of Hegelianism. Instead, according to von Balthasar, Moltmann misidentifies "realized eschatology" as the real theological enemy, and he makes the remarkably erroneous assumption that he can enlist Hegelianism, as well as other forms of Gnosticism, in a Christian war against it.

Moltmann's project of resistance to "platonizing" and "existential" realized eschatology starts with the modern Gnostic assumption that the created order has not yet been redeemed in Christ.[112] With thinkers like Joachim and Marx, Moltmann argues that humanity must await a future redemption in which peace and justice will be fully and irreversibly established on earth. There can be no real presence of the kingdom in the present epoch. In taking this position, Moltmann also necessarily removes the new covenant's vertical orientation from his theology, leaving only the old covenant's horizontal perspective, whose main religious orientation is hope for the future messianic age. Disconnecting the horizontal and the vertical dimensions of revelation in this way is, of course, a modern Gnostic tactic. Von Balthasar, however, does not think Moltmann's purpose is to perform a hostile reinterpretation of Christianity but rather to preserve a biblical understanding of God's pathos from a hostile reinterpretation by ancient philosophical doctrines of divine impassability.[113] Although he affirms this purpose, he questions the manner in which Moltmann pursues it. He suspects that Moltmann's attack on philosophies of divine immutability comes from the mythological pole of epic theology.[114] Hence Moltmann's theology remains entrapped within the logical parameters of speculative thought. This is most obvious in Moltmann's alliance with Hegelianism, but also in his avowed agenda of bringing Christianity back to its biblical roots through the use of Ernst Bloch's atheistic "gnosticism."[115] Von Balthasar considers this entire project wildly misguided. Bloch's philosophy, he believes, is inherently antibiblical because it "is a radically secularized Messianism" that interprets the incarnation, not as the axis of history, but as simply one historical moment in the "unstoppable 'linear' movement [of history], since redemption lies exclusively 'in the future.'"[116] Moreover, Bloch's thought could not possibly return Christianity to its biblical roots because it takes as its basic axiom the belief that Jesus did not complete his mission on earth but only inaugurated a process toward its full establishment. Von Balthasar charges Moltmann's "theology of hope" with uncritically assimilating this "secular Messianism," and with consequently wrongly assuming that "realized eschatology" is Christianity's enemy.[117]

This line of reflection indicates that Moltmann's theology has been infected with the false either/or dichotomy of Gnostic epic theology: either God is vertically distant from and sublimely unconcerned with the turmoil of history or God is entangled in linear world history and inescapably suffers along with it. Moltmann recognizes that the first option is clearly incompatible with the Christian belief that God is love; so he decides for the second option. Yet, in order to preserve a doctrine of hope, Moltmann then makes a predictable move: he repeats in new terms Origen's doctrine of universal salvation (*apokatastasis*).[118] In so doing, he narrates salvation history as the story of how the God of love undergoes suffering on the cross in solidarity with those who suffer in history, and in the process both God and world develop together toward perfection so that, in the end, both God and all of creation will be redeemed and fully united in love.[119] Noting the rhetoric of "certainty" in all of Moltmann's discussions of this point, von Balthasar labels the "theology of hope" as a "kind of triumphalism" that speculatively erases all the contingencies that arise from the interaction of divine and human freedom.[120] Von Balthasar is convinced that an ethos of resignation must necessarily haunt and subvert every attempt Moltmann makes to develop a theology of praxis.[121] By putting an exclusive emphasis on the cross, and virtually ignoring the redeemed goodness of creation and the freedom from cosmic determinism that results from the resurrection, Moltmann makes it difficult to see how the "new political theology" he promotes can amount to anything but moralism.[122] Moreover, the latent "triumphalism" of his eschatology subtly contradicts his calls for activism by encouraging an attitude of existential indifference to the current state of the world. Von Balthasar also believes that Moltmann's ability to resist speculative forms of epic theology is severely handicapped by his neglect of the Gospel of John as a theological resource.[123] Had Moltmann understood the Johannine theology of revealed glory, he would not have overlooked the "nuanced" Johannine conception of realized eschatology. Instead, he argues, Moltmann mistakenly assumes that John teaches an other-worldly genre of realized eschatology, and hence, despite his consistent assertion of the Johannine theme that God is love, Moltmann's "theology of hope" avoids the Fourth Gospel. This hermeneutic bias allows Moltmann's theology to drift into speculative mythological "panentheism" that undermines its best theological intentions.

This presentation of Moltmann as a collaborator with Gnosticism does not tell the whole story of von Balthasar's interpretation, however.

There is also a soft critique of Moltmann in *Theo-Drama*. Von Balthasar grants that, despite the near saturation of Moltmann's theology with Hegelian assumptions, it is not Moltmann's intention to disseminate an unreconstructed version of Hegel's thought. The presence of these intentions illustrates that Moltmann has at least some (however minimal) critical distance from Hegel. Von Balthasar does see in Moltmann some inchoate gestures of resistance that could possibly have some theological value if properly developed.[124] For example, he lauds him for maintaining that Christian praxis is neither guaranteed success nor able to avoid sharing in the suffering of the cross; Christians must not delude themselves into believing their efforts will construct the kingdom of God on earth.[125] This at least indicates that Moltmann has some critical distance on the humanistic titanism of Marxism, as well as on the totalitarian political systems of the right that have arisen from Hegelianism. On at least this one point, von Balthasar thinks Moltmann has shown more caution than liberation theology.[126] Also, in a direct contrast to Hegel, Moltmann believes in the personal resurrection of Jesus from the dead, and he believes that human persons can legitimately hope for their own resurrection in Christ.[127] Moltmann also gets credit for recognizing that hope for the resurrection of individual persons is the basis for Christianity's opposition to social-political injustice; because Christians are not resigned to death as their fate, neither can they resign themselves to injustice and oppression as if these were part of cosmic necessity. Another positive element in Moltmann is his apparent opposition to Joachim's trinitarian theology. For Moltmann, Christ and the church are not surpassed by an age of the Spirit, but rather they exist together in history in a common mission to deliver the "perfected kingdom" to the Father at the end of time.[128] This might imply in Moltmann a doctrine of the interpenetration of the trinitarian persons in salvation history that would contradict Joachim's trinitarian theology of sequential historical epochs. Moltmann's case on this point is helped by the fact that he interprets the cross "not only as on atoning event between God and the world but above all as the eminent, and indeed the only, locus of God's trinitarian revelation in the world."[129] This could indicate a degree of difference between Moltmann and Joachimite discourse. Moreover, all these positive points suggest that a critical distance could open up between Moltmann and his Gnostic influences. There are four conditions for the development of these points into adequate gestures of resistance to Gnosticism: (1) a willingness to accept the "two-natures" doctrine of the incarnation as a paradox that reconciles time and eternity, and creation and redemption, in mutually affirming coexistence; (2) an accurate interpretation of Johannine realized eschatology that understands how its nuances allow it to affirm Christ as the complete fulfillment of Old Testament messianic expectation prior to the full establishment an earthly kingdom of universal righteousness; (3) a willingness to at least question his "really naïve"[130] assumption that the traditional theological doctrine of the immanent Trinity necessarily implies a static, abstract deity absolutely detached from creation; and (4) a stronger doctrine of the church as the site God's maximal divine disclosure in and openness to participation by the finite, temporal order.[131]

Nevertheless, the soft critique does not express von Balthasar's final position. The soft critique is based on conditions that Moltmann himself consistently rules out. Even if it were possible for Moltmann to clarify his theology in a way that might avoid some of its Gnostic implications, von Balthasar sees few internal resources in it capable of correcting its Marxist rejection of realized eschatology and his Hegelian rejection of the immanent Trinity. Moltmann's interest in rehabilitating Hegel and Bloch as Christian theologians could prove to be a constant source of heterodox mischief in theology. But there are some inchoate resources for facilitating Moltmann's movement from his Gnostic milieu. If Moltmann reflected more carefully the ontological implications of his belief in the resurrection, his affirmation of creaturely personhood, his non-Joachimite economic trinitarianism, he could possibly come to an appreciation of a genuinely monotheistic doxological interpretation of Christianity. This, of course, remains hypothetical. We can only conclude that von Balthasar's critique of Moltmann is characterized primarily by a fundamental ambivalence.

### Notes

1. For a detailed and cogent discussion of these points of agreement, see Eamonn Conway, *The Anonymous Christian—A Relativized Christianity?* (Frankfurt: Peter Lang, 1993).

2. Conway, *The Anonymous Christian—A Relativized Christianity?* 38. Conway rightly observes that "Balthasar's critique of Rahner shows a familiarity with all his major works, and occasionally Balthasar builds upon some particular concept of Rahner." Conway mentions as an example here that Balthasar's doctrine that the individual must have full freedom to accept or reject God's offer of salvation. See Rahner's *Foundations of Christian Faith: An Introduction to the Idea of Christianity* (New York: Crossroad, 1989), 133, and von Balthasar's *Dare We Hope "that all men be saved?"* (San Francisco: Ignatius Press, 1988), 32. Conway then adds that von Balthasar and Rahner collaborated on several theological works (he lists them on p. 38 n. 7). He also quotes von Balthasar making the following statement: "I consider Karl Rahner, taken from an overall perspective, to be the strongest theological potential of our time . . . in 1939 we worked together on a plan for dogmatics which later became *Mysterium Salutis* . . ." (quoted from "Geist und Feuer, *Herder Korrespondenz*, 30, 1976, 75-76).

3. In 1978 von Balthasar made the following remarks about Rahner: "It is true that Karl Rahner is inclined to filter all questions through the prism of his own method but, on the other hand, his pastoral concern enables him to see all problems—theological and secular—in their realistic complexity, and to accept other than his own attempts of solution" ("Current Trends in Catholic Theology," *Communio: International Catholic Review* [Spring, 1978]: 85).

4. *TD1*, 28-31.

5. Ibid., 28-29.

6. Ibid., 29. For an extremely well-documented and carefully argued critical examination of von Balthasar's critique of Rahner's theology of the anonymous Christian, see Conway's *The Anonymous Christian—A Relativized Christianity?* The merit of Conway's approach is that he puts this entire issue in the historical and conceptual context of von Balthasar's overall theology as he formulated it over several decades.

7. Along these lines, it is interesting to note that von Balthasar criticizes Karl Barth and Rahner for precisely the same reason: neither adequately appreciates the historical perspective offered by historical-critical exegesis. "With Barth, the neutral 'historico-critical method' is not merely set aside as a baneful by-product (as in Bultmann . . .). It is simply regarded as obsolete and put out of action: in sovereign power, the word of God interprets itself directly to faith, scorning all critical exegesis" (*TD3*, 62). With regard to Rahner's theology he writes, "As in Barth, the system remains essentially untouched by the questionings of the historico-critical method, bordering on a Christology constructed along a priori lines" (*TD3*, 63).

8. Certainly this is not to suggest that von Balthasar believes that the Catholic Rahner has failed here to the same degree as the Protestant Bultmann. Indeed, von Balthasar is careful to note that Rahner's theology of "history" is "partly parallel and partly in opposition to" the theology of "event" represented by Bultmann (*TD1*, 28).

9. See *TD3*, 410ff.

10. Ibid., 411.

11. Ibid., 411 n. 18.

12. *TD4*, 222. See Rahner's *Grundkurs des Glaubens* (Herder, 1976), 288ff., 310ff. (Eng. trans. *Foundations of Christian Faith: An Introduction to the Idea of Christianity* [New York: Crossroad, 1989]).

13. *TD3*, 411-12.

14. Ibid., 413. Von Balthasar again charges Rahner with relativizing the Christ-event later when he writes that the provocation of "Jesus' word and actions is so final that it constitutes a historical event that cuts world history in two, thus making it impossible to relativize the event by the use of transcendental theology (K. Rahner)" (*TD4*, 427).

15. Ibid., 413-14.

16. *TD4*, 273. Von Balthasar bases his arguments here largely on *Foundations of Christian Faith*, but he also relies on several volumes of the *Theological Investigations*.

17. Ibid., 274. This claim echoes von Balthasar's earlier assertion that Hegel's understanding of Christianity "jettisons" the aspects which are the most significant.

18. See *TD4*, 274. Von Balthasar is quoting here Rahner's *Theological Investigations*, XII, 26.

19. *TD4*, 274-75.

20. Ibid., 275.

21. Recall that von Balthasar thinks Hegel also holds this philosophical position (*TD1*, 62; cf. 322).

22. *TD4*, 276.

23. On this point von Balthasar asserts that Christ's word of salvation "is not an implicit word that merely becomes explicit; it is not something transcendental of which man is 'conscious,' which, when it meets a form expressed in categories that are adequate, becomes the object of 'knowledge'" (*TD3*, 421).

24. Von Balthasar finds evidence for this point in Rahner's suggestion that he and Adrienne von Speyr had a "gnostic" theology of the Trinity (*TD5*, 13). This inability to distinguish his own theology from Gnosticism indicates to von Balthasar that Rahner did not have a clear sense of the true nature of the post-Christian antagonist.

25. *TD4*, 64-65.

26. For a detailed discussion of the relations between the pre-Christian, the Christian, and the post-Christian, see *TD2*, 346-426. The one very important exception von Balthasar makes to this either/or between Christian and post-Christian players is postbiblical Judaism. Even though it originates in pre-Christian history and has a pre-Christian character, Israel retains "an eminently theological role among the actors in the drama" (*TD4*, 428; cf. *TD3*, 361ff.).

27. *TKB*, 55, 326-63.

28. See, for example, Fergus Kerr's contention in *Balthasar at the End of Modernity* that the positive significance of von Balthasar's work is "its opening towards the theology of Karl Barth" (3). Kerr adds that *The Glory of the Lord* "surely owes far more to Barth than to Adrienne von Speyr" (6). This is true but misleading nonetheless. It certainly owes far more to de Lubac than to Barth. Kerr seems on the way to granting this when he observes that von Balthasar draws from the "quasi-patristic" strands in Barth's theology (10). Later he seems to grant this point fully when he observes that von Balthasar praised Barth for essentially taking sides with de Lubac in the Catholic controversy over the relationship of nature and grace (11).

29. *GL1*, 53-56.

30. Ibid., 153.

31. Ibid., 380-90; see also 480.

32. *TD1*, 26. In his discussion of the trends in modern theology, von Balthasar identifies the theology of "event" with the "early" theology of Karl Barth. However, the criticisms he offers of Barth here recur elsewhere without the qualification of "early" or "late" Barth. He also identifies the theology of "event" with Rudolf Bultmann. I have already discussed his criticisms of Bultmann in an earlier chapter so my focus here will be exclusively on Barth.

33. Ibid., 27.

34. See, for example, his discussion of Barth in *TD5*, 238-39.

35. *TD1*, 27-28.

36. "By saying that all sins are swallowed up in the Cross, Barth has left himself open to the charge of teaching apokatastasis, but he has always dismissed this charge with the (perhaps not very convincing) observation that salvation history is not yet concluded and that he is only stressing that God's word must be consistent with itself right to the end" (*TD5*, 238; cf. 319).

37. *TD1*, 27.

38. *TKB*, 198, 200.

39. Von Balthasar makes this same point about Barth's doctrine of election in *TD3* when he describes him as a theologian who "gives the order of grace a prior-

ity over the order of creation [and] places such one-sided emphasis on God's will to give himself in Christ that the human response pales into relative insignificance" (253). In *GL5* von Balthasar argues that Barth asserts a triumphalist doctrine of universal salvation "against all possible objections by His creatures" (*GL5*, 475-76).

40. *TD5*, 285.

41. *TKB*, 198-99.

42. Further, Barth's failure here is the direct result of his failure to consistently understand that the incarnation is the presupposition for the analogy of being, not its negation. Cf. *TKB*, 201-2; *GL5*, 466; *TD1*, 28; *TD4*, 308.

43. *TD3*, 62.

44. Ibid., 68.

45. Cf. *TD3*, 273, 343; *TD4*, 267, 407.

46. *GL5*, 466.

47. Ibid., 475-76.

48. *TD3*, 471, 478-88; *TD5*, 205-9.

49. Ibid., 480; *TD5*, 207.

50. Ibid., 483.

51. Ibid., 485.

52. *TD4*, 144.

53. *TD5*, 230.

54. Ibid., 238.

55. It must be readily acknowledged that von Balthasar himself often creates the impression that he is offering a polemical blanket condemnation of all liberation theologians without distinction. More often than not he is guilty of grotesquely oversimplifying and wildly generalizing in his interpretations of liberation theology. Indeed, he rarely troubles himself to comment on particular theologians in this movement, and he almost never bothers to make nuances or qualifications about particular writers. The one possible exception in *Theo-Drama* comes in a footnote where he briefly mentions several authors he has culled from a secondary source. See *TD5*, 180. Although this cavalier hermeneutic practice gives rise to what I believe are inaccurate associations and misleading overgeneralizations, I will leave it unchallenged here in this chapter. My point in this section is not to criticize von Balthasar's critique of liberation theology, but simply to present it as an illustration of his fundamental theological concerns.

56. Craig Arnold Phillips makes precisely this charge against von Balthasar's theology. See "From Aesthetics to Redemptive Politics: A Political Reading of the Theological Aesthetics of Hans Urs Von Balthasar and the Materialist Aesthetics of Walter Benjamin" (Ann Arbor, Mich.: UMI Dissertation Services, 1993), 166ff. I will return to Phillips's argument in the next chapter. In an even less-careful reading of von Balthasar's theology, Leonardo Boff accuses his theology of the cross of being fideistic and mythological, and hence ahistorical, individualistic, and oblivious to the meaning of Christian faith for the sufferings of people in history. See *Passion of Christ, Passion of the World*, trans. Robert R. Barr (Maryknoll, NY: Orbis Books, 1987), 108-15.

57. I will rely on Erasmo Leiva's English translation of von Balthasar's essay "Liberation Theology in Light of Salvation History," which can be found in a collection edited by James V. Schall, *Liberation Theology in Latin America* (San Francisco: Ignatius Press, 1982), 131-46. Henceforth this essay will be cited as LTSH. This essay was originally published in German under the title "Heilsgeschichtliche Überlegungen zur Befreiungstheologie" in *Theologie der Befreiung* (Einsiedeln:

Johannesverlag, 1977). This date of publication situates the essay on liberation theology between the publication of *TD2* in 1976 and *TD3* in 1978 and *TD4* in 1980. It is thus no coincidence that these three texts of *Theo-Drama* show a high degree of congruence with the 1977 essay in their several respective discussions of liberation theology.

58. LTSH, 131.

59. *TD4*, 482.

60. *TD3*, 45.

61. LTSH, 140.

62. In addition to his explicit assertions of this point (ibid., 131, 132-33, 140), von Balthasar makes it a central theme in sections entitled "Liberation and Salvation in the Old Testament," "The Structure of Israel and the Structure of the Church."

63. *TD3*, 367.

64. *TD4*, 441-42.

65. LTSH, 133, 138, 142-46.

66. Ibid., 144.

67. Cf. *TD2*, 40. See also *GL5*, 593.

68. This worry is obviously evident when von Balthasar writes, "Christian evangelization can and, indeed, should always begin with direct proclamation to the poor of this deeper liberation [from the power of sin and death], and with a corresponding pronouncement to the rich and the oppressors. From this point onwards, and as far as possible *without violence*, following the example of Christ, progress can be made to political and social liberation as well" (LTSH, 139; italics added). This is not to say that von Balthasar opposes on principle war or the use of violence for self-defense (*TD4*, 485-87). On the question of "Christian revolution" and why he has misgivings about it, see *GL7*, 530.

69. *TD2*, 425; cf. LTSH, 144.

70. *TD3*, 45; cf. LTSH, 132, 143-44.

71. *TD4*, 440-41.

72. Ibid., 441.

73. Ibid., 441-42.

74. Ibid., 482.

75. Ibid., 482. At the end of LTSH von Balthasar remarks that "The urgency of the practical concerns of liberation theology is not called into question by any criticism that may be made of it" (146).

76. *TD4*, 478.

77. Ibid., 479.

78. Ibid., 481.

79. Ibid.

80. Von Balthasar, LTSH, 133-34.

81. *TD4*, 480.

82. Ibid., 478.

83. Ibid., 482.

84. Ibid., 478.

85. Ibid.

86. *TD5*, 178-80.

87. *GL7*, 129. He adds later in this same text that several of Jesus' parables "are thus first of all illustrations of the grace of God which is united with the poor against the rich" (137).

88. "It is worth pointing out . . . that, as far as the Latin American *liberation theologies* are concerned, the Christian imperative of active political transformation of social structures is practically never linked with the topic of hope. Rather it is a response to the appeal for loving solidarity with the poor and oppressed as practiced and commanded by Christ" (*TD5*, 180).

89. *TD5*, 176.

90. *TD2*, 70.

91. Ibid., 71.

92. The "enemy" referred to in this passage is certainly Gnosticism. Von Balthasar's assertion that the competition between rival systems of absolute meaning has "political implications" is just one clue to this point (*TD1*, 74).

93. *TD4*, 482.

94. Ibid., 483.

95. Ibid., 487. Von Balthasar insists that "Jesus sides with the poor, fulfilling the Old Testament's pronouncements concerning God's saving actions. . . . The Church, too, must by preference side with the poor: its best members have always done so" (LTSH, 143-44).

96. This perspective is clear in the condescending comments von Balthasar made in 1978: "I feel that the combined efforts of theology in the United States and Europe should also be directed toward helping the Latin American theology of liberation, which often becomes self-seeking and confused. I mean helping to clarify it with a sympathetic understanding of its genuine claims. Teilhard de Chardin saw the future of theology as supranational, global, but he did not recognize the concerns of liberation theology. We must include them in our theological thinking, but in doing so we must show greater discernment than our South American brothers do. Usually, their analysis of the social situation is based impulsively on Marxist categories of 'exploiting' and 'exploited countries.' . . . The tragic situation is more complex and we must show them that" ("Current Trends in Catholic Theology," *Communio* [Spring, 1978]: 84-85).

97. See *TL3*, 34.

98. *TD4*, 321.

99. *TD5*, 173, 227.

100. *TD4*, 227, 322-33.

101. Ibid., 295.

102. Quoting from Moltmann's *The Crucified God*, von Balthasar demonstrates that Moltmann believes the following: on the cross "the Father himself is forsaken, death is located in God, and Jesus' death on the Cross is 'God's death and God's suffering.' . . . The most profound communion between Father and Son is 'expressed at the very point where they are most profoundly separated, when Jesus dies on the Cross, forsaken by God and accursed.' 'In the Christ-event', therefore, in the genuinely Hegelian manner, salvation is to be defined as a 'negation [expiation] of the negation [sin]'" (*TD4*, 322; cf. 295). The passages quoted here are from *The Crucified God* (London: SCM Press, 1974), 192, 215, 190, 261, 230.

103. Moltmann, *The Crucified God*, 246; quoted in *TD4*, 321.

104. Moltmann, *The Crucified God*, 249; quoted in *TD4*, 322.

105. *TD5*, 228.

106. Ibid., 322, 229.

107. Ibid., 228. Cf. Moltmann, *The Trinity and the Kingdom of God*, (London: SCM Press, 1981), 38-39, 46, 106.

108. Von Balthasar also observes here that Moltmann "on several occasions . . .

warns the reader not to engage in polemics against the Neoplatonic doctrine of emanations" (ibid., 229; cf. *The Trinity and the Kingdom* 54, 113). We are told later that Moltmann "cannot envisage a God without the world" (*TD5*, 231). Although von Balthasar does not make this point here, he could have also argued that Moltmann's proclivity for ontological monism is made possible by his polemical rejection of monotheism. In what seems to be a clear case of the Gnostic dichotomy between the Old and New Covenants, Moltmann argues extensively that monotheism is an inherently heretical discourse that gives rise to religious authoritarianism and political oppression, and thus it must be rejected in favor of the grace and freedom made known in New Testament trinitarianism (Moltmann, *The Trinity and the Kingdom of God*, 129ff., 191-202). Therefore, it certainly would not have come as a surprise to von Balthasar in his reading of this text that Moltmann holds up Joachim of Fiore as the model for how monotheism can be "overcome" by trinitarianism (*The Trinity and the Kingdom of God*, 202-222).

109. *TD5*, 228-229.

110. See Moltmann, *The Trinity and the Kingdom of God*, 166, 107, 109. Von Balthasar had also noted earlier that, in contrast to Hegel, Moltmann takes the resurrection of Jesus "seriously" (*TD5*, 170).

111. See the footnote on *TD4*, 323. See also his discussion of Moltmann's claim that he does not conceive of the relationship of God and the world in a way that confuses them, as in pantheism. Von Balthasar then quotes a passage from this book that seems to put into question the seriousness of Moltmann's resistance to pantheism: "God the Spirit is also the spirit, the all-embracing atmosphere, the structure, the true content, the energy of the universe. . . . The evolution and the catastrophes of the universe are also the movement and the experience of the Spirit of creation" (*Gott in der Schöpfung* [Munich, 1985], 30; see *TL3*, 390).

112. *TD5*, 168.

113. *TD4*, 295.

114. For example, von Balthasar notes that Moltmann tries to fit Abraham Heschel's reflections on God's "pathos" into his own "system." But this cannot work, he explains, because "Heschel explicitly rejects any attempt to interpret the prophetic utterances in terms of Western metaphysics. . . . God's *pathos* has nothing whatever to do with any mythological suffering, dying and rising God. . . . Rather, it is his 'moral abhorrence' of the failure of his people (or of individuals) to respond to his covenant" (*TD4*, 344).

115. *TD5*, 168-74. In his theological aesthetics, von Balthasar brands Bloch's philosophy as a type of gnosticism that proves that "gnosis and atheism go together, and that they are in fact *the* alternative to Christian trinitarian theology" (*GL7*, 510).

116. *TD5*, 170.

117. Von Balthasar argues that Moltmann consistently "misinterprets genuine realized eschatology. The only content he will acknowledge in it is either 'mystical' (no doubt in Schweitzer's sense), enthusiastic (Paul asserts his theology of the Cross against the Corinthians) or, finally existential (Bultmann)" (*TD5*, 174).

118. Ibid., 171.

119. Ibid., 168.

120. Ibid., 174-75.

121. Ibid., 172.

122. *TD4*, 296.

123. *TD5*, 169.

124. Cf. ibid., 227.
125. *TD5*, 171-72; see also 180 n. 16.
126. Ibid., 180.
127. Ibid., 170.
128. Ibid., 170.
129. Ibid., 172.
130. See *TD4*, 323.
131. See *TD5*, 168-70. This last point about the church is, of course, both the presupposition and the implication of the first three conditions. Von Balthasar is following Henri de Lubac here. In the conclusion of *THdL* von Balthasar discusses de Lubac's book *La Posterité spirituelle de Joachim de Flore*. Von Balthasar points out that in this book de Lubac identifies Moltmann as an heir to Joachim's intellectual legacy. (De Lubac also associates him with Ernst Bloch.) As is the case for all Joachim's heirs, Moltmann must deal with the following question: "In the eyes of universal history, must the Church be understood as the next-to-last reality, the work of the second Person of the Trinity, just as creation and the Old Testament were the works of the first Person—a work that will be overtaken by an age of the Spirit, long-awaited, hoped for, and still to come? Or is she, as the one, holy Catholic and Apostolic Church, invested with the Spirit of the Father and the Son, the final and definitive reality, filled with internal potentialities that will unfurl across the ages, embracing them until the end?" (*THdL*, 124-25).

# Chapter VII

# Theodramatics and the Doxological Rule of Resistance

In the previous chapters I reviewed von Balthasar's criticisms of theologies he considers insufficiently resistant to hostile reinterpretation by modern Gnosticism. In this chapter I will broaden this discussion by examining the analogical resources he derives from dramatic theory for defending a *corpus triforme* theological system. I have already mentioned that he uses the theme of dramatic tension to interpret salvation history in terms of Irenaeus's distinction between true and false gnosis. Examining von Balthasar's other analogies between *corpus triforme* Christology and dramatic theory will shed additional light on the Irenaean assumptions shaping his assertion of specific norms in theology. Achieving clarity on this point is essential for creating the possibility of internal critique that measures von Balthasar's theology by the same standards he uses to evaluate other theologians. For example, does von Balthasar always successfully avoid confusion between his theological aesthetics and the "aesthetic myths" of Gnosticism opposed by Irenaeus? If one were to make a case that von Balthasar's theology is itself Gnostic (and Karl Rahner has suggested this[1]), or that it is at least guilty of insufficient resistance, then this case could only be made plausibly if one kept in mind how his use of analogies from dramatic theory theologically regulates his use of aesthetic analogies. Following this discussion I will sketch the doxological rule of resistance to Gnostic reinterpretations of Christianity implied by his deployment of dramatic theory in theology. This sketch will provide a synopsis of the internal logic of von Balthasar's theology. Whether or not he consistently follows his own logic is a question that I will raise in the last chapter.

## Theodramatic Theology Against Epic Gnosticism

Given that throughout the over 3,500 pages of *The Glory of the Lord* von Balthasar vigorously argued for the central importance of aesthetic

categories in theology, it is understandable that the reader might be per-
plexed when he shifts to the entirely new analogical genre of dramatic
theory in *Theo-Drama*. If the aesthetic categories of form and splendor
really function as adequate analogical indicators of sacramental paradox, why then does von Balthasar suddenly change analogical genres by
introducing dramatic theory into his theological project? Rather than
dealing directly with this question, many commentators have chosen to
evade it subtly by isolating a particular theme in *Theo-Drama* and then
arguing that dramatic theory in general does indeed provide an apt analogical point of entry for understanding it. A primary example of this
interpretive strategy can be seen in authors who isolate the theme of the
metaphysical unity between the transcendentals of the beautiful and the
good in *Theo-Drama*, and then argue—accurately if somewhat
vaguely—that for von Balthasar the dramatic action of the theater analogically indicates the need for Christian praxis in salvation history in
order to pursue the good.[2] Another, more directly theological candidate
for isolated treatment in such a strategy has been the theme of the relationship between human freedom and grace.[3] Certainly these themes are
extremely important in *Theo-Drama*, but neither alone nor together do
they provide a fully adequate explanation for the transition from aesthetic to dramatic categories. The first task of this chapter, therefore,
will involve clarifying the agenda of von Balthasar's project in theodramatics by showing how it both continues and develops his project in
theological aesthetics. I will contend in this chapter that an essentially
Irenaean theological agenda also guides von Balthasar's analogical
deployment of categories drawn from dramatic theory, holding his theodramatic approach together with his theological aesthetics in one common effort to retrieve a doxological theology of the *corpus triforme*.

There are several textual cues early in *Theo-Drama* to indicate that
von Balthasar assumes and uses an organic model to explain the transition from theological aesthetics to theodramatics. For example, in *TD1*
he asserts that theodramatic theology presupposes an existential and
aesthetic "pre-understanding" of life as inherently dramatic.[4] In *TD2*
von Balthasar describes the transition according to an organic four-stage
movement: (1) aesthetic form interprets itself to the contemplative
observer; (2) this self-interpretation expresses an intelligible word,
thereby opening up a world of meaning that is both illuminating and
alluring; (3) the world of meaning opened by the beautiful form non-
coercively calls upon its hearer to learn its language—that is, its ordered
pattern of meaning; (4) once the hearer has learned the aesthetic form's
language of meaning, she possesses the freedom to think and act out of
her new literacy; the hearer experiences the encounter with the self-

interpreting form as an election to a personal mission because the world of intelligibility opened by the form challenges the hearer to respond by ordering her life according to the form's pattern of meaning.[5] According to this organic model, contemplation and doxology are intrinsically connected with praxis because, as the theological aesthetics consistently attempted to show, a contemplative receptivity to the form is the condition for the possibility of an action, as well as the measure of this action's content and direction. The most concise statement of von Balthasar's commitment to an organic model comes when he asserts in *TD2* that "it is important to reflect on the way 'aesthetics' opens up to and moves across into 'dramatics,' even in the realm of intramundane phenomena."[6] He offers yet another example of the organic model a little later in this text when he explains that because the beautiful is teleologically oriented toward freedom and the good, it is also true that election to a personal mission is "latent" in aesthetic form.[7] He reiterates this point when he asserts that his task in *Theo-Drama* is simply to make explicit what was implicit in his theological aesthetics.[8] I contend, however, that this organic implicit-explicit model simplifies the meaning of the transition from theological aesthetics to theodramatics.

Von Balthasar offers another explanatory model to explain the union of his aesthetics and dramatics. I will call this model the dramatic organic model. This model grants a relative priority to the organic explanations present in *Theo-Drama*, but it is also distinct from the organic explanation because it is more sophisticated in its account of the differences between a pretheological and a theological movement from contemplation to action. If we look closely at how von Balthasar's organic explanation in *Theo-Drama* actually functions, then we will see three significant differences. First, the form under contemplation in theological aesthetics is the form of the incarnate Word and not simply an impersonal worldly form indifferent to the personal identities of those who contemplate it. *Theo-Drama* consistently works with the following theological aesthetic model: the eternal tripersonal God presents itself in the historical form of Jesus Christ, interpreting itself in this form as the mystery of the Father's Word of love to creation; this Word of love becomes meaningful to those who accept it and allow the Holy Spirit— who is the intelligible meaning proceeding freely from the love between Father and Son—to educate them into a free response. Second, as the first point implies, the issue is not for von Balthasar simply that a latent personal praxis is born fully mature out of contemplation of a form. Rather, contemplating the Christ-form gives birth to a praxis that undergoes a highly personal guidance and development under pedagogical guidance by the Trinity. Third, this personal development, this education into one's finite freedom by the Spirit, means that one is given a unique role to play on the stage of history. Unlike the latent praxis in any worldly form, therefore, the praxis that arises from contemplation of the Christ-form grants horizontal history absolute meaning as the indispensable site of salvation. One is not simply elected to a personal mission outside of any context, but instead one is elected to cooperation with Christ as he carries out the Father's plan to redeem the entire created temporal order. The more one cooperates with Christ in this mission, the more one is drawn back to contemplation of him as the primary and central historical agent of the Father's plan. As one is drawn to ever-deeper levels of contemplation, one is educated into ever-deeper levels of freedom and ever-more profound missions of love in the overall plan of salvation history. The organic model is not linear but circular, or perhaps a spiral in which one's contemplative understanding and worldly praxis develop together toward higher levels of wisdom and love. These three differences between the organic explanation and the dramatic organic explanation indicate that the organic model alone does not sufficiently account for the kind of strong Irenaean doctrine of providence von Balthasar wants to articulate in *Theo-Drama*. Once *The Glory of the Lord* sets in place the holistic aesthetic unity of revelation, grace, and faith, the task for von Balthasar in *Theo-Drama* is to show how the doxological unity of faith, hope, and love that follows from it is intrinsically related to the church's mission in salvation history. To really make the link between the revelation of divine love in history, on the one hand, and the unity of this revelation with grace and a developmental praxis of faith, on the other, von Balthasar relies on the more theologically sophisticated dramatic organic model.

Von Balthasar assumes throughout *Theo-Drama* that if theology attempted to work with aesthetic categories without opening out to dramatic theory, then it would be in danger of degenerating into an iconic, static, and purely contemplative theology. Although aesthetic categories have the potential to express the integration of contemplation and action (rapture and response) that occurs in the encounter with revelation, this potential needs to be activated through the use of complementary analogical categories.[9] In other words, von Balthasar is addressing the tendency toward abstraction in aesthetic discourse, a tendency he was also concerned with addressing throughout *The Glory of the Lord*. He is fully aware that aesthetic categories are in themselves unstable, hovering between the conflicting pull of an ethos of resignation and a practical ethos of response. It is because of this awareness that he can criticize the "aesthetic" when it becomes detached from the dramatic, yielding a decadent type of aesthetic theology that pretends to be concrete but in fact has only perception and no praxis.[10] Von Balthasar thus insists that aesthetic categories have only a *relative* adequacy in theology. In making his proposals for supplementing them with dramatic theory, he focuses his arguments on the themes of history, praxis, and the good. His goal is to gain for himself a measure of authority as a theologian committed to the antispeculative principle that praxis in the concrete realm of history must be the starting point for theological reflection. Establishing this authority, he believes, will allow him to outmaneuver theologies of praxis and history on their own territory. This will give the critical readers of *The Glory of the Lord* a new perspective on his theological project, one that will allow them to see more clearly the historical relevance of and political implications for Christian praxis that follow from a *corpus triforme* Christology.

In von Balthasar's theological aesthetics the purpose was to retrieve and repristinate a doxological understanding of divine mystery. *Theo-Drama* has the same goal. In both cases, a doxological understanding of divine mystery necessarily implies making the economy of salvation history theology's starting point and consistent object of concern. I will begin by discussing the theological vision informing von Balthasar's interpretation of dramatic theory. As I have been arguing, this vision is fundamentally agonistic: he uses dramatic theory in theology because he believes that the realm of history is an arena of conflict in which the church must struggle for its conception of the good in the midst of a situation of competition, hostility, and obstruction. In other words, for von Balthasar, dramatic theory functions not only as an analogical indicator of the need for Christian praxis in history but also as an indicator of the embattled nature and context of this praxis.[11] Therefore, the "theodrama" of history does not refer only to Christian action on the world stage but, more specifically, to the fact that this action occurs in the context of a competitive historical struggle between protagonists and antagonists over incommensurate symbolic systems, conflicting claims of absolute truth, and rival conceptions of the good. Von Balthasar's argument in *Theo-Drama* is therefore concerned with defending all three corollaries of *corpus triforme* Christology.

With regard to the second corollary, the unity of old and new covenants, the analogy of a "theater of the world" allows him to present history from creation to eschaton as one narrative of salvation history played before the eyes of the creator. This analogy involves applying the Irenaean promise-fulfillment schema to the "theater-of-the-world" image so that the trinitarian theodrama of history can be interpreted in terms of two basic "acts": the old and the new, the preparation and the completion, the preredemption and redemption. With this second modification, the incarnation of the Word in Jesus becomes illuminated as the axis of history, with all that comes before and after it being bathed in the light of the trinitarian metanarrative of history it reveals. In Irenaean terms, the interactions of all the various players throughout history receive meaning from their place in the overall trinitarian "rhythm" and "harmony" of history revealed in Christ.[12] A christocentric interpretation of the theater of the world also sees a coherent unity between the old and the new covenants in which the latter gives full meaning to the former.[13] Moreover, it sees the entire pre-Christian pagan world as a preparation for the light of trinitarian meaning fully bestowed in Christ.[14] The whole thrust of von Balthasar's argument here is that the theater-of-the-world analogy can be used as a theological weapon to defend the *corpus triforme* corollary of the unity of old and new covenants in salvation history from hostile reinterpretation in terms of epic theology.

The unity of the covenants, however, is also a unity in difference. Von Balthasar accounts for his difference by drawing an analogy between the incarnate Word's entry into history and the star actor's dramatic entry onto the stage. This analogy is theologically valuable because it preserves the unity of the covenants by indicating that history is a dramatic narrative. The analogy is useful because it also accounts for the difference between the first and second phases of the *corpus triforme* process. For example, the Word's entry into his human role in Jesus reveals for the first time that God is a Trinity. Von Balthasar explains that the Word's role in Jesus demonstrates for both the audience and the other actors that the dramatic action of salvation history is authored by the Father and directed by the Spirit. The analogy of role suggests another difference between the covenants. Von Balthasar argues that no human actor can identify with a role with the same degree of ontological unity-in-difference as the fully divine Word identifies with his fully human role.[15] This point allows von Balthasar to quantitatively distinguish Jesus and the Jewish prophets. The Word's role in the drama of salvation history is to disappear so totally into his role that the trinitarian love of creation is revealed in his performance, which paradoxically exposes Jesus as the divine Son acting out a role assigned by the Father. Moreover, analogically interpreting Jesus' mission as part of a larger trinitarian play on the world stage allows Christians to see their lives as roles assigned by God. Thus, von Balthasar argues, in coming to this understanding of history as a "world stage," Christians find that they are not merely puppets of the gods but instead free actors who are given roles within the wider trinitarian drama. This illuminates the basic dividing line between true and false gnosis: true gnosis focuses on Christ and thus sees history as a monotheistic-trinitarian drama, whereas false gnosis is not christocentric and hence lacks a truly dramatic perspective on history.

Von Balthasar's use of dramatic theory is also directed toward defending the first corollary of the *corpus triforme*, the unity of creation and redemption. In *The Glory of the Lord*, he articulated this corollary of *corpus triforme* Christology in terms of the unity of form and splendor, which expressed the sacramental unity of finite particularity and non-finite universal meaning. In *Theo-Drama* von Balthasar uses categories drawn from dramatic theory to expand the capacities of the aesthetic form-splendor model. This expansion is evident not only in Christology (with the Christ-form read as a dramatic theatrical form) but also in anthropology. The limited time-frame of a drama performed on stage analogically indicates that human life must be lived in the shadow of death and that therefore it is necessary to decide about how to direct one's temporal existence.[16] The analogy of a dramatic "role" has not only christological but also anthropological relevance. A dramatic role, a limited part played for a particular narrative purpose but yet possessing significance for the overall drama, indicates that the finite life of an individual or of a particular people can nevertheless disclose meaning that has relevance for the whole of history.[17] This yields a sense of real freedom for the actors in history. Von Balthasar defines human nature as free participation in the Word's role in obedience to the Father's script and the Spirit's direction. In following the lead of the Word and playing their own God-given roles, therefore, human persons are enabled to achieve their own humanity. Becoming human thus means turning away from slavery to impersonal fate and turning toward Christ, who reveals a transcendent author and director involved in creation to guide humans into their finite freedom. Obviously, then, von Balthasar strictly regulates his analogies from dramatic theory with a monotheistic trinitarianism in which Christ is both the exclusive point of divine immanence and the site of God's Otherness. In this sense, a stage play mirrors the sacramental potential of creaturely human existence to mediate the redemptive light of absolute and eternal meaning. Through carrying out divinely appointed missions in the midst of ambiguous temporal situations, individuals and communities become sacramental forms with meaning for all of salvation history. In von Balthasar's theodramatic Christology, the role of Jesus Christ on the world stage transforms his finite existence into a sacramental form revealing the absolute meaning of history. Insofar as the human institution of the church shares in the Christ-form, its sacramental forms also reveal this absolute meaning.

It is important, however, to realize that von Balthasar is not simply suggesting that finite temporal reality is simply one possible way to mediate meaning. Rather, his point is that just as dramatic meaning comes only through the actual narrative performance of roles on the stage—there is no supplementary dramatic intelligibility gained by peering behind the stage or beyond the actors' roles—so too eternal absolute meaning is accessible to us in history only through the missions of individuals and communities on the world stage. This is the direct implication of the unity of creation and redemption in *corpus triforme* Christology: no matter how tempting it may be to bypass the ambiguities of the finite, material, bodily, and temporal in favor of a purely spiritual and eternal understanding of redemption, humans have no access to spiritual meaning and truth except as these are embodied by the incarnate Christ's redemptive role on the stage of creation. The analogy of dramatic role provides a resource for analogically indicating that the vertical gift of redemption in the Christ-event does not supersede humanity's embodied nature or creation's horizontal history but rather irradiates them with spiritual meaning by glorifying the full nature of created human persons, enabling them to glorify God in return by sharing in Christ's temporal mission of redemption.[18]

Von Balthasar also deploys the dramatic categories of author, actor, and director in order to connect a theology of history with theology of creation.[19] A theodramatic interpretation of the unity of the old and new covenants presupposes a trinitarian understanding of Christ's mission in salvation history. This is the reason why von Balthasar insists on maintaining the unity of creation and redemption. Jesus' earthly life indicates that he knew his role in the Father's plan to glorify creation— that is, the script for salvation history[20]—and he knew that this role was to be the central actor bringing the Father's doxological vision "from above" to life on the world stage. This Christology allows von Balthasar to articulate his recapitulation Christology in which Christ mediates trinitarian divine freedom "from above" to creatures from within their own bodily and finite nature, thereby redeeming them "from below" by empowering them to become actors freely playing divinely assigned roles on the world stage. Playing such a role means that believers carry out their own divinely given personal missions in history through their participation in Christ's own mission from the Father. This empowerment into a role/mission implies the aesthetic dynamic of being enraptured by a beautiful form and transported out of the private sphere of the self. In the theodrama of history, the incarnate Word's performance is captivating precisely because it models the doxological nature of creaturely existence, thereby drawing believers into a pattern of existence in which they embody in their own lives the unique roles that the Father has assigned them from before creation.[21] This dynamic is guided by the

Spirit, the "director" of the theodrama. But in order to avoid misunderstandings about the relationship of Christology and pneumatology on this point, it is necessary to underline how important the primacy of a sacramental christocentrism is in von Balthasar's thinking.

Von Balthasar argues in his excursus on *Against Heresies* that Irenaeus's soteriology is strongly committed to both an anthropology of human body-soul unity and a Christology that emphasizes Christ's full-bodily humanity as the site of the invisible Father's self-expression in creation. It is precisely this emphasis that leads Irenaeus to interpret redemption in terms of the divine Word's full recapitulation of human finitude and death. For Irenaeus, Christ is able to communicate the transcendent and omnipotent love of the Father only by undergoing suffering and death. The obedience of the Son in fully recapitulating human reality gives the Father the opportunity to resurrect him, thereby revealing that the love of God is able to heal and perfect the created order because it is stronger than even the power of death. As von Balthasar reads it, the starting point for Irenaeus's doxological theology is clear: a recapitulation Christology maintains that only the revelation of infinite love in the visible Christ-form redeems human persons by liberating them into their finite freedom as embodied souls created with a unique personal identity. This liberation occurs through playing one's own unique role in Christ's redemptive mission of perfecting the entire created, temporal order.[22] The Spirit is never found a priori lying latent in human nature; in Irenaeus's logic, the a priori presence of the Spirit in human nature would imply that humans are themselves divine, a position he rejects. Von Balthasar emphasizes this aspect of Irenaeus's theology, contending that he consistently argues for the indispensable unity of the sacramental Christ-form and the Spirit. For Irenaeus, redemption does mean receiving the "gift of freedom" in the Holy Spirit, but this freedom does not mean being liberated from the aesthetic power of the Christ-form. On the contrary, for Irenaeus, the gift of the Holy Spirit facilitates "our assimilation to the Son's attitude toward the Father, namely, elasticity in his hands, . . . childlikeness, . . . [and] simplicity," all of which Irenaeus contrasts with "presumptuous Gnostic theology."[23] Irenaeus is resisting the belief that humans can "deduce God" or speculatively construct "some overall totality" capable of embracing both the divine and the nondivine.[24] On the contrary, the totality of religious meaning in Christ can only be known through an a posteriori contemplative receptivity that begins with the epistemic humility proper to creatures in their relationship with the creator. This is why von Balthasar uses the compound term "Christ-Spirit" in describing Irenaeus's highly christocentric pneumatology.[25]

It is also important to recognize that von Balthasar does not believe that Irenaeus is arbitrary or idiosyncratic in insisting that humans have no access to the Holy Spirit prior to or independent of the Christ-form. On the contrary, Irenaeus's christocentric pneumatology is a direct consequence of his commitment to the biblical notion of a "radical opposition between the Creator-being and the created being."[26] If creatures are to have any chance of knowing God, then God must take on a creaturely form. Although God can become human, humans cannot make themselves divine—if they could, they would not need redemption. Hence humanity is radically dependent on God for redemption, a redemption, moreover, that respects their nature as finite, sensory, and temporal. Like most other church fathers, Irenaeus interprets the biblical theologoumenon of the radical opposition between creator and creature in terms of a doctrine of creation out of nothing.[27] Only a theology of creation out of nothing can maintain, without running the risk of degenerating into a type of pantheistic monism and divine/cosmic determinism, that redemption is a pure gift of grace that perfects the finite, temporal order in general and creaturely personhood and freedom in particular.[28] Following Irenaeus's doxological theology on this point, in his theodramatic hermeneutics, von Balthasar describes the Christian system of meaning in terms of its opposition to the totalizing perspective offered in monistic systems. Monism's totalizing perspective fails to meet a doxological standard because it wrongly assumes that one can stand above the interaction between God and humanity and rationally describe it as a "system that can be viewed and grasped as a whole."[29] This assumption clearly contradicts Irenaeus's insistence on epistemic humility and contemplative receptivity to the incarnate Christ. The implication for a theodramatic theology of history is that knowing the trinitarian metanarrative necessarily requires forfeiting any pretense to having a reference point outside the frame of history, and instead accepting the "paradox" that in the "contingent fact" of the incarnation of the Logos in Jesus "the sphere of the eternal touches the temporal sphere, and this point alone can spread meaning that is ultimate. . . ."[30] For Irenaeus, this christocentric perspective allows one to realize that the divine belongs to a completely different ontological order than creation, and thus that "it is only in the successive revelation of the Word, up to his incarnation, that man learns who God really is," namely, infinite, free, uncreated, and personal.[31] Following Irenaeus on this point, von Balthasar contends that it is only in the revelation of this ontological difference between God and creation that humans learn the truth about their own nature as finite, free, and personal creatures dependent on God for their very existence.[32]

This point raises the question of how *corpus triforme* Christology understands the pre-Christian religious world. Von Balthasar does not think that before Christ pagan antiquity was completely without religious truth. Rather, he thinks the incarnation recontextualizes its truth within a monotheistic and trinitarian theology in which the freedom of human persons is no longer threatened by cosmic determinism.[33] This ultimately means that the pagan cosmos is resacralized within the sacramentality of Christ's risen body, the church. Von Balthasar explains this point as follows:

> Bodily Resurrection and Ascension are not dis-incarnation but a transformation of the entire human form, spirit and body, into a pneumatic mode of existence. The divine Pneuma is the power behind this transformation, making sure that the definitive descent of the Word becomes sacramental, for all times. This is what comes about in the bodily life of the Church, effected by the personal Incarnation of the Word. In virtue of his physical nature, the Son can fashion mankind as his 'body' (1 Cor 12:27) by means of his Eucharist (1 Cor 10:16f.): he pours his 'fullness' into a vessel, which is formed by this very act of pouring (Eph 1:23). Thus the movement toward enfleshment is completed by becoming ecclesial, and even cosmic. . . .[34]

Therefore, for von Balthasar (following Irenaeus), the pneumatic and sacramental unity of "Christ-Spirit" and the church completes the synthesis of the *corpus triforme* system of meaning. Again, this tight unity of Christology and pneumatology is necessary in order to avoid a highly privatized conception of redemption in which each individual is redeemed solely through the indwelling of the Spirit within his or her own soul. On the contrary, von Balthasar follows Irenaeus's lead in holding that redemption in Christ blossoms into harmonious social communion. In redeeming the created order, Christ redeems the social relationships among creatures, because these relationships are intrinsic to created human nature. In his theodramatic hermeneutics, von Balthasar articulates this ecclesial understanding of redemption in terms of the historical process of the church's receiving and enfleshing of the Word in its biblical canon and sacramental life. This process is inherently concerned with the nonspeculative personal interactions of the tripersonal God and personal human creatures on the world stage. Von Balthasar uses the term *communio* to describe this dramatic interaction, a word he also uses with reference to Irenaeus's understanding of the unity between the Christ-Spirit and the church.[35] *Communio* implies for von Balthasar that the historical totality of the Christ-form interprets itself through the Spirit in the historical context of the church, and therefore all true knowledge of God is inherently connected with personal participation in the "eucharistic-ecclesial Body" of Christ as it plays its role in the theodrama of history.[36] Through this participation in Christ's historical mission, the church is able to reflect his glory into the world.[37] In other words, because the church is a sacramental community with a distinct historical mission, it is a living element of the *corpus triforme* with a direct stake in maintaining the unity of salvation history, and the unity of creation and redemption.

Playing its assigned role in the *corpus triforme* Christology requires that the church incarnate a christocentric doxological ethos in creation. This incarnational mission in the theodrama of history requires that the church work, through its sacramental, eucharistic praxis, to open each of its members to the direction of the Holy Spirit.[38] The Holy Spirit is the director who trains believers in receptivity to Christ, and in doing so guides them into the freedom of playing their own unique roles in the theater of the world.[39] In receiving Christ's grace and playing the role it assigns, von Balthasar argues, an individual is liberated into her created nature and becomes a "theological person."[40] Further, insofar as one becomes a "theological person" under the direction of the Spirit of the risen Christ, one also becomes a *homo ecclesiasticus*, a unique person with a distinct role to play in the ecclesial community's efforts to transform the entire created order into a doxological liturgy of worship and justice.[41] In other words, there is a directly proportional relationship between one's growth into the uniqueness of one's personal identity and one's participation in the ecclesial community. The individual is given a uniqueness that comes from the absolute uniqueness of God and Christ; it cannot be deduced from the community or found there antecedently, although the community can count on this uniqueness as something that enriches it and is specifically designed for it.[42] This point makes it clear that for von Balthasar the church nurtures both the individual's direct encounter with Christ and the communal context of such encounters. This is why he believes that the singular mark of the church's doxological and trinitarian character is that the individual and the community are neither set in opposition nor merged into an identity, but instead are enabled to exist in a relationship of mutually affirming self-giving and receiving. This harmonious relationship between individual and community is guided and contextualized by the Christ-form and never by the Spirit alone, independent of the ecclesial community or the other elements of the incarnate *corpus triforme*. This is because it is primarily the incarnate Christ—and not solely the Spirit—who is, in von Balthasar's terms, "the matrix of all possible dramas."[43]

As the site of the *corpus triforme* of the risen Christ, the church draws human persons into a sacramental drama of redemption that is eucharistic and ecclesial.[44] Thus Irenaeus's opposition to sectarian elitism and emphasis on the public nature of the church is also highly significant for von Balthasar's own ecclesiology.[45] This commitment to the visible, sacramental church guides the discussion of dramatic theory in *TD1*, where von Balthasar uses terms such as "beholding" and "contemplative" to refer to the audience's relationship to the aesthetic form of a theatrical drama.[46] The audience's nonneutral, contemplative awareness forms a "communion" between the author's vision, the actor's visible embodiment of the vision on the stage, and the audience's cooperation in the presentation of the vision.[47] Unlike the audience at the theater, however, the audience of the theodrama of salvation history "participate" in the play through the guidance of the Spirit, who calls them out of their spectator positions and onto the stage. Von Balthasar's use of dramatic theory here anticipates later discussions in *Theo-Drama* of an ecclesiology in which the director Spirit trains the audience members of the church to overcome the fear, horror, and grief that results from witnessing the reality of tragedy on the world stage—a reality that often gives rise to an ethos of resignation—and instead to open themselves to being struck and enraptured by the divine mystery revealed in Christ's incarnation, cross, and resurrection. In being led by the Spirit into contemplation of the entire *corpus triforme*, believers are thereby led into the paschal mystery, where they learn that creation has been redeemed from the "pitiless destiny" of fate, and they are now free to live in the "acting area" within history opened by Christ.[48]

This "acting area" is also an arena of conflict. As I explained in both chapter 1 and chapter 5, von Balthasar believes that over the course of time there is an increasing polarization between the church and its enemies that eventually becomes a full "theodramatic war." This war results from the fact that the more the church lives in the "acting area" made possible by the overall aesthetic power of the *corpus triforme*, the more it incarnates a christocentric doxological ethos in creation, thus provoking fierce opposition from antidoxological, anti-incarnational forces.

### The Doxological Rule of Resistance

This section will outline six basic theological principles that constitute von Balthasar's doxological rule of resistance. All of the rule's content has already been discussed in terms of his analogical use of the aesthetic categories of form and splendor and his extensive use of dramatic theory. The doxological rule, however, is distinct from the *corpus triforme* system in the specificity of its theological function. In an agonistic historical context, the constructive christological proposal of the *corpus triforme* system necessarily generates a rule of resistance that proscriptively and prescriptively governs theological discourse to prevent it from deviating from the *corpus triforme* standard. This section summarizes the doxological rule in terms of six theological principles. Von Balthasar himself does not explicitly formulate a rule of resistance in these terms. But the content of the rule formulated here does circulate below the surface of his first order discourse of constructive theological proposals for *corpus triforme* Christology. When von Balthasar is positively describing Christianity's agonistic historical context, this first order discourse spawns a second order discourse of negative principles and methodological admonitions to prevent theological aberrations from the positive norm. A clear example of this is his statement of principles and methods in his "theodramatic hermeneutics."[49] Working from this discussion, as well as from my earlier discussions of related themes, I will distill and delineate six theological principles that von Balthasar presupposes are necessary for maintaining Christianity's integrity and identity in its rivalry with Gnostic discourse. The first two are intrinsic to the notion of aesthetic form that is at the basis of *corpus triforme* theology. These two principles are, therefore, regulative of the remaining four principles of the doxological rule. The remaining four principles, as I will show, are derived from each of the three corollaries of the *corpus triforme* system.

The first principle is that a philosophically derived negative theology must not be allowed to supplant the revelation of supernatural mystery in Christ.[50] A theological aesthetics centered on the totality of the *corpus triforme* must always have priority over all areas of theology, including, especially, the theology of vertical divine transcendence. This must be the case, von Balthasar believes, because the historical "fact" of the incarnation is the deepest and most permanent source of infinite divine mystery in the finite order.[51] There are two theological assumptions at work here: (1) the transcendent creator God of Jewish monotheism is the same God who became fully incarnate in Jesus Christ, and (2) humans have no access to this transcendent creator God other than the incarnate Christ. Therefore, contrary to philosophical theories of transcendent mystery, theology can only speak of divine transcendence and mystery insofar as it contemplates the capacious reality of the *corpus triforme*. Therefore, von Balthasar believes that if a theology is to succeed in genuinely focusing on divine mystery, it must be christocentric in a distinctively contemplative (i.e., not speculative) sense.

The second principle of the doxological rule of resistance is that theologians must allow God's self-revelation in Jesus Christ to interpret itself in the lives of believers through the work Holy Spirit.[52] The full content of the Christ-form is supplied by the "totality principle" of the incarnation; the Christ-form interprets itself as the *corpus triforme*.[53] This second principle of the doxological rule is the key to understanding both von Balthasar's resistance to speculative reinterpretations of Christianity and his belief that contemporary Christian theology has shown insufficient resistance to these reinterpretations. Even if modern theologians have not consciously affirmed modern Gnosticism's willed deviance from the *corpus triforme* standard, von Balthasar worries that they have internalized, to one degree or another, Gnostic suspicions about the aesthetic principle that Christ will interpret himself.[54] As a corrective to this internalization, he insistently advocates that contemporary theology unify both intellectual reflection and spiritual contemplation, and historical-critical exegesis and dogmatics.[55] An important implication of this point is that von Balthasar rules out what he calls an "integralist or fundamentalist" conception of revelation: the primary content of revelation cannot be confused with a list of propositions to be believed or moral norms to be lived, however valid these may be in themselves as pointers to revelation.[56] Revelation interprets itself in the holiness of a personal life that is transparent to divine love, and thus cannot simply be reduced to dogmas or moral rules.

The third principle of the doxological rule of resistance is derived from the second corollary of the *corpus triforme*. The unity of the two covenants lies primarily in their monotheistic, christocentric understanding of the God-world relationship. The third principle, therefore, holds that Christian theology must always maintain that the eternal divine realm and the temporal created realm are separated by an absolute ontological gap, and this absolute gap is bridged but not erased by Christ's mission of redemption in salvation history. In Christ, the eternal both participates in time and opens itself to participation by temporal creatures; the meaning of salvation in Christ is the divinization of creation through the mutual indwelling of God and creation.[57] In other words, the incarnate Word interprets itself through the Spirit as the ontologically asymmetrical yet mutual glorification of time and eternity, finitude and the infinite, and the human and the divine. Irenaeus is the primary source for von Balthasar's thinking on this point. In this doxological approach, there is a directly (and not inversely) proportional relationship between a theology focused on the temporal created order and one focused on the eternal God: the more deeply one understands the revelation of God's eternal, tripersonal inner life in the temporal Christ-form, the more deeply one comprehends the meaning of human personhood, finitude, and history. This third doxological principle, therefore, is the uniting of *The Glory of the Lord*'s sacramental theology of revelation, *Theo-Drama*'s theology of salvation history, and *Theologik*'s trinitarian pneumatology in a common resistance to Gnostic rationalism. In refusing biblical monotheism, Gnostic "epic" theology will not allow a theocentric perspective to coexist in union with a cosmocentric or an anthropocentric perspective; in epic theology, either God is totally absorbed into the cosmos or the human soul, or God is totally banished from nature and human religiosity. In either case, epic theology inevitably negates Christianity's understanding of salvation as the asymmetrical yet mutual exchange of love between a free, personal God and free, personal beings created in God's image. The third principle, therefore, summarizes von Balthasar's resistance throughout the entire trilogy to this epic either/or perspective.

The fourth principle of the doxological rule of resistance is derived from the first corollary of the *corpus triforme*. In the unity of creation and redemption, the dynamism of finite freedom is liberated and perfected through its participation in the ever-greater mystery of God.[58] The fourth principle, therefore, is the principle of the "ever-greater."[59] Von Balthasar also refers to this idea as the "Johannine comparative." In John's Gospel, he argues, believers are drawn forward by the alluring and glorious mystery of Christ into "ever-greater" levels of spiritual understanding. For John, the glory of Christ's mystery neither compels the intellect nor coerces the will. Instead, the glory of the divine love in Christ continually fascinates and draws one toward a deeper comprehension of the depths of divine mystery, and hence toward a deeper experience of freedom in allowing one's self to be drawn into God. "In John we find two things at the same time: a relentlessness, which, just where the highest point seems to have been reached, directs our attention to an even higher region; and a great calm, which regards this 'greater' dimension (capable of infinite upward expansion) as the natural presupposition of the manifested *Gestalt*, indeed, as the latter's own inner form."[60] This principle of the "ever-greater" illustrates that deviance is not determined by the wide scope of a particular theological claim; there is no predetermined line beyond which a claim can be accused of saying "too much." The standard for measuring the legitimacy of theological claims is qualitative not quantitative. A question he asks of any theological claim (no matter how expansive or restrictive) is whether it is authentically rooted in the spiritual dynamic of contemplative faith or whether it is based only on an exclusively cognitive understanding. If a theological claim proceeds from contemplative participation in the ever-greater mystery of Christ, von Balthasar is willing to ratify it, even if it goes beyond what contemporary academic theologians consider the boundaries of legitimate theological discourse.

The fifth principle of the doxological rule of resistance is also derived from the unity of creation and redemption. According to this principle, theology must recognize and affirm the free praxis of faith that results from contemplation of and desire for the ever-greater mystery of the *corpus triforme*.[61] Any theology that advocates an exclusively contemplative ethos subverts the supernatural dynamism of human faith because it aborts the concrete works of love that flow from authentic contemplation. The synthesis of faith and love, contemplation and action, is the outward sign that one is accessing deeper levels of the ever-greater mystery of God. This principle is the logical conclusion of von Balthasar's insistence that neutrality impedes genuine spiritual understanding.[62] As I argued in earlier chapters, by privileging praxis in theology, he believes he is continuing Irenaeus's practice of correlating religious knowledge with freedom rather than with propositional statements or metaphysical speculation. He believes no form of worldly beauty can generate a doxological praxis capable of sustaining itself in the face of wickedness, tragedy, and death. Only the presence of absolute divine love in Christ can give humanity hope, and hence the ability to overcome an ethos of resignation.[63] The internal logic of the Christ-form, therefore, cannot be defined by a theory, but rather it must be lived to be understood. Living this internal logic implies a divine pedagogy in which one is trained by divine love into ever-deeper levels of finite freedom, and thus into ever-deeper levels of practical love for others. This point is the basis for von Balthasar's conviction that holiness must be a primary factor in evaluating the legitimacy of any theological claim.[64]

The sixth principle of the doxological rule of resistance is derived from the third corollary of the *corpus triforme*, namely, the unity of Christ and church. According to this principle, any legitimate Christian theology or praxis must originate in the context of the church and be fully accountable to its historical mission. Von Balthasar believes that the church's mission in history is to bring the entire world under the mystagogical guidance of the Father's "two hands," the Son and the Spirit.[65] It is extremely important for him that this mission be understood in universal terms because otherwise the prior five principles could be misinterpreted as fostering an esoteric, elitist, and sectarian religiosity. In both rejecting neutrality and insisting on the public nature of theology and praxis, von Balthasar is following Irenaeus, for whom the church is an "esoteric mystery" while at the same time "the most public and anti-sectarian body known to history."[66] The paradoxical public esotericism of the church results from the self-interpreting nature of trinitarian revelation. The self-interpretation of the Word through the Spirit does not occur in a vacuum—it occurs in particular times and places through the lives of receptive believers who allow themselves to be formed by participation in Christ's paschal mystery. Therefore the church must actively live out its faith through works of love in the midst of human suffering and injustice, thereby challenging the dehumanizing forces of human sin with theological hope focused on Christ. Hence if the church's activity of challenging dehumanizing forces is to have any degree of efficacy, it must maintain its own constant openness to the Holy Spirit's guidance and initiate others into this openness.[67]

## Notes

1. Rahner has remarked that "there is a modern tendency (I do not want to say theory but nevertheless a tendency) as much with Balthasar as with Adrienne von Speyr (naturally more with the latter), but also independent from them with Molt-mann, which conceives of a theology of the death of God, which seems to me to be basically gnostic. Said rather primitively, to become extracted from my dirt and mess and my doubt, it is of no use if God—to put it crudely—is just as dirty" (Karl Rahner, *Im Gespräch* 1, 245–46; quoted in Eamonn Conway, *The Anonymous Christian—A Relativized Christianity?* [Frankfurt: Peter Lang, 1993], 128).

2. This is the approach Angelo Scola takes in his book *Hans Urs von Balthasar: A Theological Style* (Grand Rapids, Mich.: Eerdmans, 1995). Scola focuses attention on *Theo-Drama*'s argument that the ecstasy inherent to the encounter with Beauty leads one into a life of active commitment to Good (see pp. 40–42).

3. Edward Oakes in *Pattern of Redemption* proposes this explanation for the deployment of dramatic categories in *Theo-Drama*. Oakes contends that von Balthasar is attempting to force a "paradigm shift" in the way theologians deal with the thorny problem of the relationship between grace and free will (cf. 217ff.). Oakes also rightly recognizes that in this "paradigm shift" von Balthasar is "building on the foundation he laid in the Aesthetics" (218). However, Oakes's dual desire to emphasize the uniqueness of von Balthasar's approach and to characterize him as a critic of patristic theology (at one point Oakes asserts that von Balthasar's theology can be read as "a startlingly anti-patristic polemic"; cf. 109) obscures his ability to recognize that von Balthasar's perspective is neither novel nor antipatristic but rather is grounded in a particular strand of patristic thought, a strand whose progenitor is Irenaeus.

4. *TD1*, 17.

5. *TD2*, 21–37. Von Balthasar summarizes this movement from contemplation of the beautiful to responsive action as follows: "The power of aesthetic expression is never an overwhelming power but one that liberates. If we lack receptivity to it, we can blindly pass by the most magnificent work of art. All the same, its power is greater than the kind of power that can put people in chains; it does not fetter, it grants freedom. It illuminates, in itself and in the man who encounters it, the realm of the transcendent word and hence of all meaning, the realm of an infinite dialogue. But, again, this dialogue does not consist primarily of formulated words but in the confrontation and communing of lives. What speaks in the work of art cannot, indeed, directly impart this same language to the recipient. But if he does not know this language, it *is* possible for him to learn it through diligence and practice. The work's freedom can educate us to the freedom of seeing and responding" (*TD2*, 29).

6. *TD2*, 23.

7. Ibid., 31. Von Balthasar briefly outlines this point as follows: "God only shows himself to someone, only enraptures him, in order to commission him. Where this is not taken seriously, where the aesthetic fails to reveal the ethical that lies within it, such rapture is degraded to a prettifying excuse (*"ravissant"*). Where a thing of beauty is really and radically beheld, freedom too is radically opened up, and decision can take place" (31).

8. Ibid., 35. Von Balthasar expands on this assertion by observing that "in the real Christian life, dramatically lived out, there is no moment of pure orthodoxy distinct from and prior to orthopraxy. 'Doxy,' rather, is simply an internal factor in the transition from divine to human 'praxis,' in the realm of christological dramatic action" (68–69). Along these lines, he adds that "by an inner necessity, the 'aesthetic' form tends directly toward the dramatic" (ibid., 77).

9. If theology remained only in the aesthetic plane, he insists, there is a danger that its categories would become essentialist and thus "cause the picture of Christ to ossify into an icon" (ibid., 21).

10. "Thus it is a basic Christian requirement that existence should represent itself dramatically. . . . We can say, 'Lord, Lord!' in the depths of spirituality and mysticism, we can 'eat and drink with him' sacramentally, but it is all in vain if we do not carry out the will of our heavenly Father. . . . Neither faith, contemplation nor kerygma can dispense us from *action*" (*TD1*, 22).

11. See, for example, Marc Ouellet, "The Message of Balthasar's Theology to Modern Theology" (*Communio* 23/2 [Summer 1996]: 270–99). Ouellet rightly argues that *Theo-Drama* offers the following "message" to modern theology: God's absolute love is "supremely alive above history but [also] supremely engaged in the vicissitudes of this history of salvation" (298). However, although formally correct, Ouellet's interpretation of *Theo-Drama* has abstracted its "message" from its context in von Balthasar's wider contention that the church must engage in a dramatic struggle on behalf of these truths against hostile and rival systems of meaning that seek to deny and/or subvert them.

12. See *GL2*, 60–62, 66, 71, 73, 76–77, 82. Von Balthasar essentially repeats this discussion of Irenaeus in his excursus on *Against Heresies* (*TD2* 147–49).

13. Cf. *TD2*, 251; *TD3*, 361ff.

14. See *TD4*, 443–44.

15. Ibid.; *TD1*, 292–96.

16. Cf. *TD1*, 344–45.

17. Ibid., 250–251.

18. See ibid., 190, 256, 344–45; *TD3*, 527ff.

19. Von Balthasar contends that the unity of the author, actor, and director in dramatic theory is "a perfect metaphor for the economic Trinity in the theo-drama" (*TD3*, 532). On the working out of this trinitarian analogy between author, actor, and director in his interpretation of dramatic theory, see *TD1*, 268–305.

20. The "script" for salvation history is not the letter of Scripture (*TD2*, 109–15) but rather God's plan for the glorification of creation from before the beginning of time. According to von Balthasar, the content of this script is described in the first chapter of Ephesians (see *GL7*, 161, 178, 282–83, 392–93, 397, 405). This chapter also receives a great deal of attention in *Theo-Drama* as the "script" of salvation history. In this script, all creatures were created through the eternal Word from before the creation of the world, and hence all human creatures find their true identity in and through the Word's incarnation and temporal mission. Cf. *TD2*, 21, 50, 88, 89, 118, 266, 277, 279, 303, 308, 344, 412–13; *TD3*, 39 and 157.

21. Von Balthasar holds that in the theodrama of salvation history, Christ "is not only the main character but the model for all other actors and the one who gives them their own identity as characters" (*TD3*, 201; cf. also 230–82, 525–35).

22. *TD2*, 142–44.

23. Ibid., 144.

24. Ibid., 142.

25. Ibid., 148.

26. Ibid., 142.

27. "The (essentially unrefined) formula 'creation out of nothing' has been current since the first Christian centuries. In order to express the same thing in a positive way, some of the Fathers tried to say that the divine act of will is the 'substance out of which' created things were made. Thus Irenaeus: '*substantia omnium voluntas ejus*' (*AH* 2.30.9)" (*TD2*, 264–65).

28. Von Balthasar explains that the concrete meaning of humanity's glorification in Irenaeus's theology is that Christ, by revealing the Father's love, redeems by liberating human persons into their own finite freedom, a liberation that works by "persuasion" and never by "compulsion" (*TD2*, 149). This central theme of theodramatic hermeneutics receives further development in *TD2*. In a discussion of the effort of patristic theology to defend the Christian notion of finite freedom against "the determinism and fatalism of the ancient world," von Balthasar elaborates on this point (and further signals its proximity to his own position) by singling out Irenaeus as the progenitor of the baseline patristic position on the relationship between finite and infinite freedom. He quotes from Irenaeus, *Against Heresies,* arguing that the human person was "created in autonomy (*idian exousian*) from the beginning . . . so that he can follow God's counsel (*gnomê*) freely, without compulsion (*AH* IV, 37, 1)" (215, 216). He then adds that for Irenaeus once humanity has been given its own finite freedom, infinite freedom will not exercise coercion over it because "it is the mark of infinite freedom that it does not use force." This conclusion leads to what von Balthasar refers to as one of Irenaeus's favorite pedagogical themes, namely, that God allows the misuse of finite freedom so humans can learn that their ultimate fulfillment can come only from following God's guidance. In Irenaeus's pedagogical doctrine of God's loving forbearance, von Balthasar continues, "redemption came so late in history [because] man's experience needed time to ripen (IV, 38, 1–4)" (217). It seems clear that von Balthasar spends a great deal of time exegeting this Irenaean theme of providential guidance precisely because it is one of his own favorite theological themes, as is evident later in *TD2* when he offers his own theology of "infinite freedom" working to "facilitate finite freedom" (*TD2*, 260–71).

29. *TD2*, 115. These rational descriptions usually take the form of highly sophisticated but closed and nondramatic systems of cosmological and/or anthropological meaning. Cf. 115, 119, 125.

30. Ibid.

31. Ibid., 143.

32. Cf. ibid., 399–400.

33. See *TD4*, 475; cf. 401, 443–44. In *TD2* he contends that in biblical religion, God has "dedivinized nature" so that humanity will not turn away from God and toward images of God or toward itself. Christ alone is the now image of God for us (417).

34. *TD2*, 412. For Irenaeus too, von Balthasar notes, the church is a "pneumatic and institutional" unity of universal and concrete, a "vessel" into which Christ pours his resurrected human body, thereby renewing this vessel throughout history (140, 148).

35. Ibid., 127–28, 148.

36. Ibid., 101, 112.

37. Ibid., 126.

38. *TD3*, 527.

39. Cf. *TD1*, 298ff.; *TD3*, 533–34.

40. Von Balthasar argues that "the individual who receives the Word acquires a new quality: he becomes a *unique person*. This category only comes to light in the biblical-Christian dispensation. . . . The 'person' only shines forth in the individual where the absolute Unique God bestows an equally unique name on him (unique because it is chosen by God), a 'new name which no one knows except him who receives it' (Rev 2:17)" (*TD2*, 402).

41. Ibid.; cf. 402ff.

42. Ibid., 414–15.

43. *TD3*, 162.

44. *TD2*, 409–10.

45. "The contrast between the secret tradition of the Gnostics (secret and therefore uncontrollable and arbitrary) and the public character of the church—in the provable apostolic succession and the exposition of the faith given by the bishops and presbyter—is absolutely fundamental for Irenaeus" (*SI*, 10–11).

46. See *TD1*, 308, 351.

47. Ibid., 285.

48. *TD3*, 535, 130–34; see also *TD1*, 312.

49. *TD2*, 91–136.

50. *TL2*, 88.

51. Ibid., 115.

52. See *TL3*, 57–87, 268–79.

53. Cf. ibid., 91, 141ff.

54. Ibid., 125.

55. *TD3*, 59ff. All of von Balthasar's criticisms of the historical-critical method as a form of "rationalism" are intended to make this point. Cf. *TD4*, 459–61.

56. *TD2*, 99.

57. *TL3*, 169–74.

58. *TD2*, 189–316; *TL3*, 245–52.

59. *TD2*, 128. It is also a central Irenaean theme. See *AH* 4.20.5. See *TD2*, 140–41.

60. Ibid.

61. *TD1*, 16, 33–34; *TD2*, 21–37, 68–69, 78, 128, 292; *TD3*, 527.

62. *TD4*, 12.

63. *TD1*, 320. See also *GL7*, 509–13, 521, 526–28.

64. It is important to note that asserting that personal holiness is a "primary" factor in evaluating the legitimacy of theological claims does not imply for von Balthasar that it is the exclusive factor. Of course, he thinks it is possible and legitimate to repeat theological truths originally formulated by others. In such cases the burden of proof for theological legitimacy depends on one's ability to trace one's claim back to the holy person or canonical text from which it arose. Even in the case of theological repetition, however, he thinks context and intention matter a great deal. For example, von Balthasar insists that "the same proposition can bear a different charge in the mouth of Augustine and in that of Jansen" (*TD2*, 101).

65. See *TL3*, 153–55; 234–44.

66. *GL2*, 87.

67. *TD5*, 176–78.

# Chapter VIII

# Opening the Possibility of Internal Critique

In the introduction I asserted that the goal of this study is to make possible an evaluation of von Balthasar's thought on its own terms. Several scholars have offered critiques of von Balthasar's work, but many of these critiques fail to persuade because their analyses either overlook or misunderstand the core theological commitments animating von Balthasar's intellectual project. An internal critique based on what von Balthasar actually argues will always be more effective than one based on misinterpretations of his work. It is impossible, however, to evaluate von Balthasar by his own standards if they are not clearly defined and accurately ranked in order of conceptual priority. Although von Balthasar himself does not explicitly lay out his presuppositions, I have attempted to explicate and prioritize them in order to allow for criticisms of his work without resorting to accusing it of being covertly monist or inadvertently dualist.

There are many possible lines of internal critique that could be profitably pursued in the field of von Balthasar studies. He is a brilliant theologian, but he is not always consistent, coherent, or rhetorically balanced. In what follows I will suggest two areas of his theology that illustrate his fallibility. The first deals with trinitarian theology and the second with political theology. In both cases the internal critiques will be general and relatively soft. There are other areas of his theology, such as his polemical rhetoric against Judaism, that might yield harsher internal critiques. I will focus here only on trinitarian and political theology to demonstrate how an internal critique might be carried out.

## Trinitarian Theology and the Doxological Rule of Resistance

One of the most theologically interesting aspects of *Theo-Drama* is its application of an essentially Irenaean theological perspective to modern trinitarian theology. Von Balthasar contends that if trinitarian theology can be wrested away from the deforming grasp of Joachim's and Hegel's Gnostic reinterpretation, it can then become the key for reestablishing the doxological rule of resistance in the defense of the Christian understanding of the God-world relationship. Yet, many commentators on *Theo-Drama* have not fully recognized or addressed the anti-Joachimite and anti-Hegelian strategy at work in von Balthasar's trinitarian theology. Yet, an awareness of this strategy provides the necessary context for understanding what von Balthasar is trying to achieve and avoid in his trinitarian theology. Recognizing his strategy is crucial to seeing that his trinitarian theology facilitates rather than impedes the formulation of an anti-Gnostic theology. The focus in this section, therefore, will be on the function of the doxological rule of resistance as an interpretive tool for understanding von Balthasar's strategy of resistance to Gnostic trinitarianism. I will also indicate some of the ways in which applying this interpretive tool enables us to avoid several basic hermeneutic errors when reading von Balthasar's trinitarian theology. For example, J. B. Quash argues that von Balthasar is an "epic" thinker who does not adequately escape Hegel's influence.[1] Similarly, both Leonardo Boff and Karl Rahner have expressed criticisms of von Balthasar's trinitarian theology of the paschal mystery that fail to distinguish it from Moltmann's Hegelian-influenced theology of the cross.[2] The doxological rule can be a hermeneutic resource for avoiding these mistaken readings; at the same time, it can create the possibility of an internal critique that addresses the concerns underlying them.

Working within the parameters of the first two principles of the rule, von Balthasar maintains that a theology of trinitarian mystery must originate in and refer back to the incarnation, cross, and resurrection of Christ.[3] Any trinitarian theology that deviates from a cataphatic and aesthetic norm risks either treating the mystery of the Trinity as an inscrutable philosophical proposition that is totally beyond all comprehension and thus without any direct relevance to the life of faith or lapsing into mythological "pseudo-logical speculations" about the God-world relationship.[4] In both cases, theology surrenders the soteriological meaning of the Trinity to Gnostic epic reinterpretation. It is an act of resistance, therefore, when von Balthasar insists that "there is only one way to approach the trinitarian life in God: on the basis of what is manifest in God's kenosis in the theology of the covenant—and hence in the theology of the Cross—we must feel our way back into the mystery of the absolute. . . ."[5] Von Balthasar maintains that in the Son's mission in history, he presents himself as "the definitive 'interpretation' (Jn 1:1) of God the Father" who, despite his revelation in the Son, remains transcendent above history.[6] Jesus is both "the Father's perfect unveiling" and the origin of "the gift of the Spirit," who bestows the "eyes of faith" for seeing the Father in the Son.[7] The incarnate Son points to the eternal Father from whom he comes and whom he obeys, and to the eternal Spirit who raises him from the dead and whom he sends from the Father after returning to him. Thus, working with the first and second principles, von Balthasar holds that

> it is only on the basis of Jesus Christ's own behavior and attitude that we can distinguish such a plurality in God. Only in him is the Trinity opened up and made accessible. . . . We know about the Father, Son and Spirit as divine "Persons" only through the figure and disposition of Jesus Christ. Thus we can agree with the principle, often enunciated today, that it is only on the basis of the economic Trinity that we can have knowledge of the immanent Trinity and dare to make statements about it.[8]

Therefore in the positive revelation of Christ we see the interpenetration of all three trinitarian persons and the Trinity's immanence in and transcendence above history.

All this is in opposition to what von Balthasar refers to as Joachim's and Hegel's "nonsensical" doctrine of a "successive revelation of the three Persons."[9] Against this doctrine, he argues that "the Persons in God will never appear on stage as individual Persons, that is, as divine Persons in isolation."[10] It is true, he acknowledges, that there is "progressive revelation of the Trinity" in salvation history. But this cannot be interpreted as the sequential unfolding of the divine persons, as Joachim and Hegel thought.[11] *Theo-Drama*'s use of dramatic theory in its trinitarian theology (Father as author, Son as central actor, Spirit as director) can only be adequately understood as a strategy of resistance against Gnostic trinitarian discourse. The point of this analogical system is to articulate a doctrine of the interpenetration of the three trinitarian persons, and thereby contest the Gnostic assertion that they can be isolated into discrete historical epochs.[12] Moreover, the doctrine of trinitarian interpenetration must also be read as von Balthasar's application of the fourth, fifth, and sixth principles of the doxological rule. For Joachim, dividing the persons of the Trinity into historical epochs meant dividing the epoch of the Son and the church from the epoch of the Spirit. This implied for him a spirituality of "infinite progress" into the mystery of God that took one beyond Christ, beyond the sacramental, institutional church, and into a life of absolute freedom in the Spirit. Von Balthasar affirms the notion of a spirituality of "infinite progress" into the ever-greater divine mystery as a patristic theme (he names Irenaeus, Gregory of Nyssa, and Augustine as its proponents). But, contrary to Joachim, he applies the fourth principle and maintains that this progress does not lead beyond the trinitarian persons; rather, it leads into an ever-greater participation in their eternal mutual love and self-giving.[13] Further, according to the fifth and sixth principles, he holds that this participation leads to the church's praxis of cooperation with Christ's mission of initiating the created order into the mystery of inner-trinitarian love.

This point brings us to von Balthasar's ratification of Rahner's axiom about the unity of the economic and the immanent Trinity. His agreement with Rahner, however, is qualified. If Rahner's axiom is to have full efficacy as a strategy of resistance to the post-Christian effort to reduce the Trinity to a purely temporal plane, von Balthasar thinks, then it will have to be interpreted in accordance with the third principle of the doxological rule. According to the first two principles, the positive reality of the economic Trinity interprets itself as the *epistemological* source of the immanent Trinity. But according to the third principle of ontologically asymmetrical mutual glorification of God and creation, the immanent Trinity is the *ontological* source of the economic Trinity.[14] To interpret Rahner's axiom in only epistemological categories would be to leave trinitarian theology open to a "Hegelian process theology" that fails to maintain the ontological difference between God and creation.[15] Von Balthasar believes that maintaining this distinction is necessary for preserving the dramatic seriousness and spiritual ultimacy of salvation history. Hence he frequently attacks as epic "mythology" Hegel's assertion that the Trinity needs creation to avoid being "static," "abstract," "self-enclosed," and isolated from the seriousness of love.[16] He thinks this monistic rejection of the immanent Trinity leads to precisely the opposite conclusion than the one Hegel had intended: asserting that God needs the world to be a dynamic God of love ultimately leads to a nondramatic, epic theology that directly contradicts the biblical understanding of divine love as the gift of life.[17] To make this point, von Balthasar argues that in the paschal mystery, the trinitarian persons interpret themselves as (1) absolute personal love and dynamic freedom in their eternal relations, (2) absolute personal love and dynamic freedom in their temporal mission to redeem creation, and (3) transcendent above the cosmic laws of fate, tragedy, and death even in the incarnate Word's full recapitulation of creaturely suffering, tragedy, and death. I will briefly examine these points to show that they illustrate how von Balthasar applies the doxological rule of resistance against Gnostic trinitarian discourse.

It is a leitmotif of *Theo-Drama* that God does not need the world to become a dynamic Trinity of love.[18] The anti-Hegelian intention of this point is clear when read in the context of von Balthasar's frequent contention that God created the world for no reason other than absolute freedom and infinite love and not out a sense of deficiency or imperfection—the world is not a necessary emanation from God, an accidental "fall" from God, or an alienated dimension of God's own divine self.[19] Entirely independent of creation, salvation history, or the event of the cross, God exists as an eternal dynamic Trinity of ontological self-giving and self-receiving in absolute love and infinite freedom.[20] Again in an attempt to refute Hegelian dialectical theology, von Balthasar explains that these intratrinitarian relations constitute a "primal divine drama" that "surpasses all possible drama between God and a world."[21] In this divine drama of the immanent Trinity, the Father "risks" himself in the total self-giving of his divine essence to the Son.[22] In experiencing the "poverty" and "powerlessness" of an eternal *kenosis* that pours out the very divinity of the Godhead, the Father shows the dynamic "recklessness" and absolute magnanimous wealth that defines him as God.[23] The Son, in turn, responds to his gift of divine being from the Father with an equally dynamic "recklessness" that returns the gift of divinity to the Father.[24] The Spirit proceeds from within this "total reciprocal self-giving," and "selflessly" participates in it. This perichoresis constitutes a trinitarian "blood circulation" of divine life.[25] The reckless self-giving of the immanent Trinity becomes visible in the economic Trinity, when God freely opens the divine circuit for participation by creation. In the paschal mystery, we see this free self-giving between the trinitarian persons in eternity played out on the world stage in the form of an intra-divine prayer.[26]

In making such strong claims about the inner life of the eternal Trinity, von Balthasar is endeavoring to bring the first, second, and third principles of the rule into conjunction with the fourth, fifth, and sixth principles. He is convinced that everything he asserts about the imma-nent Trinity can be verified by a life of practical, ecclesial holiness cen-tered on contemplation of the paschal mystery, as well as of the entire *corpus triforme* pattern of meaning it discloses. This point allows us to avoid thinking that his trinitarian theology is chronically speculative. But it does not rule out the possibility that there might nonetheless be acute instances of speculation in his theology of the Trinity.[27] But any attempt to identify these acute instances in an internal critique must take into account that von Balthasar always qualifies the first, second, fourth, and fifth principles according to the third and sixth principles. In other words, all his assumptions about the symbiosis of trinitarian rev-elation, personal spiritual growth, and practical holiness are contextu-alized by his presupposition about the ontologically asymmetrical yet mutual glorification of creator and creation, and the doxological vision and mission of the church in history.[28] Let us briefly examine two test cases to illustrate this point.

Von Balthasar's views on the unity between the eternal *kenosis* of the Father and the temporal *kenosis* of the Son have led some commentators to conclude that his trinitarian theology is almost Gnostic because it fails to maintain the theological tradition's doctrine of the ontological gap between creator and creation.[29] There are several passages in *Theo-Drama* that, if read out of context, could affirm this conclusion. For example, von Balthasar argues that the Son's temporal mission is "taken up" into his eternal procession, "rendering it timeless."[30] Further, he closely connects the creation of the world with the eternal procession of the Son. "The world can only be created within the Son's 'generation.' . . . Accordingly . . . *processio* here is seen to be *missio*, up to and including the Cross. . . ."[31] He also asserts that "the world only has its place within that distinction between Father and Son that is maintained and bridged by the Holy Spirit. . . . Everything temporal takes place within the embrace of the eternal action as its consequence."[32] These passages could easily be misread as advocating a Neoplatonic doctrine of emanation. But if we are aware of how the second, third, and sixth principles of the rule operate in von Balthasar's trinitarian theology, it will be possible to avoid misreading these passages as expressions of speculative monism. Von Balthasar believes that monistic trinitarianism (as in Hegel) undermines both the New Testament's doxological soteriology of freely offered and freely accepted divine love and the traditional christological orthodoxy's affirmation of the unity-in-difference of divine and human natures and wills in Christ. He thinks that confusing creation with divine emanations inevitably results in a monophysite Christology and a soteriology of creaturely absorption into the divine.[33] If the incarnate Word is allowed to interpret itself it communicates that human persons are ontologically distinct from but analogically congruent with the divine. Working within the parameters of the doxological rule (and within the internal logic of Johannine theology), he believes that the incarnation reveals that human persons are created in the image and likeness of the Trinity in general, and the second person in particular. The Son's eternal procession is the "prototype" and "blueprint" of the creation not in a univocal sense but in the analogical sense that creation has genuine autonomy from God, just as the Son has genuine autonomy from the Father. Moreover, human creatures in particular are created to be free, unique persons capable of a doxological relationship with God, just as the Son is a free, unique trinitarian person whose essence is a doxological relationship with the Father and the Spirit.[34] Therefore, in redeeming creation through its integration into the realm of eternal intratrinitarian love, God does not negate the personal uniqueness and creaturely freedom of human persons but rather affirms them by connecting them to their ontological source in the eternal personal uniqueness and freedom of the Trinity. There is a directly proportional relationship here between a theology of the eternal Trinity and a theology of creaturely freedom and praxis in history.

At this point the sixth principle comes into play. For von Balthasar, a synthetic doxological discourse of the immanent Trinity and the economic Trinity is not speculative and esoteric but instead ecclesial. This is because it is the mission of the eucharistic church in post-Easter history to foster the directly proportional relationship between eternity and time in Christ.[35] In collaboration with the Son in his earthly mission, the mission of the church is to make the eternal Father's love visible in time through the institution of a doxological human community of love and reckless self-giving. The church is the economic manifestation of the eternal trinitarian relations.[36] Analogously to the Son, who glorifies the Father in thanksgiving for his divine being and life, the church's essence is to glorify God actively through its thanksgiving for creaturely life and freedom.[37] The church is intrinsically trinitarian because its members were created in the image of God. In Christ, through the indwelling of the Spirit, a human person becomes a child of the Father and hence a "theological person." Becoming a "theological person" means being "de-privatized" in the sense that, like the Son, one "is taken over for God's salvific purposes for the world."[38] One becomes, in other words, *homo ecclesiasticus* in the *imago Trinitatis*.[39] This point is directly connected to von Balthasar's resistance to Gnostic theories of redemption that equate salvation with the erasure of the individual and his or her freedom. The church's mission, von Balthasar believes, is to perfect the finite freedom of each of her members through doxological "incorporation" into the Trinity's community of love.[40]

This point leads to the second test case. Does the incorporation of the created order into the eternal Trinity mean that von Balthasar's God suffers, changes, and is generally contaminated with finitude and death? Answering this question requires understanding his nuanced effort to bring the principles of rule into a balanced, mutually qualifying relationship.[41] As I have shown, the third doxological principle rules out a God who is entangled in the suffering and change of the finite order. Von Balthasar refuses to accept notions of divine passibility and mutability as they are defined in the Gnostic mythology of Joachim and Hegel.[42] But, based on the mutually qualifying interrelations of the first, second, and third principles, he does not necessarily rule out the possibility of a theological discourse of divine mutability and suffering. He writes, "we do well to avoid speaking of 'God's immutability,' precisely because it is essential to keep before us his absolute freedom, manifested in his plan for the world as a freedom to pursue his (trinitarian) freedom."[43] For von Balthasar, the danger with a doctrine of immutability is that it often presupposes the epic, monistic deity of ancient philosophical metaphysics. In this way of thinking, God becomes so utterly detached from the creation and so absolutely static that the incarnation becomes impossible, petitionary prayer becomes meaningless, and the New Testament's trinitarian theology of the paschal mystery becomes unthinkable.[44] He thinks that doctrines of divine impassability are similarly plagued with metaphysical presuppositions incapable of respecting the first two principles of the doxological rule. Hence, we find von Balthasar making the following strong assertions: on the cross there is an "interweaving of Christ's sufferings and the suffering of the Trinity"; and God's "blood circulation" in the eternal Trinity "is the basis for there being a 'death' in God."[45] In other passages he is more cautious, asserting only that the "possibility" of "intramundane experience and suffering . . . is grounded in God"; and "there is something in God that can develop into suffering."[46] He is also careful to distance his position from the heresy of "patripassianism."[47] He is fully aware of the dangers in his nuanced position but insists nevertheless on maintaining it in order to resist epic discourse.[48] The issue for von Balthasar, therefore, is not necessarily content but genre. If theology assiduously avoids an explanatory mode of discourse and relies on the doxological rule in its entirety, then a discourse of divine suffering and change is permitted. For example, in opposition to Hegel's trinitarianism, and in accordance with the first two principles of the rule, von Balthasar insists that any discourse of divine suffering and change must include a strong focus on Jesus' personal, bodily resurrection as a vitally important sign of God's power to overcome death and preserve the integrity of individual personhood.[49] With regard to the third and fourth principles, theology must recognize that the "ever-greater" mystery of God "is not a matter of temporal process, . . . [but] surpasses all we can mean by separation, pain and alienation in the world and all we can envisage in terms of loving self-giving, interpersonal relationship and blessedness."[50] Therefore, God does not change in essence, but rather God's essence is to be dynamic trinitarian self-giving. It is possible for creation and the economy of salvation to "enrich" God and bring him "new joy," but only if this is understood to mean that God lacked nothing prior to this "new and changed dimension" in the divine life.[51] Finally, with regard to the fifth and sixth principles, theology can maintain a doctrine of divine "immutability" only if it refers to a biblical conception of God's unwavering providential care for and absolute loving fidelity toward the creation.[52] For von Balthasar, maintaining this point is the necessary condition for preserving a vibrant ecclesial praxis of "reckless" trinitarian self-giving from degenerating into existential resignation to impersonal fate and dehumanizing social-political forces.[53] As we will now see, this point has important implications for political theology.

### Political Theology and the Doxological Rule of Resistance

As chapter 6 demonstrated, although von Balthasar does not think liberation theology is necessarily a Gnostic theological movement, he does find it guilty of insufficient resistance to Gnostic reinterpretation. In terms of the doxological rule of resistance, he finds not just liberation theology but all types of political theology very weak in their ability to defend the Christian system of meaning. With regard to the first and second principles, he believes political theology tends to impose meaning on the Christ-form rather than respond to its self-interpretation.[54] Often this means that political theology overlooks the reality of the cross and pursues "worldly well-being" as if the meaning of discipleship were exclusively defined by the successful exercise of political and economic power on behalf of the poor and oppressed.[55] Further, political theology is insufficiently critical of theories of historical "progress" and "evolution" that arise from Marxism's secularized old covenant messianism.[56] Political theology also leaves Christianity vulnerable to Gnostic reinterpretation because its anticontemplative understanding of praxis renders it hostile toward any theological discourse that emphasizes the contemplation of positive mystery. As a result, it is incapable of recognizing the social and political relevance of the theology of grace presupposed by the third and fourth principles of the doxological rule.[57] Further, without a strong doctrine of grace grounded in a trinitarian theology of the paschal mystery, political theology cannot effectively apply the fifth principle against Gnostic discourse because its own discourse of praxis will inevitably swing between two extremes: either (1) the discourse of praxis will be essentially Pelagian and resemble more a will-to-power than Christian practical holiness; the morality espoused by political theologies is often puritanical and emphasizes coercion and violence over love and reconciliation[58] or (2) the discourse of praxis will be eroded by the painful reality of serious failures, tragedy, and death, and will eventually degenerate into an existential ethos of resignation. Finally, with regard to the sixth principle, von Balthasar suspects that political theology presupposes an ecclesiology that strongly gravitates toward a type of Constantinianism that is unable to distinguish state power from ecclesial mystagogy. Much of his concern about the insufficient resistance of political theology is based on his anxiety that the identity of the church will be submerged in the power dynamics of an authoritarian or totalitarian state.[59] When this anxiety is waxing in this thought, von Balthasar seems to rule out the very notion of a Christian political theology as an oxymoron.[60] When this anxiety is waning, he grants that although political theology may be "necessary" in some sense, it is inherently hostile to a Christian spirituality of sharing in the suffering of Christ and must be "constantly" reminded of the difference between worldly power and faith.[61] As this acknowledgment that political theology might be "necessary" suggests, however, von Balthasar's thinking on this issue is more nuanced and ambiguous than his hyperbolic criticisms suggest.

As I discussed in chapter 6, von Balthasar affirms liberation theology's basic goals and intentions, and he thinks it has theological resources at its disposal for overcoming its deficiencies.[62] Just as the presence of heterodox trinitarian options on the theological landscape does not imply for him that Christians ought to avoid trinitarian reflection altogether, neither does the presence of heterodox political theologies imply for him the impossibility of a Christian political theology. This raises some important questions, however. Why is there an anti-Hegelian trinitarian theology of resistance in *Theo-Drama* but not an anti-Marxist political theology of resistance? Why are von Balthasar's critical discussions of political theology not accompanied by any attempt to formulate a constructive alternative grounded in the doxological rule in general, and in the sixth principle in particular? Some commentators try to answer such questions by arguing that there is no political theology in von Balthasar's writing because his theological presuppositions rule it out as an impossibility. Within this group of commentators, some consider the absence of a political theology in von Balthasar a virtue of his approach, and some consider it a vice. The latter group interprets his criticisms of political theology as a sign of an underlying systematic bias against political interpretations of Christian faith. Conversely, another group of commentators argue that the absence of a developed political theology in *Theo-Drama* is a lacuna that aborts the trajectory of its theodramatic project. Briefly reviewing some of the arguments in these debates will help us get a clear idea of how an internal critique of von Balthasar on this issue might be formulated.

Craig Arnold Phillips and Frederick Christian Bauerschmidt interpret the absence of a political theology in von Balthasar as sign of a systematic theological bias against political interpretations of Christian faith.[63] Both authors identify von Balthasar's systematic correlation of soteriology, trinitarian theology, and Christology as the root cause of what they take to be his ahistorical and apolitical theology. According to Phillips, von Balthasar "does not differentiate sufficiently between the history of human suffering and the intra-Trinitarian history of God."[64] On Phillips's reading, von Balthasar's trinitarian theology works with a "Platonic model of time and eternity" that reduces all of salvation history to an illusory nonreality that plays itself out in the internal life of the eternal Trinity.[65] As a result of his Platonism, von Balthasar illegitimately thinks theology can "avoid a material and political analysis of human suffering and oppression" by focusing instead on a discourse of the eternal Trinity's suffering on the cross.[66] Hence, von Balthasar's trinitarian soteriology fosters an ahistorical and individualistic notion of Christian praxis that "has more to do with personal redemption from sin and from the finality of death than with emancipation from human oppression and social degradation."[67] Bauerschmidt essentially echoes this line of criticism. Although his argument is more nuanced, he ultimately agrees with Phillips in his contention that von Balthasar's understanding of Christianity is "inevitably apolitical."[68] Like Phillips, Bauerschmidt takes issue with von Balthasar's trinitarian interpretation of the cross. He caustically accuses it of being "banal" because it depoliticizes the meaning of Jesus' death.[69] By so strongly emphasizing the cross as the revelation of the eternal Trinity, he contends, von Balthasar's theology eclipses the fact that the cross also "reveals human sin in its paradigmatic form as a politics founded on the killing of the just by the unjust in the name of 'order.'"[70] Bauerschmidt also asserts that von Balthasar's overemphasis on the eternal Trinity in his theology of the cross results in an intrinsically individualistic conception of faith. It might be possible to develop a theodramatic political theology out of von Balthasar's theology, Bauerschmidt suggests, but only if it is corrected on several major points. First, contrary to von Balthasar's ahistorical and individualistic approach, a theodramatic political theology must recognize "that Jesus has given his followers a way that is, by God's grace, in fact *livable*—albeit stumblingly—in this world, and livable not just for individuals, but for the community of disciples as a whole."[71] Second, a theodramatic political theology would have to correct the trinitarian interpretation of the cross with an ecclesiology that interpreted it historically as the creation of a community of disciples dedicated to nonviolent political action. Von Balthasar simply failed to understand that Jesus' death created a community of nonviolent disciples who pose a distinctively political threat to any order that bases its survival on the use of violence. Third, and most important, a theodramatic political theology would have to reject von Balthasar's privileging of eternity over time. Bauerschmidt complains that, for von Balthasar, "ultimately the horizontal dimension must be subordinated to the vertical. . . . The horizontal axis is superseded by the vertical, and the eschaton's vertical interruption of history seems to have little horizontal effect."[72] Bauerschmidt laments that in this "prioritizing of the vertical over the horizontal" the meaning of Christian faith becomes "so thoroughly internalized that it can avoid the imperative to manifest crucified love to the world by means of a historically and communally embodied tradition."

It is possible to validate many of Phillips's and Bauerschmidt's concerns about von Balthasar's lack of a fully developed political theology. It is a mistake to assume, however, as Phillips does, that von Balthasar's trinitarianism has a Platonic, other-worldly disdain for the notion of a distinctively Christian praxis in history oriented toward challenging economic and political injustice. Nor is it correct, as Bauerschmidt assumes, that he was theologically incapable of drawing any political implications out of his trinitarian theology of the cross. Both Phillips and Bauerschmidt overlook two fundamental elements of von Balthasar's theology that lead them to overstate their cases against him: (1) they fail to see the doxological structure of his trinitarian theology; and (2) they fail to notice that he understood salvation history in political and agonistic terms.

With regard to the first point, both commentators make the flawed assumption that von Balthasar thinks of the vertical and horizontal in either/or terms; they assume that because von Balthasar grants ontological priority and chronological initiative to the eternal and divine, he must necessarily minimize the religious value of history and finitude. Contrary to this assumption, and in accordance with the third principle of the doxological rule, von Balthasar understands the vertical and the horizontal in terms of a doxological relationship of mutual but asymmetrical affirmation. It is precisely this doxological perspective that enables him to resist any attempt to set internal faith and external works in history against each other in an inversely proportional relationship. The relationship is directly proportional: the deeper the internalization of vertically bestowed divine grace, the more perfect one's praxis of creaturely love on earth. Moreover, a theology focused on the eternal Trinity and a theology focused on praxis in history are, for von Balthasar, completely symbiotic; asserting that for him an emphasis on the former implies an underemphasis on the latter is a sign that one has profoundly failed to understand the meaning and function of the doxological discourse in his theology.

With regard to the second point about von Balthasar's distinctively political understanding of salvation history, it seems that both commentators ignore the multiple ways in which the fifth and sixth principles of

the doxological rule guide his thinking. Phillips in particular intentionally ignores as mere "hypocrisy" the numerous passages in *The Glory of
the Lord* and *Theo-Drama* where von Balthasar insists that Christian
faith cannot be merely about the individual soul but absolutely must be
about praxis in the social, economic, and political realms.[73] To his
credit, Bauerschmidt recognizes more clearly than Phillips the role of the
fifth principle in von Balthasar's theology. Yet he fails to grasp adequately its connection to the other five principles. As a consequence, he
mistakenly argues that von Balthasar failed to conceive of Christian discipleship in political terms. A clearer awareness of *Theo-Drama*'s agonistic interpretation of salvation history might have led Bauerschmidt to
rethink this claim. For example, von Balthasar gives a resolutely political interpretation to the church's "theodramatic war" against its modern Gnostic enemy.[74] He contends that a *civitas diaboli* arises out of the
Gnostic rejection of Christ as the sole source of genuine human freedom.[75] This *civitas diaboli* first took the form of the "quasi-religious
pagan state" that persecuted the early church for its resistance against
it.[76] Later, through the influence of modern Gnostic discourse, it took
the form of a purely atheistic "absolutist state" that rivaled the church
by deceiving humanity with the specious promise of "total autonomy"
for all through freedom from God.[77] This later, Gnostic *civitas diaboli*,
von Balthasar argues, was foretold in the book of Revelation's descriptions of "Babylon the Great" (Rev. 17:5). This new Babylon will be the
tool of the Antichrist for waging a political war against the *civitas Dei,*
the community of disciples who form the Christian church.[78] In a passage that further demonstrates his political interpretation of Christian
discipleship, von Balthasar makes the following dark warning: "The
Antichrist's total power will necessarily be earthly and political. . . . The
total embrace of political power means that there can be no remaining
sanctuary, nowhere to emigrate to; this obliges the Christian to take his
stand publicly."[79] Notice that von Balthasar explicitly enjoins on Christians the necessity of political engagement—he absolutely rules out a
sectarian retreat from politics.

Given his resolutely political conception of Christian discipleship,
why did von Balthasar not develop his own theodramatic approach into
an explicit political theology? Gerard O'Hanlon supplies the most plausible answer to this question. He generally disagrees with critics who
charge that von Balthasar's interest in the eternal Trinity results in an
"excessive spiritualisation" of theology that risks undervaluing "the
reality and importance of creation in its temporal, historical and social
dimensions."[80] He grants that some of these criticisms may have relative
merit, particularly given "the dangers of downgrading temporality

which are inherent in some of the ways in which [von Balthasar] for-
mulates an understanding of the relationship between time and eternity."[81] But O'Hanlon further qualifies his already nuanced cautions on
this point by noting that von Balthasar's image of God includes "the full
reality of human existence, including evil and the cross."[82] Moreover,
unlike Phillips and Bauerschmidt, he takes seriously both von Balthasar's warnings about the potential dangers of political theology and his
appeals for a socially and politically active faith that seeks to convert
"structures" and not just hearts.[83] Nonetheless, O'Hanlon has some
reservations about what he sees as von Balthasar's excessively constric-
tive approach. His warnings about the dangers of political theology,
O'Hanlon notes, are "very helpful," but they can also be "emasculating
and theologically . . . questionable."[84] His warnings are helpful insofar
as they subvert an overly optimistic and dangerously simplistic conception of what raw political power can achieve in the realm of human
morality. "We are well cautioned against a Marxist utopian view,"
O'Hanlon remarks, "especially in so far as it involves an anthropology
which sacrifices the individual to the group project. It is good to be
reminded that there is a discontinuity between history and what God
has prepared for us at the end, as the cross of Christ indicates. . . ."[85]
These warnings, however, are questionable insofar as they presuppose
"a dichotomy between human and theological hope, based on the primacy of the spiritual, the kingdom of God, over the material, the Earthly
City."[86] The result of this dichotomy in von Balthasar is not necessarily
a healthy theological realism about politics, O'Hanlon thinks, but an
"arbitrary" restriction on what God's grace might successfully achieve
by working through faithful men and women whose lives are centered
on the incarnate Christ.[87]

O'Hanlon provides a cogent hypothesis about why, despite his
appeals for a socially and politically active faith, von Balthasar does not
develop a theodramatic political theology: "Balthasar's distance from
the socio-economic is much more a matter of personal sensibility than
theological judgment."[88] Had von Balthasar lived in an impoverished
and destitute part of the world, instead of in his wealthy and "highly cultivated, educated Swiss milieu," O'Hanlon argues, pastoral issues would
have compelled him to develop the economic and political implications
of his theology. O'Hanlon offers this apt commentary:

> From one who is so conscious of the reality of evil there is a curious lack
> of engagement with the great modern structural evils. Granted every pri-
> macy to individual conversion, can we really afford to be so lacking in a
> hermeneutic of suspicion with regard to social evils? Can we, precisely
> from the Christian perspective, avoid sharing the anger of those oppressed

by unjust structures, and, with every respect for realism and complexity, avoid joining in the search for more just replacements? Can we view in-built, systematic, grave disparities in economic and social status with any-thing less than urgent attention? In this sense, while accepting Balthasar's caution that theology is not competent to change structures, one regrets any serious attempt in his work to engage in the kind of social analysis in an inter-disciplinary way which would allow theology to contribute in this area. After all, if art, music, drama, philosophy and so on may be dialogue partners for theology, why not economics and politics?[89]

This is a very astute critique, but O'Hanlon slightly exaggerates his case when he asserts that von Balthasar fails to examine "in-built, sys-tematic" economic structures, and that his theology lacks a hermeneu-tic of suspicion regarding social evils. It is important to distinguish acute and chronic failures on this point. Clearly von Balthasar applies a hermeneutic of suspicion to the structural evil of Marxist totalitarian-ism. But, because of his own privileged socio-economic context, he was not consistent in applying his hermeneutic of suspicion to other extremely pernicious structural evils—he simply did not go beyond his critique of Marxism to ask the obvious question of whether the theoret-ical presuppositions of capitalism might be inherently Gnostic. This is unfortunate, since he certainly had the theological perspective for ask-ing this question. For example, von Balthasar complains that in post-Christian (that is, Gnostic) discourse freedom is seen as only "one element among many. From above, the individual appears as one ele-ment within the history of a nation or of mankind, within a cosmic evo-lution. Whether in the terms of Idealism, Naturalism or Socialism, the individual with his tragedy becomes the expression of particular 'condi-tions' that 'are not as they should be' and prevent men from being good . . . [and] if at all possible, these conditions should be changed."[90] It is interesting to notice that liberal capitalism—with its rhetoric about inevitable market forces, economic progress, and the providential "invisible hand" of free trade—is not named here. One may reasonably ask why not.[91]

O'Hanlon's critique is unassailable, therefore, if it is taken as an inter-nal critique that points to an area in which von Balthasar's theology fails on its own terms. Von Balthasar's failure to interpret the economic theories of global capitalism through the lens of his sophisticated *corpus triforme* theology results in his own insufficient resistance to reinterpre-tations of salvation history in terms of the redemption of the human race by the free market through an inevitable process of infinite economic growth.[92] This does not imply, however, that he was oblivious to the potential for evil in global capitalism. For example, von Balthasar's exegesis of the book of Revelation strongly suggests that he could have developed his theology into a critique of the Gnostic presuppositions and practices of global free trade. He explains that in the book of Revelation,

> . . . evil, the rejection of love, is compelled to assume a perverse outward shape of love, manifested in the Arch-Whore of Babylon, "mother of harlots and of the earth's abominations" (Rev. 17:5), with whom "the kings of the earth have committed fornication, and the merchants of the earth have grown rich with the wealth of their wantonness" (Rev. 18:3). Here love is perverted into pleasure and the accumulation of wealth, just as Paul sees licentiousness and greed together (Eph. 4:19; 5:3; Col. 3:5). Indeed, the accumulation of wealth—the complete opposite of God's attitude—is by far the predominant element in the great dirge on the Fall of Babylon; it is primarily the "merchants of earth" who lament Babylon's desolation and burning, for all the products of their worldwide trade were designed to increase and glorify its harlotry (Rev. 18:9-24).[93]

It is lamentable that von Balthasar never applied the results of this biblical exegesis to a critical engagement with thinkers such as Adam Smith, Friedrich Hayek, or Milton Friedman, or even Ayn Rand, who blends pagan religiosity with capitalist ideology.[94]

This critique leads us to the conclusion that it is more accurate to see the absence of a developed, fully articulated political theology in von Balthasar as a self-subverting lacuna rather than as a logical outcome of a systematic bias against political interpretations of Christian faith. His theology does not lack the necessary constitutive elements of a political theology, but, for idiosyncratic rather than theological reasons, it does fail to consistently and explicitly synthesize, amplify, and apply them. Nevertheless, this failure should not be allowed to obscure the intrinsic and necessary connection between doxological theology and political theology. Von Balthasar's theology is implicitly political because it is explicitly doxological. We need not go "beyond" it to develop a political interpretation of faith. The doxological model of theology has the flexibility and spaciousness to include a political theology, which in turn can stretch the doxological model to its fullest potential.

## Notes

1. See "'Between the Brutely Given, and the Brutally, Banally Free': Von Balthasar's Theology of Drama in Dialogue with Hegel," *Modern Theology* 13:3 (July, 1997), 293–318. Quash's conclusions are problematic because his method highlights formal similarities and ignores as irrelevant the overall anti-Hegelian agenda in von Balthasar. Quash highlights such things as von Balthasar's reading of Shakespeare's *Measure for Measure*, and some of his assertions about the communion of saints (303–5, 309). Aside from whether these are in fact examples of "epic" think-

ing in von Balthasar, I am not convinced that Quash succeeds in proving that such acute instances of speculation qualify as a chronic form of Hegelianism. The root problem is Quash's refusal to take von Balthasar's explicit anti-Hegelian arguments seriously. For example, after arguing that von Balthasar borrows the categories of epic, lyric, and dramatic from Hegel (which is true enough), he asserts that von Balthasar's "particular debate [with Hegel] is entirely secondary here to the work of creative theology" (296). Quash advocates overlooking von Balthasar's disagreements with Hegel on the grounds that they are merely "imaginative" polemics rooted in a caricature of Hegel (296, 300).

2. For Boff's critique of von Balthasar on this point, see his *Passion of Christ, Passion of the World: The Facts, Their Interpretation, and Their Meaning Yesterday and Today*, trans. Robert R. Barr (Maryknoll, N.Y.: Orbis Books, 1987), 104–16. Karl Rahner generally shares Boff's view that von Balthasar and Moltmann are engaged in basically the same theological project (see chapter 7 n. 1). The basic mistake in both Boff and Rahner is that they read parts of von Balthasar's theology out of the whole context. Von Balthasar does share some things in common with Moltmann, but by applying the doxological rule to this question, we can avoid confusing him with Moltmann.

3. *TD4*, 319.

4. *TD5*, 14.

5. *TD4*, 324.

6. *TD3*, 506.

7. Ibid., 507.

8. Ibid., 508. Hence von Balthasar affirms Karl Rahner's axiom, "'The economic Trinity is the immanent Trinity and vice versa." See *TD4*, 320; *TD5*, 224–225. He contends that the starting point in the economic Trinity necessarily implies that "only with great caution should we adduce analogies from the Trinity from outside Christianity. Such analogies lack the 'economic' basis and can easily appear as a mere collection of cosmological principles . . . that does not get any farther than tritheism, or else they stay at the level of modalism, speaking of three aspect of the One . . ." (*TD3*, 508).

9. Ibid., 512.

10. Ibid., 505.

11. Ibid., 512; cf. *TD2*, 127–28.

12. Von Balthasar argues that even prior to the coming of Christ into history, God worked as a united Trinity of interpenetrating persons (*TD3*, 513).

13. For an extensive discussion of this point, see *TD5*, 373–487.

14. *TD3*, 157, 508; *TD4*, 320–23. See also von Balthasar's essay, "Creation and Trinity," *Communio: International Catholic Review* (Fall 1988): 285–93.

15. *TD4*, 325; cf. *TD3*, 508; *TD1*, 319.

16. See *TD4*, 325, 326–27; *TD5*, 245, 508–9. Von Balthasar also faults Moltmann for making this same point. He quotes Moltmann in *The Crucified God* asserting that "the Trinity is not a closed circle in heaven but an open eschatological process for men on earth, with the Cross as its origin" (quoted in *TD4*, 322). Catherine Mowry LaCugna also shares Hegel's opinion that holding a doctrine of the immanent Trinity necessarily implies an understanding of the Trinity as "locked up in itself and unrelated to us. . . ." See *God For Us: The Trinity and Christian Life*, (San Francisco: HarperCollins, 1991), 2.

17. Recall here the passage from Hegel's *Philosophy of Religion* where he defines

God's "infinite love" as follows: "Infinite love is seen in that God has identified him-self with what is alien to him in order to kill it" (12:246–51; quoted in *TD1*, 60).

18. See, for example, *TD3*, 529; *TD4*, 323, 324; *TD5*, 507, 245. Von Balthasar is again following Irenaeus on this point, whom he quotes from *Against Heresies* arguing that "the God of love did not need man, but man needed the glory of God" (4.16.6; *TD2*, 118). He later adds that, "God does not need the world to confirm him as God or to provide him with a series of stages to go through and so perfect himself; indeed, he does even need the world to reveal to himself the possibilities of his omnipotence: '*Non quasi indigens Deus hominis*' (Irenaeus, *AH* IV, 14,1)" (*TD2*, 261).

19. See *TD2*, 245, 256, 260–62; *TD4*, 327; *TD5*, 508–9. Irenaeus is again a pri-mary source for von Balthasar on this point. He mentions Irenaeus as teaching the doctrine of "creation out of nothing" (*AH* 2.10.4) and his view that the world was made out of a "divine act of will" (2.30.9) (*TD2*, 264–65).

20. It is the very nature of God to exist dynamically as a Trinity of "limitless self-giving," "dialogue," "wonder," "adoration," and "letting-be" (see *TD2*, 243–44, 256–59; see also *TD4*, 324–26).

21. *TD4*, 325–27.

22. Ibid., 328.

23. Ibid. See *TD2*, 256–57; *TD3*, 518; *TD4*, 323–24; *TD5*, 516.

24. *TD5*, 245–46.

25. Ibid., 246.

26. See *TD2*, 259–60, 296–98; *TD3*, 510–11, 517–19, 522; *TD5*, 244, 509, 516.

27. We cannot but question, for example, whether the following speculative pas-sage, in which von Balthasar feigns insider knowledge of detailed trinitarian con-versations that took place prior to the creation, indicates an extremely serious breakdown of epistemic humility: "From all eternity the divine 'conversation' envis-ages the possibility of involving a non-divine world in the Trinity's love. This con-versation has always included the preliminary stages that will be necessary: the creation of a finite freedom in its twofold relation (to God and to other free crea-tures), which, however 'cannot perfectly fulfill love.' If finite freedom is to be drawn into divine freedom, what is needed is, first, the incarnation of the Son, which in turn draws the Church and, through her, the world 'into the multiplicity of the Son's rela-tionship with the Father and the Spirit,' and then, secondly, the Cross, which opens a path whereby men can get beyond their refusal and allow themselves to be drawn into God. . . . This means that the creature's alienation was always considered as a possibility in the divine conversation, as was the overcoming of this alienation through the Son's blood on the Cross, in anticipation of all other means of salva-tion" (*TD5*, 509–10).

28. For Irenaeus, he explains, seeing God means simply seeing "the revelation of the Father in the Son through the Spirit, that is, the triune God's being for us. Thus, on the one hand, all revelation is God's becoming visible, and faith hangs on those encounters in which God has been seen; similarly the Church's tradition (working backwards) hangs on the 'autoptics,' the eyewitnesses" (*GL2*, 46).

29. This is the gist of Gerard Loughlin's reading of von Balthasar. See "Erotics: God's Sex," in *Radical Orthodoxy: A New Theology*, ed. John Milbank, Catherine Pickstock, and Graham Ward (New York: Routledge, 1999). Asserting that von Balthasar is a theologian "for whom theological agnosticism is almost utterly for-eign" (157), Loughlin charges that his theology of the relationship between the

immanent and economic Trinity is "surreal," and may be in danger of falling into
"Gnostic mythology" (145, 155). Loughlin grants that it is legitimate for von
Balthasar to maintain a close connection between the immanent and economic Trinity, but he thinks it is surreal "to suppose that in the economic Trinity . . . we see the
inner economy of the immanent Trinity" (145). In particular, Loughlin argues that
the gender analogies used in von Balthasar's theology of the immanent Trinity are
not derived from reflection on the economic Trinity, but instead are imported from
human cultural biases. Hence von Balthasar is guilty of a "failure to maintain the
'greater unlikeness' between God and humankind," and a "failed *analogia entis*"
(157). Loughlin may possibly have identified an acute instance of von Balthasar violating the second principle of the doxological rule, but this does not mean he chronically violates the third principle.

30. *TD3*, 513. This assertion is very close to exactly what von Balthasar criticizes
in Moltmann as an illegitimate Hegelian influence. Von Balthasar remarks that, for
Moltmann, "The 'immanent' *processio* of the Son (within the Trinity) is identified
with his 'economic' *missio*. Thus we have arrived at Hegel's view in his *Phenomenology*" (*TD5*, 228).

31. *TD4*, 326.

32. Ibid., 327.

33. Following Irenaeus, von Balthasar holds that it is "the stupendous goal of
God's dealing with man [that] man is not consumed by and absorbed into a God
who remains sole and alone but is finally given the freedom to perform his true role;
he is given an exemplary identity and a mission . . ." (*TD4*, 61). See also *TD2*, 260.

34. See *TD2*, 270, 292; *TD5*, 277, and *TD2*, 261–63, 267; *TD3*, 526–27.

35. *TD5*, 511.

36. *TD3*, 527; *TD2*, 283.

37. *TD4*, 326; *TD5*, 509.

38. *TD3*, 527.

39. Ibid.

40. *TD5*, 518ff.

41. For lucid discussion of this question, see Gerard O'Hanlon, *The Immutability of God in the Theology of Hans Urs von Balthasar* (Cambridge: Cambridge University Press, 1990). O'Hanlon has a good sense for the operation in von Balthasar
of what I am calling the third principle of the doxological rule. He writes, "Balthasar
has identified and developed the similarity, within dissimilarity, of the created and
divine spheres in their analogous relationship (revealed primarily in Christ) in such
a way that he may speak about a supramutability and suffering in God which are
clearly not identical with and yet relate positively to created change and suffering.
In this way he avoids the appearance (common in other approaches) of a 'split' in
God, whether between God in himself and God in the other, or between the economic and immanent realms, or between the human and divine natures in Christ,
while being able to maintain the distinction proper to the divine transcendence"
(170).

42. Von Balthasar writes, ". . . the Trinity must not under any circumstances be
described as a 'becoming' (since, despite the order of origin, Father, Son and Spirit
are coeternal) . . ." (*TD2*, 261). Elsewhere he explains that God "can and will get
involved in this world but without becoming entangled in its confusion. The drama
that takes place before him . . . is not his own 'process.' Otherwise he would have
to redeem himself; he would have to be both Redeemer and Redeemed, which is self-
contradictory" (*TD3*, 529).

43. *TD2*, 280.

44. See *TD2*, 294–98, 302.

45. *TD5*, 245–46.

46. *TD4*, 324, 327–28.

47. *TD2*, 49.

48. Von Balthasar writes, "To think in such a way is to walk on a knife-edge: it avoids all the fashionable talk of 'the pain of God' and yet is bound to say that something happens in God that not only justifies the possibility and actual occurrence of all suffering in the world but also justifies God's sharing in the latter, in which he goes to the length of vicariously taking on man's God-lessness. The very thing that negative ('philosophical') theology prohibits seems to be demanded by the *oikonomia* in Christ: faith, which is beyond both yet feels its way forward from both, has an intuition of the mystery of all mysteries, which we must posit as the unfathomable precondition and source of the world's salvation history" (*TD4*, 324).

49. Cf. *TD3*, 530.

50. *TD4*, 325–26.

51. Ibid. See also *TD2*, 302; *TD3*, 522–23.

52. See, *TD2*, 277–80.

53. "The trinitarian God, and he alone, never changes into mere 'fate' but accompanies his creature in such a vital manner that, in doing so, he can also attract and call him to a more intimate fellowship, encourage him to bolder action, entice him to play a unique role" (*TD2*, 296).

54. *TD3*, 28–29.

55. "Success is not one of the names of God, or of Christ, or of his Church," von Balthasar curtly comments (*TD5*, 177; cf. 178–79). See also *TD2*, 71; *TD3*, 452ff.; *TD4*, 483–84.

56. See *TD1*, 37–40; *TD4*, 431; *TD5*, 176–77; *GL7*, 182.

57. This is why he accuses liberation theology of being a type of "monism" (*TD3*, 367).

58. See *GL7*, 531; *TD4*, 485.

59. He explicitly makes the connection between Constantine and "modern political theology" in *GL7*. He argues that Constantinianism is "discredited by the New Testament." This is because the exercise of state power is inherently non-Christian. "The only thing possible for the Christian is to fill the structures of the state with Christian spirit and life, and thus to blunt them a little . . ." (*GL7*, 502). See also *GL7*, 495–504ff.; *TD4*, 476ff.

60. At one point von Balthasar flatly asserts that "Only within Judaism or paganism is it possible to have something like a 'political theology'" (*GL7*, 502).

61. Ibid., 531.

62. With regard to the basic goals and intentions, in *The Glory of the Lord* von Balthasar defines Jesus' "message" as "the establishment of a just order upon earth that is worthy of man, the struggle against injustice and inhumanity" (*GL7*, 129). He then adds that "Jesus' authority does not relieve mankind of the exertion to assume full concreteness: now that his word and example have been among us, active human love—individual and social, personal and acting through structures— cannot be postponed" (*GL7*, 129). In *Theo-Drama* he qualifies this point but does not retract it. See in particular *TD4*, 487; *TD5*, 176, 178.

63. Craig Arnold Phillips, "From Aesthetics to Redemptive Politics: A Political Reading of the Theological Aesthetics of Hans Urs Von Balthasar and the Materialist Aesthetics of Walter Benjamin" (Ann Arbor, Mich.: UMI Dissertation Services,

1993), 155–66. Frederick Christian Bauerschmidt, "Theo-Drama and Political Theology," *Communio: International Catholic Review* 25/3 (Fall 1998): 532–52.

64. Phillips, "From Aesthetics to Redemptive Politics," 159.

65. Ibid., 174. See also ibid., 121–86.

66. Ibid., 159.

67. Ibid., 167–68.

68. Bauerschmidt, "Theo-Drama and Political Theology," 549. It must be noted that, contrary to Phillips, Bauerschmidt does see in von Balthasar's theodramatics "a conceptual framework" for understanding "the distinctively 'political' character of Christian existence" (533). Bauerschmidt also notes that von Balthasar affirms political theology for deprivatizing faith, emphasizing the ecclesial character of faith, and highlighting the mission of the church to the whole world (535). However, he believes that systematic biases in von Balthasar's theology prevented him from developing these points into a political theology. Indeed, these biases tend to erase the elements of von Balthasar's theology that have the most potential for development into a political interpretation of faith. Hence, he argues, we must "move beyond Balthasar's own work" to save its political implications from his own apolitical theological assumptions (542, 534). In the end, therefore, Bauerschmidt's conclusions do not differ significantly from Phillips's conclusions

69. Ibid., 548.

70. Ibid., 550.

71. Ibid., 547–48.

72. Ibid., 549.

73. Phillips, "From Aesthetics to Redemptive Politics," 180.

74. *TD4*, 437–52. Indeed, von Balthasar maintained that the idea of a competition in history between rival systems of absolute meaning necessarily had political implications. Cf. *TD1*, 74. See above, pp. 169-73. Recall especially that von Balthasar explicitly criticizes *Gaudium et spes* for not teaching clearly enough that the "combat" of Christian faith in history is not a private matter, but must occur "at the *social* level, at the level of culture and politics" (*TD4*, 481). See also *GL7*, 464, 429ff.

75. *TD4*, 433–42.

76. Ibid., 443.

77. Ibid., 443–45.

78. Ibid., 445–52.

79. Ibid., 450.

80. O'Hanlon, *The Immutability of God*, 170.

81. Cf. ibid., 101–3. O'Hanlon raises this same point in an essay on *Theo-Drama*. He writes, "The real drama in Balthasar occurs in the heart of the individual and, above all, in the life of God. But might not this indicate some justification to critics who charge him with being a-historical? Is there not a danger of being over-centered on the eternal Trinity to the relative neglect of the historical Jesus?" ("Theological Dramatics," in *The Beauty of Christ*, 107–8).

82. O'Hanlon, *The Immutability of God*, 176.

83. O'Hanlon, "Theological Dramatics," in *The Beauty of Christ*, 102–3.

84. Ibid., 103.

85. Ibid., 105–6.

86. Ibid., 106.

87. O'Hanlon's point here is fair, but also perhaps a little overstated. In a discussion of political theology and the meaning of Christian mission, von Balthasar

writes, "Naturally, the person who is sent forth as a Christian is not forbidden to have a human expectation of success. In fact, he needs it, just as Christ needed it, having renounced foreknowledge of the 'hour'" (*TD5*, 179). Further, von Balthasar holds that "Things are possible by the grace of Christ that are impossible by the world's grace and favor" (*TD4*, 478). Nevertheless, O'Hanlon is right to observe that in *Theo-Drama* the emphasis falls most consistently on admonitions against expecting success.

88. O'Hanlon, "Theological Dramatics," 108.

89. Ibid., 108–9.

90. *TD2*, 40.

91. On this point, von Balthasar could have very easily brought his theology into constructive dialogue with the political theologian Johann Baptist Metz. We find in Metz a very similar critique of the modern mixture of evolutionary thinking and utopian politics that we find in von Balthasar. In addition to the passage just quoted, see, for example, *GL7*, 508–9, where von Balthasar expresses an understanding of Christian politics that is extremely close to the one articulated by Metz in *Faith in History and Society: Toward a Practical Fundamental Theology*, trans. David Smith (New York: Seabury, 1980). Their shared assumptions about Christianity's opposition to evolutionary political theory are due to the fact that they are both avowedly monotheistic and christocentric thinkers who bring a prophetic perspective to bear on contemporary speculative and mythological heterodoxies. See, for example, Metz's fascinating essay, "Theology versus Polymythicism: A Short Apology for Biblical Monotheism," in *A Passion for God: The Mystical-Political Dimension of Christianity*, trans. J. Matthew Ashley (New York: Paulist Press, 1998), 72–91. In this essay, Metz argues against "the new mythological thinking" prevalent today that retrieves ancient "gnostic" attempts to reinterpret Christianity as a religion of timelessness. Among other numerous points of agreement, Metz, like von Balthasar, praises Irenaeus for his resistance against Marcion, and equates Hegel's theology with "gnosticism" (86). The connections between Metz and von Balthasar could be further elaborated, but unfortunately this task is beyond the scope of the present work.

92. In an intriguing and provocative book, David L. Schindler has attempted to bring von Balthasar's theological perspective to bear in a critique of several Catholic advocates of a capitalist "spirituality of wealth creation." See *Heart of the World, Center of the Church: Communio Ecclesiology, Liberalism, and Liberation* (Grand Rapids, Mich.: Eerdmans, 1996), 89–143.

93. *TD4*, 452.

94. John Milbank's arguments about the theological presuppositions of secular reason and modern free market economic theory could be brought into constructive dialogue with von Balthasar on this point. See *Theology and Social Theory: Beyond Secular Reason* (Cambridge, Mass.: Basil Blackwell, 1991), 9–45. The starting point of this dialogue could be the connection between von Balthasar's understanding of post-Christian discourse and Milbank's contention that "'scientific' social theories are themselves theologies or anti-theologies in disguise" (3).

# Conclusion

The French liturgist and sacramental theologian Louis-Marie Chauvet uses the felicitous term "(arch-)sacramentality" to describe the nature of Christian existence.[1] This term captures well both the internal logic of von Balthasar's theology and what he seeks to defend as normative theological discourse through his retrieval of Irenaeus's doxological discourse. On von Balthasar's reading, for Irenaeus it is axiomatic that a religious commitment to the fundamental sacramentality of existence cannot be sustained in the absence of a rigorously monotheistic theology of trinitarian revelation in Christ. Von Balthasar's theology is worthy of scholarly attention precisely because it takes this point seriously and challenges contemporary theology to take it seriously as well. As I have demonstrated, far from being esoteric, careless, idiosyncratic, and polemical, von Balthasar's doxological defense of trinitarian monotheism is characterized by a remarkably systematic approach to theological reflection, an immense respect for critical thinking and open intellectual dialogue, and a commitment to fair, balanced evaluations of those with whom he disagrees. For this reason, he offers a formidable scholarly defense of the (arch-)sacramentality of Christian existence against what he sees as the modern Gnostic war against the *corpus triforme* system of meaning. Like Irenaeus, he interprets Gnosticism not simply as a rejection of the incarnation, but, at a deeper level, a rejection of biblical monotheism. Von Balthasar learns from Irenaeus that when a religious discourse disconnects creation from redemption, the disconnection of the old covenant from the new covenant and the disconnection of Christ from the church are not far behind. Contemporary theologians seriously committed to a sacramental understanding of Christianity ought to engage von Balthasar's theology in a correspondingly serious dialogue on this point. One need not ratify every argument he makes to recognize the reality of the danger he identifies and to consider thoughtfully the merits of the theological resources he marshals against it.

### Notes

1. Louis Marie Chauvet, *Symbol and Sacrament: A Sacramental Reinterpretation of Christian Existence*, trans. Patrick Madigan and Madeleine E. Beaumont (Collegeville, Minn.: Liturgical Press, 1993), 2.

# Bibliography

## Primary sources

### Books

Balthasar, Hans Urs von. *Church and World*. Trans. A. V. Littledale and Alexander Dru. New York: Herder & Herder, 1967.

———. *Convergences: To the Source of Christian Mystery*. Trans. E. A. Nelson. San Franciso: Ignatius Press, 1983.

———. *Explorations in Theology 1: The Word Made Flesh*. Trans. A. V. Littledale. San Francisco: Ignatius Press, 1989.

———. *First Glance at Adrienne von Speyr*. San Franciso: Ignatius Press, 1981.

———. *The Glory of the Lord: A Theological Aesthetics: Volume I: Seeing the Form*. Trans. Erasmo Leiva-Merikakis. San Francisco: Ignatius Press, 1982.

———. *The Glory of the Lord: A Theological Aesthetics: Volume II: Studies in Theological Style: Clerical Styles*. Trans. Andrew Louth, Francis McDonagh, and Brian McNeil, C.R.V. San Francisco: Ignatius Press, 1984.

———. *The Glory of the Lord: A Theological Aesthetics: Volume III: Studies in Theological Style: Lay Styles*. Trans. Andrew Louth, Brian McNeil, C.R.V., John Saward, Rowan Williams, and Oliver Davies. San Francisco: Ignatius Press, 1989.

———. *The Glory of the Lord: A Theological Aesthetics: Volume IV: The Realm of Metaphysics in Antiquity*. Trans. Andrew Louth, Brian McNeil, C.R.V., John Saward, Rowan Williams, and Oliver Davies. San Francisco: Ignatius Press, 1989.

———. *The Glory of the Lord: A Theological Aesthetics: Volume V: The Realm of Metaphysics in the Modern Age*. Trans. Andrew Louth, Brian McNeil, C.R.V., John Saward, Rowan Williams, and Oliver Davies. San Francisco: Ignatius Press, 1991.

———. *The Glory of the Lord: A Theological Aesthetics: Volume VI: Theology: The Old Covenant*. Trans. Brian McNeil. San Francisco: Ignatius Press, 1991.

———. *The Glory of the Lord: A Theological Aesthetics: Volume VII: Theology: The New Covenant*. Trans. Brian McNeil. San Francisco: Ignatius Press, 1989.

———. *In the Fullness of Faith: On the Centrality of the Distinctively Catholic.* Trans. Graham Harrison. San Francisco: Ignatius Press, 1988.

———. *Love Alone: The Way of Revelation.* Trans. Alexander Dru. London: Burns & Oates, 1968.

———. *The Moment of Christian Witness.* Trans. Richard Beckley. New York: Newman Press, 1969.

———. *My Work in Retrospect.* Trans. Brian McNeil, C.R.V. San Francisco: Ignatius Press, 1993.

———. *Mysterium Paschale: The Mystery of Easter.* Edinburgh: T&T Clark, 1990.

———. *New Elucidations.* Trans. Sr. Mary Theresilde Skerry. San Francisco: Ignatius Press.

———. *The Office of Peter and the Structure of the Church.* San Francisco: Ignatius Press, 1986.

———. *Our Task: A Report and a Plan.* Trans. John Saward. San Francisco: Ignatius Press, 1994.

———. *Prayer.* San Francisco: Ignatius Press, 1986.

———. *The Scandal of the Incarnation: Irenaeus Against the Heresies.* Trans. John Saward. San Francisco: Ignatius Press, 1990.

———. *Theo-Drama: Theological Dramatic Theory: Volume I: Prolegomena.* Trans. Graham Harrison. San Francisco: Ignatius Press, 1988.

———. *Theo-Drama: Theological Dramatic Theory: Volume II: Dramatis Personae: Man in God.* Trans. Graham Harrison. San Francisco: Ignatius Press, 1990.

———. *Theo-Drama: Theological Dramatic Theory: Volume III: Dramatis Personae: Persons in Christ.* Trans. Graham Harrison. San Francisco: Ignatius Press, 1992.

———. *Theo-Drama: Theological Dramatic Theory: Volume IV: The Action.* Trans. Graham Harrison. San Francisco: Ignatius Press, 1994.

———. *Theo-Drama: Theological Dramatic Theory: Volume V: The Last Act.* Trans. Graham Harrison. San Francisco: Ignatius Press, 1998.

———. *Theologic: Volume One: The Truth of the World.* Trans. Adrian Walker. San Francisco: Ignatius Press, 2000.

———. *Theologik: Erster Band: Die Wahrheit Der Welt.* Einsiedeln: Johannes Verlag, 1985.

———. *Theologik: Zweiter Band: Die Wahrheit Gottes.* Einsiedeln: Johannes Verlag, 1985.

———. *Theologik: Dritter Band: Der Geist Der Wahrheit*. Einsiedeln: Johannes Verlag, 1987.

———. *The Theology of Henri de Lubac: An Overview*. San Francisco: Ignatius Press, 1991.

———. *A Theology of History*. New York: Sheed and Ward, 1963.

———. *The Theology of Karl Barth: Exposition and Interpretation*. Trans. John Drury. San Francisco: Ignatius Press, 1992.

———. *The Truth Is Symphonic: Aspects of Christian Pluralism*. Trans. Graham Harrison. San Francisco: Ignatius Press, 1987.

———. *Razing the Bastions: On the Church in This Age*. San Francisco: Ignatius Press, 1993.

### Articles

Balthasar, Hans Urs von. "Creation and Trinity." *Communio: International Catholic Review* (Fall 1988): 285-93.

———. "Current Trends in Catholic Theology." *Communio: International Catholic Review* (Spring 1978): 77-85.

———. "Earthly Beauty and Divine Glory." *Communio: International Catholic Review* (Fall 1983): 202-6.

———. "God Is His Own Exegete." *Communio: International Catholic Review* (Winter 1986): 280-87.

———. "In Retrospect." *Communio: International Catholic Review* (Fall 1975): 197-220.

———. "Liberation Theology in Light of Salvation History." Pp. 131-46 of *Liberation Theology in Latin America*. Ed. James V. Schall, S.J. San Francisco: Ignatius Press, 1982.

### Secondary Sources

Bauerschmidt, Frederick Christian. "Theo-Drama and Political Theology." *Communio: International Catholic Review* (Fall 1998): 532-52.

Beeck, Frans Jozef van, S.J. *God Encountered: A Contemporary Catholic Systematic Theology, Volume One: Understanding the Christian Faith*. San Francisco: Harper and Row, 1989.

———. *God Encountered: A Contemporary Catholic Systematic Theology, Volume Two/1: The Revelation of the Glory*. Collegeville, Minn.: Liturgical Press, 1993.

Boff, Leonardo. *Passion of Christ, Passion of the World*. Trans. Robert R. Barr. Maryknoll, N.Y.: Orbis Books, 1987.

Carabine, Deirdre. "The Fathers: The Church's Intimate, Youthful

Diary." In *The Beauty of Christ: An Introduction to the Theology of Hans Urs Von Balthasar*. Ed. Bede McGregor, O.P. and Thomas Norris. Edinburgh: T&T Clark, 1994.

Chapp, Larry Scott. *The God Who Speaks: Hans Urs von Balthasar's Theology of Revelation*. San Francisco: International Scholars Publications, 1996.

Chauvet, Louis Marie. *Symbol and Sacrament: A Sacramental Reinterpretation of Christian Existence*. Trans. Patrick Madigan and Madeleine E. Beaumont. Collegeville, Minn.: Liturgical Press, 1993.

Conway, Eamonn. *The Anonymous Christian—A Relativized Christianity?* Frankfurt: Peter Lang, 1993.

Cunningham, David S. *These Three Are One: The Practice of Trinitarian Theology*. Malden, Mass.: Blackwell Publishers, 1998.

de Lubac, Henri. *Augustinianism and Modern Theology*. New York: Crossroad/Herder & Herder, 2000.

———. *Catholicism: Christ and the Common Destiny of Man*. Trans. Lancelot C. Sheppard and Elizabeth Englund. San Francisco: Ignatius Press, 1988.

———. *The Drama of Atheist Humanism*. Trans. Edith M. Riley. New York: Sheed & Ward, 1950.

———. *The Mystery of the Supernatural*. Trans. Rosemary Sheed. New York: Herder & Herder, 1967.

———. *Theological Fragments*. Trans. Rebecca Howell Balinski. San Francisco: Ignatius Press, 1989.

Duffy, Stephen J. *The Graced Horizon: Nature and Grace in Modern Catholic Thought*. Collegeville, Minn.: Liturgical Press, 1992.

Gawronski, Raymond, S.J. *Word and Silence: Hans Urs von Balthasar and the Spiritual Encounter Between East and West*. Grand Rapids, Mich.: Eerdmans, 1995.

Henrici, Peter, S.J. "Hans Urs von Balthasar: His Cultural and Theological Education." In *The Beauty of Christ: An Introduction to the Theology of Hans Urs Von Balthasar*. Ed. Bede McGregor, O.P. and Thomas Norris. Edinburgh: T&T Clark, 1994.

Hunt, Anne. *The Trinity and the Paschal Mystery: A Development in Recent Catholic Theology*. Collegeville, Minn.: Liturgical Press, 1997.

Kannengiesser, Charles. "Listening to the Fathers." *Hans Urs von Balthasar: His Life and Work*. Ed. David L. Schindler. San Francisco: Ignatius Press, 1991.

Kehl, Medard, and Werner Löser, eds. *The Von Balthasar Reader*. New York: Crossroad, 1982.

Kerr, Fergus. "Foreword: Assessing this 'Giddy Synthesis.'" In *Balthasar at the End of Modernity*. Ed. Lucy Gardner, David Moss, Ben Quash and Graham Ward. Edinburgh: T&T Clark, 1999.

Komonchak, Joseph A. "Theology and Culture at Mid-Century: The Example of Henri de Lubac." *Theological Studies* 51/4 (December 1990): 579-602.

LaCugna, Catherine Mowry. *God For Us: The Trinity and Christian Life*. San Francisco: HarperCollins, 1991.

Leahy, Breandán. *The Marian Principle in the Church According to Hans Urs von Balthasar*. Frankfurt: Peter Lang, Europäischer Verlag der Wissenschaften, 1996.

———. "Theological Aesthetics." In *The Beauty of Christ: An Introduction to the Theology of Hans Urs Von Balthasar*. Ed. Bede McGregor, O.P. and Thomas Norris. Edinburgh: T&T Clark, 1994.

Loughlin, Gerard. "Erotics: God's Sex." *Radical Orthodoxy: A New Theology*. Ed. John Milbank, Catherine Pickstock, and Graham Ward. New York: Routledge, 1999.

McCool, Gerald. *Nineteenth-Century Scholasticism: The Search for a Unitary Method*. New York: Fordham University Press, 1989.

———. *From Unity to Plurality: The Internal Evolution of Thomism*. New York: Fordham University Press, 1989.

McIntosh, Mark A. *Christology from Within: Spirituality and the Incarnation in Hans Urs von Balthasar*. Notre Dame: University of Notre Dame Press, 1996.

Metz, Johann Baptist. *Faith in History and Society: Toward a Practical Fundamental Theology*. Trans. David Smith. New York: Seabury, 1980.

——— "Theology versus Polymythicism: A Short Apology for Biblical Monotheism." *A Passion for God: The Mystical-Political Dimension of Christianity*. Trans. J. Matthew Ashley. New York: Paulist Press, 1998.

Milbank, John. *Theology and Social Theory: Beyond Secular Reason*. Cambridge, Mass.: Basil Blackwell, 1991.

Moltmann, Jürgen. *The Crucified God*. London: SCM Press, 1974.

———. *The Trinity and the Kingdom of God*. London: SCM Press, 1981.

Nichols, Aidan. *From Newman to Congar: The Idea of Doctrinal Development from the Victorians to the Second Vatican Council*. Edinburgh: T&T Clark, 1990.

———. *No Bloodless Myth: A Guide Through Balthasar's Dramatics*. Washington, D.C.: Catholic University of America Press, 2000.

————. *Say It Is Pentecost: A Guide Through Balthasar's Logic*. Washington, D.C.: Catholic University of America Press, 2001.

————. "Thomism and the Nouvelle Théologie." *The Thomist* 64/1 (January 2000): 1-19.

————. *The Word Has Been Abroad: A Guide Through Balthasar's Aesthetics*. Edinburgh: T&T Clark, 1998.

Norris, Thomas. "The Symphonic Unity of His Theology: An Overview." *The Beauty of Christ: An Introduction to the Theology of Hans Urs von Balthasar*. Ed. Bede McGregor, O.P. and Thomas Norris. Edinburgh: T&T Clark, 1994.

Oakes, Edward T. *Pattern of Redemption: The Theology of Hans Urs von Balthasar*. New York: Continuum, 1994.

O'Donnell, John, S.J. "Hans Urs von Balthasar: The Form of His Theology." In *Hans Urs von Balthasar: His Life and Work*. Ed. David L. Schindler. San Francisco: Ignatius Press, 1991.

————— "The Logic of Divine Glory." In *The Beauty of Christ: An Introduction to the Theology of Hans Urs von Balthasar*. Ed. Bede McGregor, O.P. and Thomas Norris. Edinburgh: T&T Clark, 1994.

O'Hanlon, Gerard F. *The Immutability of God in the Theology of Hans Urs von Balthasar*. Cambridge: Cambridge University Press, 1990.

————. "Theological Dramatics." In *The Beauty of Christ: An Introduction to the Theology of Hans Urs von Balthasar*. Ed. Bede McGregor, O.P. and Thomas Norris. Edinburgh: T&T Clark, 1994.

O'Regan, Cyril. "Balthasar and Eckhart: Theological Principles and Catholicity." *The Thomist* 60/2 (April 1996): 203-39.

————. "Balthasar: Between Tübingen and Postmodernity." *Modern Theology* 14 (July 1998): 325-53.

————. *Gnostic Return in Modernity*. Albany: State University of New York Press, 2001.

————. *The Heterodox Hegel*. Albany: State University of New York Press, 1994.

————. "Newman and von Balthasar: The Christological Contexting of the Numinous." *Eglise et Théologie* 26 (1995): 165-202.

————. "Von Balthasar and Thick Retrieval: Post-Chalcedonian Symphonic Theology." *Gregorianum* 77/2 (1996): 227-60.

Ouellet, Marc. "The Message of Balthasar's Theology to Modern Theology." *Communio: International Catholic Review* (Summer 1996): 270-99.

————. "Paradox and/or Supernatural Existential." *Communio: International Catholic Review* (Summer 1991): 259-80.

Phillips, Craig Arnold. "From Aesthetics to Redemptive Politics: A

Political Reading of the Theological Aesthetics of Hans Urs Von Balthasar and the Materialist Aesthetics of Walter Benjamin." Ann Arbor, Mich.: UMI Dissertation Services, 1993.

Popper, Karl. *The Open Society and Its Enemies*. Princeton, N.J.: Princeton University Press, 1950.

Quash, J. B. "'Between the Brutely Given, and the Brutally, Banally Free': Von Balthasar's Theology of Drama in Dialogue with Hegel." *Modern Theology* 13:3 (July 1997): 293-318.

Rahner, Karl. "Anonymous Christianity and the Missionary Task of the Church." *Theological Investigations, Volume XII*. Trans. David Bourke. New York: Seabury, 1974.

———. "The Concept of Mystery in Catholic Theology." *Theological Investigations, Volume IV*. London: Darton, Longman, and Todd, 1963.

———. *Foundations of Christian Faith: An Introduction to the Idea of Christianity*. New York: Crossroad, 1989.

———. *The Trinity*. Trans. Joseph Donceel. New York: Herder & Herder, 1970.

———. "The Two Basic Types of Christology." *Theological Investigations, Volume XIII*. New York: Seabury, 1975.

Riches, John. "Balthasar and the Analysis of Faith." In *The Analogy of Beauty: The Theology of Hans Urs von Balthasar*. Ed. John Riches. Edinburgh: T&T Clark, 1986.

———. "The Biblical Basis of Glory." In *The Beauty of Christ: An Introduction to the Theology of Hans Urs Von Balthasar*. Ed. Bede McGregor, O.P. and Thomas Norris. Edinburgh: T&T Clark, 1994.

Roten, Johann, S.M. "Marian Light on Our Human Mystery." In *The Beauty of Christ: An Introduction to the Theology of Hans Urs Von Balthasar*. Ed. Bede McGregor, O.P. and Thomas Norris. Edinburgh: T&T Clark, 1994.

———. "Two Halves of the Moon: Marian Anthropological Dimensions in the Common Mission of Adrienne von Speyr and Hans Urs von Balthasar." In *Hans Urs von Balthasar: His Life and Work*. Ed. David Schindler. San Francisco: Ignatius Press, 1991.

Saward, John. "Youthful Unto Death: The Spirit of Childhood." In *The Beauty of Christ: An Introduction to the Theology of Hans Urs Von Balthasar*. Ed. Bede McGregor, O.P. and Thomas Norris. Edinburgh: T&T Clark, 1994.

Schindler, David. *Heart of the World, Center of the Church: Communio Ecclesiology, Liberalism, and Liberation*. Grand Rapids, Mich.: Eerdmans, 1996.

Scola, Angelo. *Hans Urs von Balthasar: A Theological Style*. Grand Rapids, Mich.: Eerdmans, 1995.

Simon, Ulrich. "Balthasar on Goethe." *The Analogy of Beauty: The Theology of Hans Urs von Balthasar*. Ed. John Riches. Edinburgh: T&T Clark, 1986.

Tracy, David. *The Analogical Imagination: Christian Theology and the Culture of Pluralism*. New York: Crossroad, 1981.

———. *Blessed Rage for Order: The New Pluralism in Theology*. New York: Seabury, 1975.

Viladesau, Richard. *Theological Aesthetics: God in Imagination, Beauty, and Art*. New York: Oxford University Press, 1999.

Williams, Rowan. "Rahner and von Balthasar." In *The Analogy of Beauty: The Theology of Hans Urs von Balthasar*. Ed. John Riches. Edinburgh: T&T Clark, 1986.

———. "Afterword: Making a Difference." In *Balthasar at the End of Modernity*. Ed. Lucy Gardner, David Moss, Ben Quash, and Graham Ward. Edinburgh: T&T Clark, 1999.

# Index

Abelard, Peter, 5
aesthetics
  classical, 61-62, 65, 66, 90
    and Johannine theology, 90-91
  and ethics, 65-66
  Kantian-Romantic, 61-62
  theological, 17, 21, 35, 60, 61, 62,
    66, 67, 68, 73, 95, 96, 106,
    112, 128, 134, 152, 156, 163,
    184, 187, 189, 193, 202, 229
    contrasted with aesthetic theol-
    ogy, 66-67, 73, 163
*Aeterni Patris* (encyclical), 4, 19
analogy
  aesthetic, 64
  Przywara's doctrine of, 2-3
anonymous Christian, 22, 70, 79,
    157, 158, 181, 182, 206
Anselm, 5, 45
Aristotle, 8, 9, 19, 69
Augustine, 28, 72, 107, 209, 212

Balthasar, Hans Urs von
  aesthetics in theology of, 61-69
  agreements with Rahner, 56
  critique of, 210
  criticized as apolitical and ahistori-
    cal, 219-21
  critique of Barth, 163-66
  critique of liberation theology, 166-
    74
  critique of Moltmann, 174-81
  critique of Rahner, 156-62
  education in neoscholasticism, 1-2
  erroneous interpretation of his the-
    ology, 14-15
  foundational theme of mutual glori-

fication of God and creation,
    28, 30, 100, 117, 203, 213,
    214. *See also* Irenaeus, mutual
    glorification of God and cre-
    ation in
  and Gnosticism, 33-37
  importance of Irenaeus of Lyons to,
    16-17, 27-50
  intellectual biography of, 1-11
  reception of, in theological acad-
    emy, 12-15
  and relation to Barth, 10
  and relation to von Speyr, 10-12,
    20, 21
  sided with de Lubac against Pius
    XII, 3-4
  theology of, viewed as monistic and
    dualistic, 13-14
  transition from aesthetic to dra-
    matic categories in, 190-92,
    206, 207
  union of aesthetics and dramatics
    in, 190-92
baptism, 110, 116, 124
Barth, Karl, 66, 87, 163-66
Bauerschmidt, Frederick Christian,
    219, 220, 221, 222, 223, 230
beauty
  aesthetic, 17, 27, 60-69, 96, 205,
    206
  of Christ (Christ-form), 35, 64, 66,
    67, 149
  of God, 79, 163
  Romantic understanding of, 61-69
Beeck, Frans Jozef van, 22, 47
Berengarius, 5
Bloch, Ernst, 178, 181, 187, 188

Böehme, Jakob, 166
Boff, Leonardo, 184, 211, 226
Bonaventure, 5, 45
Bouillard, Henri, 3
Bouyer, Louis, 1, 18, 69
Bultmann, Rudolph
  critique of, by von Balthasar, 121-
    23
  and Gnostic interpretation of
    Christ, 121-22

canon
  closing of, 119
  of Marcion, 75
  trinitarian and christocentric inter-
    pretation of history in, 76-77
Christ
  as aesthetic archetype, 64-69
  as divine archetype, 64, 65, 76, 94,
    98, 125
  as new Adam, 88
Christ-form, 35, 64, 69, 72, 73, 87,
    88, 90, 95, 96, 97, 98, 100,
    113, 115, 122, 124, 125, 128,
    148, 149, 161, 169, 174, 191,
    192, 195, 197, 198, 199, 200,
    203, 205, 218
Christology
  corpus triforme, 37-40, 48, 49, 51,
    53, 72, 76, 94, 109, 120, 133,
    137, 139, 189, 193, 195, 196,
    199, 200, 202
  and pre-Christian world, 199
  hostility to, 135
  recapitulation, 87-88, 105, 196,
    197
church
  as context for contemplating
    Christ, 112
  as incarnation of trinitarian love,
    124-26
  as institution, 112-13
  as institutional form of Christ, 109-
    13
  in Irenaeus, 109-10
church fathers
  and biblical hermeneutics, 118
  patristic consensus of, 9-10
  return to, 1, 4, 27, 28
  symbolic theology of, 5-6

understanding of human nature by,
    8-9
Clement of Alexandria, 3, 107
Communio (journal founded by von
    Balthasar), 12
Communist Manifesto, 152
Community of St. John, 11
Congar, Yves, 1, 18
contemplation, and praxis, 190-92
Conway, Eamonn, 70, 181, 182, 206
corpus triforme
  and the incarnation, 37
  and unity-in-difference corollaries,
    39
  Irenaean version of, 38, 39
  source of, in Alexandrian Christol-
    ogy, 37
  See also Christology, corpus tri-
    forme
covenant
  new, as advanced form of monothe-
    istic religion, 87
  old, as part of divine pedagogy, 41
covenants
  disconnection of old and new in
    Joachim of Fiore, 136
  disconnection of old and new in
    Marcion, 135-36
  old and new, differences between,
    89-101, 104
  unity of old and new, 74-77, 193,
    194, 195
creation, unity of redemption and, 53-
    73, 194
curriculum, incarnational, 80-86

Daniélou, Jean, 1, 5, 18, 19
Dante, 45
de Lubac, Henri, 1-17, 47, 53, 60,
    101, 123, 150, 163, 183, 188
  and the challenge to modern imita-
    tors of Thomas, 5-6, 8
Dionysius the Areopagite, 3, 28
doxa-logic
  of mutual glorification of God and
    creation, 51
  of von Balthasar, 16-17, 51

ecclesiology, trinitarian, 113-15